Living

at the

Back of Beyond

Also by the same author

A decade with Wilf Couldwell and his bikes

2009

Living

at the

Back of Beyond

The right of Wilfred Couldwell to identified
as the author of this work in accordance with
the Copyright, Designs and Patents Act 1988.

A catalogue record for this book is available
from the British Library.

*Cover photograph - The Ewden Beck area with Broomhead
moors and Garlic House Farm nestling in the distance.*

Wilfred Couldwell 2010

ISBN 978-0-95633-77-1-9

Published by Couldwell Publishing, Llantilio Crossenny

Printed by Clarke Printing, Monmouth

To my wife Ann who rendered unstinting support to my cause whilst I endeavoured to complete my story.

Acknowledgements

Paddy O'Connor my proof-reader who declares my work
as similar to a marathon.

My brother Lewis for corroborating my story and coming up
with priceless snippets of information.
Not forgetting his wife Jean for her valued help.

Coloured Pictures
are by kind permission of Steve Tivey,
Bolsterstone.

Profile picture
Steve and Charlotte Couldwell.

My brother in law,
Michael Williams.

Finally, not forgetting
Ric Currie for his
invaluable technical assistance.

Contents

Glossary

Introduction
'He'll only go and lois the bugger so I might as well kep it missen'!
'He will only lose it so I will have to keep it myself'.

Chapter 4
'If tha want's a sup er watter that bad, get thessen darn like ivvery wun else and have a sup, there's nowt wrong wi it it's just cawed'.
'If you want a drink of water have a a drink from that trough its the same as we use in the house, its very cold.'

Chapter 5
'When yer's gorrit art t'shed, remember to shut dooer after yer'.
'When you have got it out of the shed will you please close the door?'

'Tha noes it's a mans job spreading muck'.
It's a man's job spreading muck you know!

'We'll have to clean yon shed art sooin tha nose afore muck gets too bloody deep'
The muck in that shed is so deep we will have to clean it out soon.

Chapter 6
'Ahh can't steer yon bugger, theeres summat wrong wee it'.
Theres something wrong with the steering.

Chapter 9
'Cummon lad, oppen it so's we can all see wot' thas gorrin theer'.
Will you open it up lad so we can all see what's inside.

'I'd better tek mi car to top er thill afoor it gets so bloody bad aar carn't gerrup.
I think I ought to take my car to the top of the hill before it gets too bad.

Chapter 10
'Ahve got the little bugger, cum art a theer will tha'
Now I've got you, come out here will you.

Chapter 11
'Ha caught you little buggers agean'
Ahh I've caught you again.

Chapter 12
'That's not a bloody fox's work', he said, 'it's a badger what's dun that'.
A Fox didn't do that; it's the work of a badger.

Chapter 13
'Tha'l hav to fetch it art theesen if tha wants to have a look.
Ar've showed thee wheer it is, naar ah've got some werk to do'.
You will have to get it out yourself; I've got a lot of work waiting for me to attend to.

Chapter 14
'Well ahh don't know abart thee lad, but ahm off to bed, if tha stopping any longer thall after lock ow's up thesen, afoor tha goes wom'.
I don't know about you but I'm off to bed, if you are stopping any longer will you please lock the house door after you.

'I'll have all you'v got int pans to tek wom wi mi'.
I will take all what you have left to take home with me.

'What's up wi yer Land Rover an trailer? Use that'!
Can't your land rover and trailer do it?

Chapter 15
'If tha dunt kep middle full tha noes, it'll fall darn agean'.
If the middle is not kept full it will quickly fall down again.

Chapter 18
'Cum here Lass and have a look at that thing ower yonder'
Come here lass, what do you think that is over there?

Chapter 19
'Wheers ar lass' he Hollered, 'Cum eer a minit arve summat to show thee'
Where are you lass? Can you come here a moment I have something to show you

'Will tha put this little bugger in't oven lass' he said, 'afoor it dees'.
Will you put this pup in the oven before it dies?

Chapter 23
'Just leave the bugger it'l come back when it's hungry'.
If you leave it for now, it will come back when it's ready.

Chapter 25
'It can snow naa if it wants tha nose'
It can snow now if it wants.

'Fetch mi Glasses Lass so ahh can see oop theer'.
Will you please fetch me the glasses so I can see better?

Introduction

It all started during the summer of 1935, when my Father took on the tenancy of Garlic House Farm Ewden Bolsterstone. It was less than a year later in the middle of July 1936 when I made my noisy but eagerly expected appearance into the household of the Couldwell family.

It hadn't taken me long to discover that the best way to attract attention was to yell long and loud, there wasn't anything untoward wrong with me, I was just an attention seeker, or so my mother declared to anyone who had heard my loud demands.

To satisfy her that all was well my father had taken mother to see the doctor with me sitting on her lap in the sidecar attached to his BSA motorbike when I was two weeks old. Apparently all through the journey to our local practitioner's surgery in the small town of Stocksbridge, I hadn't uttered a yell of protest. I had just gurgled with delight, obviously enjoying the whole experience.

As was normal in families, over the next few weeks uncles and aunts came to see the new arrival (me). All the while making strange noises to add to mine as they professed to admire me, bouncing me up and down on there knees which usually succeeded in upsetting my delicate internal system.

On one of those occasions one of my fathers many brothers came to see me, and he pressed a halfpenny into my hand gently closing my fingers around the coin. But as I waved my arms around wildly in protest, the coin flew out of my hand to land on the floor, where upon the same said uncle who had given it to me picked it up and returned it to his own pocket, declaring to one and all

'He'll only go and lois the bugger so I might as well kep it missen'!

After my unknown (to me) uncle had gone, mother declared to father
'I've seen some tight buggers but that one takes the biscuit'.

The custom of giving money to an infant was a gesture of good luck. It didn't matter how much it was; it was the giving that mattered.

With the help of my mother, father gradually built up Garlic House Farm, buying stock when he could.   To have enough income coming in to live day to day, he had to continue working for Samuel Fox and Co the Steel Manufacturers of Stocksbridge.

This meant when he came home from an eight-hour shift of manually unloading pig iron all day, at the steel works. He had to start again this time as a farmer attending to cows and other animals, preparing the land for planting, or harvesting the crops he had grown.

He had his lighter moments.
Such as his cow dog that greeted him after every shift more than a mile or so from home. The dog always waited in a certain place at the side of the road; father just slowed down slightly with his motorbike and the dog would leap into the sidecar to ride the rest of the way home with its feet firmly planted on the front window surround.

He also had his moments of fun.
Willie Hague, son of Frank Hague of Barnside Farm, also worked at Fox's and in common with my father rode a motorcycle to work every day.

If they were on the same shift they would ride home together on their respective bikes when the work was done. Apparently my father and Willie would sometimes agree to have a 'race' to see who could be the first to reach a certain landmark.
Father however was handicapped in so much that he had a sidecar attached to his machine and Willies' didn't, so it wasn't an altogether fair test.

But Willie didn't always win the chase, as my father knew certain short cuts unbeknown to Willie and he utilised them to there full potential, sometimes arriving well before Willie Hague at the agreed place. This fuelled the desire to see who was the best yet again, so a new challenge was agreed.

Now we can move on to the first chapter of this book which begins in the summer of 1941 when I was just five years old attending my first day at Bolsterstone infants school.

One

Schooldays

Even though it is now almost seventy years on I can still remember my first day at Bolsterstone infants school when I was just five years old, and how I had yelled all through that first day wanting my mother, I was inconsolable. I also remember how one of my parents had to walk every day with me the mile or so to Broomhead Hall where I joined Roger Senior (a fellow pupil) to await collection by Lewis Scholey and the School Taxi.

I was later reminded by my parents about the one memorial occasion when my mother failed to get to the Hall at her usual time to collect me from the taxi, at the end of the school day. Apparently I was so disappointed I wouldn't wait for her delayed arrival, deciding instead to walk home by myself.

This entailed walking up the wide main drive from the Hall past the big greenhouses and gardens, to the main Mortimer road that went past the top.

It would seem that as soon as I had reached the main road, I could hear vehicles coming along, and they were making a tremendous noise. I was so frightened I had quickly ran across the road and squeezed under a wooden five barred gate into the grass field opposite to take shelter behind a high stone wall. Safe from the vehicles as they went roaring past on the road.

In the meantime, my mother had finally arrived in the Hall yard expecting me to be waiting for her, but I wasn't.

My mother searched everywhere she could think of, she became so panic stricken she went berserk, as she desperately looked for me. Meanwhile I had moved along the grass field heading towards where I lived - still behind the stone wall. Edging closer to where I could see our farm across the valley, until finally I couldn't get any further because of a barbed wire fence.

And there I had cowered down in the long grass to hide, and wait. I was still frightened by the noise of the vehicles as they drove past on the roadway.

Obviously my mother didn't know where I was as she franticly searched the area, so it was quite sometime later before I was discovered thoroughly scared and cold, still hiding behind the high stone wall.

Mortimer Road was at that time controlled by the American army and they didn't usually allow visitors or none military traffic to travel along it unless they had a permit or licence to do so.

It was several weeks and lots of arguing with the authorities later, before Mr Lewis Scholey and his School Taxi were allowed to drive past the armed guards at the road barrier near Midhopestones, and collect me at our farm gate, to take me to school each morning.

With me safely aboard the Taxi our next stop was Broomhead Hall to pick up Roger from where he lived with his parents in the chauffeur's cottage, from there we travelled down the extensive parkland and out through the big iron gates just down the road from Wigtwizzle.

'Wigtwizzle' is a small cluster of houses where my cousin Bernard Dyson lived. We knew him as and called him 'Bud'. Half a mile or so later along the narrow road past old Maids cottage brought us into an area known as the Kenyon hills, to collect Edmund Wainwright. Next to join us on board the taxi was Brenda Worthington from Walker edge cottage. At the next crossroads we turned left, to go past White Lee Farm to pick up Stella Wainwright from the end of her lane, then we entered the dark gloomy wooded area where Bruce Aloo lived in a cottage along the single-track road.

Bruce Aloo was never late; he was always waiting for us outside his yard gate.

Once he was safely aboard it was more or less a straight run around the Broomhead reservoir and up yew trees lane to Bolsterstone where we tumbled out of the taxi to scamper into the schoolyard. As soon as Lewis Scholey saw that we were safely inside the gate he drove away.

Before I go on I must mention Edmund Wainwright again. For Edmund refused point blank at all his parents' attempts to make him wear anything else on his feet but hob nailed boots. Big heavy hob nailed boots at that so as you can imagine he soon acquired the nickname of 'Booits Wainwright', and the name stuck for all the years I knew him. But saying that I was no better myself for footwear was sometimes a pain literally, as I remember when I first went to Bolsterstone School I wore clogs with wooden soles that had hob nails hammered into the soles instead of the usual clog irons. I recall my teacher Miss Gill telling my parents that their son Wilfred (me) made too much noise! Apparently I persisted in clomping about in the classroom, she had suggested to my parents that I was to be sent to school in 'Something more suitable'! As she put it.

My clogs were clean and polished. It was just the noise Miss Gill objected to.

Taking note of the teachers' comments my mother acquired a pair of boots for me to wear, however these also had a form of hob nails in the soles, not the tall traditional Hobnails, but a flatter version known as brag nails! And to me they were just as noisy, or were it me who managed to make just as much noise! Anyway, Miss Gill despaired, she wasn't making any headway with (Booits) Wainwright or me for we both had discovered that the wooden floor of our classroom was the ideal surface to practice the fine art of noise.

Over the years the number of people riding in the school taxi varied, especially if a parent wanted a lift somewhere. At such times the room inside became somewhat cramped, I remember quite clearly occasionally having to sit on the driver lap so that a seat was made available for the new passenger to sit on. I remember how eagerly I enjoyed the experience of being so close to the huge steering wheel of the Rolls or Daimler motor car we travelled in. And I didn't miss the opportunity of trying to help Lewis Scholey to steer the vehicle.

St Mary's C of E Primary School Bolsterstone had two teaching staff. Miss Gill the infant teacher, and Mrs Lindley who taught the older pupils.

Most of the children who attended lived in the village or came from farms in the surrounding rural area. The big room where Miss Gill taught us the infants had no ceiling, if we stared up into the shadows we could actually see the roof trusses and slates.

With all that space up above it must have made the classroom difficult to keep warm during the winter months, even though there was a large fireplace with a guard around it in our classroom.

I believe coal or coke fuelled it. The caretaker, Mrs Sampson, regularly kept it topped up during the winter months keeping us all nice and warm.

A tall stained glass window which seemed at the time to be about 10ft high with carved stone inserts just like a church window overlooked Morehall Lane, with smaller similar versions overlooking the village square, and Heads Lane.

A dividing wall separated the two classrooms, set in that wall was a pair of double doors that were normally closed but could be opened up to make both rooms into a communal classroom for special occasions.

Standing by the side of the double doors stood a battered upright piano, this was played every day by Miss Gill for morning assembly and for the occasional sing along lessons.

At the rear of the big classroom near the tall window overlooking the village square stood the Maypole with all its strings and ribbons attached.

I remember with fondness when the first of May came around each year, when we all eagerly awaited for the fully kitted Maypole to be taken outside into the playground or into the Village Square for the dancing celebrations.

If the weather was wet the Maypole stayed inside, where we celebrated just the same for there was plenty of room to dance around it, it wasn't quite as good as outside, but we didn't mind, it was still better than doing lessons.

The other classroom through the double doors was much smaller; it was where Mrs Lindley taught the older children, the room had a proper lowered ceiling with pictures on the walls and a glass fronted display cabinet with a stuffed fox and a pheasant on display. I also remember how each Monday morning we the children formed an orderly line at the front of Mrs Lindley's desk to hand over our weekly dinner and savings money.

The savings were all duly entered into our individual record books, not a huge amount I'm sure, just a couple of pence would be normal I suppose, or as much as our parents could afford anyway.

I was a pupil at Bolsterstone School from 1941- 45 where many of my days there were filled with excitement. As I became older I recall becoming tired or bored I suppose of running around aimlessly with the others, and I started to drift towards more practical things such as investigating around the outside of Mr Beevers blacksmiths shop just across the village square from the school front gate. It didn't take long for my hanging around to become noticed by the blacksmith Mr Beever. He eventually invited me inside his smithy to see if I was strong enough to operate the forge handle, I was. From then on I began to regularly help him by working the bellows. Soon I couldn't wait for the midday playtime to come around so I could help Mr Beever in his forge.

I had to be alert at all times listening for the school bell to ring ending the playtime period.

When the bell sounded I had to quickly dash across the village square through the school gate to join the back of the lineout, hoping nobody had noted my

4

late arrival.

I don't suppose the teachers liked the idea of me wandering off during playtimes as I remember quite clearly being told off and dragged back to school by my collar pretty regularly for venturing out of the school yard at dinner time. If the teachers already knew where I was what was all the fuss about? I never did understand that.

I became fascinated with a sword collection Mr Beever the blacksmith had, it was scattered around the inside of the smithy, not a tidy collection as one would suppose for many of the swords were propped in corners hanging on nails or just cluttered around the place.

Swords such as cutlasses, double edged long fighting swords, thin rapier swords. They were all swords from another century, another era. Some were in scabbards some were not, some were very shiny as if they were new or chrome plated, whereas others were rusty and worn as if they had been well used in an earlier life. Some looked heavy; some looked thin and light. Some were very long where others were short. But I never touched them or even asked if I could, but I shall always remember those swords in Mr Beevers Bolsterstone village Blacksmiths shop.

Just outside the main door of the building there was a device sunken into the floor. It was a special device for fitting metal tyres to wooden wheels, it was what the Blacksmiths or 'Wheel Wright' had used for centuries as an aid for fitting metal tyres to wheels on horse drawn vehicles. Vehicles such as stagecoach's, landaus, farm carts, traps or everyday milk floats.

Most vehicles of an earlier era were fitted with wooden spoked wheels and these had to be made or repaired by someone, aided by such a device as could be seen outside the Bolsterstone Blacksmiths workshop door.

I never saw it used but I always supposed it was still serviceable!

As we travelled in the taxi to school one morning in early 1943, it became obvious that something different had just started to happen just over the railings alongside Broomhead Reservoir. We noticed some heavy machinery starting to gather around the area where an old corn mill stood, before it had been demolished.

From that morning on every time we passed the site I tried to get an eye full of what was happening. Sometimes it was easy, as I began to make it a priority to try and sit by a window in the taxi so I could see what was going on more clearly. From my organised vantagepoint I couldn't help but notice the piles of shiny girders and construction materials stacked up awaiting attention. Soon we could see a concrete base had been established.

And then a few days later a slender steel tower started to rise from the base. I remember straining my neck through the open taxi window to gawp at the new structure, it went up and up into the sky or so it appeared to me at that time. I was absolutely mesmerised.

And when I noticed the large shiny ball on which the complete tower structure stood, I was as you can imagine awe-struck. The pylon itself tapered to a point at the bottom, and a similar point was embedded in the concrete base. Between the two components could be seen a shiny round steel ball on which the entire towers appeared to be precariously perched.

The structure itself was held in position by numerous guide wires anchored to concrete blocks embedded in the ground around the pylon. I would have liked to ask Mr Scholey if he would stop the taxi for a moment or two for me to get a better look, but I didn't dare at the time.

To add to the mystery another identical steel tower appeared across the water on the other side of the Reservoir, this further added to the excitement.

What could they be, we all wondered? No one knew. We were all puzzled.

We asked anyone who would listen but no one could enlighten us at the time.

When the second tower had been completed, we noticed a rowing boat on the reservoir with an occasional glimpse of a bigger motorised craft. Then later that same week, workmen could be seen stringing a taught cable stretching from the top of one pylon to the other one on the other side of the reservoir. As you can imagine our excitement grew by the day. One morning a trolley could be seen travelling across the top cable with workmen in it. They were attaching thin wires to the cable, with the other end of the wire left hanging down to or near to the water level; the excitement was by then becoming unbearable.

Indeed we could not concentrate on our lessons at school as we were all thinking about the journey home past the new exiting pylons that had been constructed by the side of Broomhead Reservoir. Soon blocks or heavy weights had been affixed to the bottom of the hanging wires spaced something like three foot apart. When the job was completed the whole thing looked like a curtain stretching across the Reservoir.

As we drove to school each morning the sunlight glittered on the curtain making it look magical. We were absolutely enthralled.

Lewis Scholey and all of us in the school taxi became used to seeing the spectacle each morning and evening as we travelled to and from our School. Gradually our interest waned. But wait. Another souce of interest developed.

We began to notice there were heavy caterpillar tractors working a little further along the road from the new pylons, they were levelling areas of the sloping roadside grass verges into 10ft by 10ft flat areas about 20 yards apart. A couple of weeks later all of the finished squares were concreted over to form raised platforms just above road level.

Once again we were seeing an exiting mystery unfold.

Soon all the concrete bases had what appeared to be bombs stacked on them. Well they looked like bombs to us as we travelled past them each morning; they were pointed at one end with small wings at the other. They were I suppose, about three foot long.

When the job was completed the stacks of 'bombs' formed a regimented line along both sides of the road for more than a mile, and along the road on the other side of the reservoir as far as we could see. We could see them as we travelled past in Mr Scholeys Taxi.

Naturally everyone in the area wanted to know about the newly installed pylons and the stacks of what appeared to be bombs. My Uncle Jim Dyson was at that time the farm bailiff (Manager) of the home farm belonging to Broomhead Hall; he lived in one of the cottages in the hamlet of Wigtwizzle. As Wigtwizzle was quite near to where the new workings were situated uncle Jim should by our reckoning know more about what was going on, as it was all happening on his doorstep, so to speak? Anyway when uncle Jim came to see my mother (his sister) she asked him what he thought the curtain of steel was all about, uncle Jim thought it might be to stop aeroplanes bombing the Broomhead Reservoir. He went on to say if that ever happened a disastrous wall of water could flood the area, causing havoc. Mother left it at that for as far as she was concerned she was none the wiser. As for the stacks of armaments on the concrete bases uncle Jim insisted he was as much in the dark as we were.

The pylons with the wire deterrents were in place for a couple of years as far as I can recall, it must have been 1945 or even 46, before the pylons and gantry wires were finally dismantled.

As far as the bombs along the sides of the road were concerned, they were taken away by the military, but the concrete bases were left to become eyesores before a contractor eventually came with heavy machinery to break them up and take the rubble away. It took a few years longer before the last traces disappeared. Anyone looking now for the location wouldn't know where to look for the grass verges all look the same.

Late autumn was the special time of year when all schools played conkers, and I had discovered a supply that was second to none, as when I took some to school to take part in the games they appeared to be good quality, some of them racked up high scores. The source of my supply was over a gate and along a little known footpath along the top of long bank. Long bank was an area of woodland over the wall from Mortimer Road; with the binoculars we could see the wall from our farmyard across the valley on the other side of Ewden beck.

If I walked along the narrow path until it crossed the wider footpath my Grandad Dyson used virtually everyday on his way to and from his work at Broomhead Hall. From there I was able to see the huge horse chestnut tree with its big leaves down the steep banking.
If I timed it right each year there were thousands of the green prickly Horse Chestnuts on the woodland floor beneath the tree, some already opened for me to gather pockets full of the big golden brown conkers.
Fellow pupils, who had heard about my conkers, besieged me at school. I discovered early that possessing good quality conkers always had bargaining powers, I found how to bargain with them and how to obtain certain things I wanted from the other kids through the common practice of swapping. I swapped conkers for such things as big marbles, small penknife, or even a halfpenny in exchange for a big conker already with a hole through the middle with a string attached ready for action. Not that big conkers had better records scoring against the smaller versions; I should have though it was more the opposite in fact. But I remember the other kids wanted 'big conkers' so I supplied them with what they wanted.

Earlier I mentioned somewhere about my wearing clogs when I went to Bolsterstone School, its true I did. The next footwear was equally awkward for it was a pair of boots which father had hammered brag nails into the soles. To make them last. He said.
I went to school wearing a succession of boots, until I worked out why I had to wear boots with Hobnails in the soles. My conclusion was that they all made a noise so everyone including father could tell precisely where I was at

any given moment. I began to notice other kids at school had started to wear shoes with a soft sole known as crepe, and they didn't appear to make any noise whatsoever. And I wanted a pair.

I begged and pleaded with my parents and eventually I got my wish. They bought me a pair of crepe soled shoes, just to be worn for school. Nothing else, just school!

They were absolutely noiseless, except maybe giving off a squeaking noise on some shiny surfaces, I could go almost anywhere without the slightest noise, and I loved them.

It was so strange being able to walk around at school without making any noise. When back at home it was back to the noisy boots I had to wear doing the farmwork.

The crepe-soled shoes wouldn't have lasted five minutes in the farmyard amongst the cow muck. But they were absolutely ideal for school footwear.

Two

Hospital and Doctors

Early in the summer of 1942 I was separated from my family and school friends when I was suddenly taken away into Grenoside isolation Hospital Sheffield. I was told later when I was old enough to understand that I had somehow contracted a life threatening condition known as Scarlet fever. I was nearly six years old at the time. And I had almost died, so they said.

I can still recall one of the days my parents came to see me, they were waving to me through a window directly across from my bed in the ward. They had brought a present for my birthday. But as they weren't allowed into the ward to give it to me themselves, they had had to hand it to a nurse who had brought it through to me, so my parents could watch through the window as I opened it.

Both my parents had to bend down slightly to look at me through the window as if they were standing on something outside. I remember that window quite clearly. It was tall and had long dark coloured curtains a nurse drew shut at dusk each evening and opened each morning. I also remember every morning when the nurse came to open the curtains; she also lifted the bottom half of the window up slightly, to let in some fresh air.

There was a tree outside that tall window and it waved around a lot in the wind, it relieved the boredom somewhat to watch birds flitting around amongst the branches.

All the time I was wishing I were back home at the farm with my family.

My parents were very lucky, for all the time I was confined to bed in the Grenoside fever hospital; they were brought to see me in an American Willys jeep.

Ordinarily they would have had to walk to Midhopestones village to catch the Barnsley bus to Stocksbridge.

From there they would have had to transfer to a number 57 Sheffield bus to travel to Oughtibridge village, then walk the last mile or more up the steep Joe Bone hill to where I was in the isolation hospital in Grenoside.

The road going past Garlic house farm where I lived with my parents was at the time in the control of the American army, where the military had sole jurisdiction of who travelled along Mortimer road. During this time my mother had quite a number of laying hens running around the farmyard, so she sold a few eggs at the door to help with the costs. A couple of times a week an American jeep came to the farm gate bringing a soldier to collect Hen fruit (eggs) for use in the officers kitchen.

Through these visits the commanding officer in charge of the local base came to hear of my plight; subsequently he had extended a helping hand to my parents by offering the use of an army vehicle whenever they wanted to visit me in hospital. The only complaint my mother voiced at the time (in private) was the speed at which the jeep driver persisted in travelling at over the not so smooth roads.

My father had had to hold onto to mother, holding her in a very tight grip with one arm whilst hanging on to the roll bar of the canvas topped Willys jeep with the other, to stop them both from being flung out of the bouncing vehicle. However, they held their tongue by not complaining realising that riding in a bouncing jeep was better than having to walk.

My enforced confinement in the fever Hospital at Grenoside continued for weeks, so my parents made full use of the vehicle by coming to visit me quite a number of times, each time enduring the ride with an erstwhile American racing driver.

But who were they to complain!

I recall well the day I was allowed back home to the farm after my enforced confinement. I had been released with strict instructions to my parents not allow me out of the house for a certain period of time. However, I must have avoided the instructions or escaped from the house for I remember quite well venturing out onto the road outside the farm gate without any shoes or socks on, wandering up the steep Ewden Beck hill in my bare feet allegedly looking for blackberries. The road was so hot it actually blistered my tender feet.

So I was again confined to the house for a while, this time with bandages on my sore feet.

My recovery after the bout of scarlet fever brought with it an unwanted side effect, our family doctor Dr McIntyre had told my parents not to let me take part in any exertions or it could jeopardise my safety. My parents also learned that the Dr had written a letter to my teacher Miss Gill at Bolsterstone school asking/telling her not to let me take part in any school sports or any other exerting exercise activity, even playing with the other children could be a risk!

I was terribly disappointed when I was told repeatedly to sit down on the sidelines and watch as the other kids were having fun. Quite some time elapsed before I was allowed to take part in the less rough sports at school.

Then within a year we were all relieved (especially me) to hear Dr McIntyre announce that I was fit and well enough to walk to Stocksbridge to her surgery to attend any future appointments. When we did go to see the doctor we were faced by a six-mile walk each way so the problem had to be serious or we had to grin and bear it.

I suppose I had the usual children's ailments such as chicken pox or measles whether they could be regarded as serious or not, but my own complaints were tooth ache or a sore throat not that I remember being off school because of them.

As you may well imagine it took us quite some time to walk all the way from Garlic House across the fields along footpaths and rough roadways to Stocksbridge.

By the time we got to the wide well used footpath in Stocksbridge known locally as the doctors drive I was buzzing with excitement. For I knew the outer door of the surgery had a doorknocker shaped like a lion's head with its mouth wide open as if it was roaring. I always ran the last fifty yards or so to the door to the surgery to excitedly reach up and grab the knocker to bang it loudly against the door. At the time I was just about tall enough to reach the knocker with both hands, pull it out on its hinge and swing it with gusto against the door before Mother arrived to grab my hand to stop me doing it again.

On the other occasions when the doctor actually visited our farm to attend to some family ailment, at some point she could be found standing on the flagstones outside the house door staring across the valley at the Broomhead moors with a wistful expression on her face. When asked what she was looking at she would whisper that the view from our farmhouse was almost identical to the one in bonny Scotland where she had lived when she was a young girl.

In later years Dr McIntyre became a frequent visitor to our farm when my mother became ill.

Mother' illness came about when one day she was on her way home from visiting her sister (auntie Mary) who lived at Hungerhill cottage Bolsterstone. My mother had to walk across many fields and footpaths on her way back home to Garlic house.

She had climbed to the top of one of the highest stiles, when suddenly a strong gust of wind blew causing mother to loose her balance. She fell down the steps on the other side of the wall bumping down each one in turn on her way down to the ground. Mother just about managed to struggle home before collapsing complaining about her back.

It wasn't immediately apparent the extent of the damage caused to her back. To either the doctor or the Hospital, but soon afterwards she wasn't able to walk at all especially outside the house and her condition quickly deteriorated becoming so bad in fact she became completely bed bound. I was able to help with the cooking of meals, and after I had left school I did more of the housework helped by Auntie Mary, Cousin Margaret Roebuck from Thurgoland or Cousin Agnes Dyson from Stocksbridge. Their help inside the house allowed me to do more to help father with the normal farm work.

When my brother Lewis left school he took over inside the house doing the same as I had done and that lasted until mother finally died.

Over the years doctors came quite regularly to our farm, usually when they had been summoned to attend to someone who had been injured in a road accident lower down Ewden Beck hill. On many occasions an injured person had been brought into our house and laid out on the kitchen table until a doctor arrived or an ambulance had been summoned to take them to hospital. Most of the injuries were the result of being the unfortunate victim in a crash, riding a bicycle or in a car. In the beginning mother would rip up bed sheets to try and help, with the promise of recompense later, but it didn't always happen that way.

Things such as paying for the torn up bed linen were forgotten when the injured party recovered; it was as if all their memories had been erased about who had helped them when they were in dire need of attention. Hardly anyone ever came back to offer payment or replacement of such expensive items such as bed sheets, eventually mother resorted instead to using whatever was around.

Don't get me wrong here mother did her best, but times were hard so she couldn't afford to destroy perfectly good bed sheets all of the time!
On more than one occasion mother had wrapped someone in thicker blankets, and when the ambulance had arrived to take the injured person away they had loaded the patient up still wrapped in the blanket. No recompense for the loss of our blankets was ever offered.
I remember quite well that it was we at the farm that went without.
And because I was always suffering from either a sore throat or toothache I had to have a heavy horse rug on my bed instead, if the weather was really inclement an army great coat was added for extra insulation.
When I thought about it later what might be the cause of my complaints, most of it could have been attributed to the fact we didn't have any heating at all in any of our bedrooms, in consequence they were damp.
In fact most of the rooms in our house were damp. Garlic House farm was very old and the house itself was set into the ground at the back, so I suppose rising damp had penetrated the walls and the lack of heating made the situation worse.
If anyone complained of being cold they were told to get some more clothes on! That was the standard answer to a lot of complaining by any of us.
Actually there was a small fireplace in each of the bedrooms but only the one down stairs was ever lit and that was when Mother was ill in bed.
The big black range in the kitchen was used for all our cooking; it had a hot water boiler attached to the side to supply water for such things as the daily washing up.
When the Sett Pot was lit it gave off quite a lot of heat. But it was only lit for Monday's washing day, and every other day to boil potatoes for the pigs and hens, in the winter months

----

Of course we had our share of injuries whether work related or by just playing around getting into to scrapes, and many of these minor injuries were our own fault. I suppose some of them were, but being kicked by a cow couldn't be called our own fault or for that matter being poked in the eye with a cows horn, or being swashed in the eye by a cows tail.
But I suppose being kicked into the gutter by a cow I was supposed to be

milking could have been attributed to what one call negligent. Or as father elegantly put it 'day dreaming'!

The staple remedy for most ailments such as abrasions was of course the dreaded iodine; a liberal application of that liquid from the bottle before being bound up with a bandage was the standard cure. If the dreaded iodine bottle was left out ready to apply another application it was far better to forget we had a injury at all as we tried not to limp or complain trying our very best to be normal! All the time fearing the iodine would be liberally applied again.

As far as I can recall I have never broken a limb either then or since, I have bent them or twisted them or even pulled them out of joint but never actually broken one.

Neither my brother nor me were into climbing trees. Most medical statistics suggest climbing trees is one of the most dangerous pastimes of the younger generation, so by both of us refraining from climbing trees saved everyone a lot of agro.

I can't really recall liking heights at all. What I can remember however is the long wooden ladder at home. The ladder swayed sideways alarmingly as well as in and out as I climbed it to do whatever needed doing at the top, either inside or outside the farm buildings. I wouldn't go onto the roof of a tall building, as even the thought of doing such a thing made me feel quite dizzy. I might have gone onto a single storey building roof if I was forced, but I didn't like it, I couldn't shin up drainpipes like some kids could, I don't know why I just couldn't. But I was in my element riding on a load of loose hay or straw on a cart or trailer, in a way this was just as dangerous as any roof climbing activity.

Don't get me wrong, I liked climbing things. But the situation had to be safe before I started, or I wouldn't do it. One of my favourites was walking across the top rail of five barred gates, but first I had to make sure the gate was secure and not likely to wobble when I was halfway across, or I couldn't do it. Of course I fell off many times before I became expert at the art.

Running on top of dry stone walls, was another of my many pastimes, I found the faster I ran the more likely I was to stay on top of the wall.

However when I did fall off the consequences could be quite nasty, with scrapes to my legs a common occurrence, sometimes slivers of skin from my legs could be seen attached to solid pieces of stone that I had unceremoniously landed amongst after a rapid decision to abort a run. Running on top of downhill sloping dry stone walls was to be avoided as the speed couldn't be controlled satisfactory, whereas up hill was too hard especially if the toppers were loose. I found the ideal situation was to find a wall on a level field, check it out clamber up on to the top and I would be away.

The biggest problem I found with that 'sport' however, was going back to check to see if the toppers were still in place after my run. As sometimes I would step on one that was ready to fall off, and the extra weight of my foot however brief would send it crashing down to the ground. It only took a few minutes to replace any fallen toppers back where they belonged.

My father knew of my what he called daft activities. He didn't mind as long as I kept everything in order. There was no doubt my wall running activities were great fun especially when I was a young teenager. However, one grows out of such things, especially when falling off the walls became more painful.

The older I became the more I had to look at my intended run carefully before even starting.

Later again the activity ceased entirely, to be replaced by something else more conducive to my age.

My cousin Bernard Dyson 'Bud' from Wigtwizzle had a couple of years previously, given me his rather old Ariel 350 motorbike. He explained to my parents that he had signed up for a long period in the military so when he had completed his service, and he was still interested in motorbikes he would buy a newer one anyway. He knew I was mad keen on anything to do with wheels so if my parents would allow him he wanted to give the Ariel to me for nothing.

My mother was dubious but father didn't mind as long as I was careful.

So the Ariel joined my pastime activities. I was nine years old at the time but from then on the Ariel gradually became my main past time either chasing about some rough fields or carrying out chores for father.

As long as there was petrol in the tank the Ariel motorcycle was very handy around the farm. For there were always numerous small tasks that needed doing which needed some form of transport especially if father was working in a far off field, where normally walking was the only means of getting around. With the bike I was able to cut out most if not all of the delay when such things as staples were required for a fence or gate or collecting a new share for the plough.

I remember one of the most difficult things I had to carry on the Ariel was a part roll of barbed wire. I had to wrap it securely in numerous layers of empty cow cake bags, before it was safe for me to sling it over my shoulder and take it to father who was waiting patiently for my return.

Over the many years I have ridden bikes (cycles and motorcycles), I have only had to go into Hospital once to have a motorcycle related accident attended to.

There were definitely three elements to the story, the first of course was a motorcycle, the second a rabbit hole and the a third me. The occasion was when I was riding my motorcycle over a large mound of earth, and I had to put my foot down to the ground to keep my balance, and my foot became trapped down a hole. The loss of balance dragged me off the back of the bike with my foot still trapped in the hole, the resulting damage was a knee joint pulled out of position with my leg almost turned back to front.

It was extremely painful. My knee needed urgent surgery at a Sheffield hospital; I came back home with a huge plaster cast and crutches making things very difficult for me for many weeks.

When I eventually went back to the hospital to have the plaster cast removed, I heard to talk amongst the nurses that my leg had gone bad!

All I know it had smelt terrible for a number of days before the cast was removed. I had to visit hospital a few times afterwards for the doctor to check to make sure my leg was going to be all right.

Relating that story reminds me of the day I had another motorcycle related accident. And that too was very painful at the time.

Whilst messing around one day in an area we knew as the bracken field, I had fallen awkwardly off the old Ariel. This fall resulted in my snapping off part of the handlebars where they are fixed to the front forks, effectively stopping me riding the bike for a day or two. After much searching I eventually discovered a small sized metal milking machine pipe fitted a treat.

Unfortunately the only length I could find was way too long, but as I couldn't find a hacksaw blade to shorten it with I had to make do and mend. So I fitted the much too long length of pipe so I could continue to ride the bike. I could shorten it anytime!

One of my duties in the mornings in the summer time when the cows had been milked was to escort them to a field where they could graze all day until the next milking time in the evening.

After the cows had been loosed out of the milking sheds into the holding yard the next step was for me to escort them to their daytime grazing field.

The cows knew the procedure just as well as I did, always impatient to be away the cows milled around the collecting yard until I was ready. Once we were away it was somewhat similar to Cavalry charge, with me at the front on the Ariel leading the way towards the pasture field.

They ran or galloped behind me with their tails in the air eager to be amongst the fresh grass, and sometimes I had my work cut out keeping my place at the front. If any gates had to be opened I had to have them opened before the mad rush arrived.

Anyway, that particular day I had to pass through a narrow gate, which normally didn't cause any problems except I had completely forgotten about my extra wide handlebars. In consequence both my hands clouted the stone gateposts on each side, the bike stopped dead and I sailed over the front of the bike into a pool of mud. I thought all my fingers had been smashed, they were in a right old mess, I was in agony. It was quite a while before I was able to move the bike out of the way to allow the cows to pass through the gateway. Without the bike I had great difficulty herding the milk cows into the correct grazing field.

After painfully closing the gate behind them I slowly walked (staggered) home, leaving the Ariel where it was, to let mother have a look at my hands. Fortunately, mother declared that nothing was broken but even so my hands were very painful for a long time after that unfortunate experience.

If we had lived nearer to a Hospital I would have had them checked out but we didn't.

It was quite a few weeks later before my hands had recovered sufficiently for me to even think of riding the Ariel again. In the meantime father had obtained and fitted a pair of proper handlebars to the bike. As he explained later he didn't want that to happen again as it affected my work both at school and at home.

Three

Moving on

Around the middle of 1945 my parents received a letter from my school, requesting them to go and see Mrs Lindley - Head teacher of Bolsterstone primary school – about me!

It transpired that Mrs Lindley considered that Wilfred Dyson Couldwell 'still me' was far too clever at certain subjects to remain a pupil at her school. Further to that she had already requested a place to be set aside for me to attend the newly built Junior/ Senior School in Shay house Lane Stocksbridge. And providing my parents agreed I was to attend the bigger school from the beginning of the next term.

Apparently there was a snag to the whole idea; in fact it was a big snag. The difficulty was, I would have to get out of Lewis Scholey's taxi in the village of Bolsterstone each morning, and walk the rest of the way to my new school. Then after each school day I would have to walk back to Bolsterstone, to board the taxi to ride home.

So at the age of nine I was to leave my usual school where all my friends were, and go on to join a new school where I wouldn't know anyone. This was two years earlier than I or anyone else had expected, as normally everyone had to be eleven years old before moving from Bolsterstone to the secondary modern School.

It was quite a shock for me and of course to my parents. For up till then their little boy 'me again' hadn't shown as being particularly bright. What it all meant of course was after my ninth birthday in July 1945. I was going to have to get out of the relatively comfortable school taxi in Bolsterstone village. To make my own way, on my own, on foot via the paved public footpath down three fields through numerous small swing gates, along Spink Hall lane, and walk all the way down Shay house lane to the big new school in Stocksbridge.

Which was I supposed considerably more than a mile. And I was using all the short cuts I knew about. However it was quite a bit further by the road, probably three miles or more, and it was a good job it was too for I had to more or less race the school taxi each and every day from then on.

It was easy walking from Bolsterstone each morning going to school, for one thing it was all 'literally all' down hill, so walking or running wasn't a problem, I could be there almost as quick as the taxi. The problem was later in the day when it was time to go home.

As I wasn't allowed to travel with the others in the taxi from my new school I had to get to Bolsterstone by myself under my own steam literally (so to speak).

For the first few weeks, I remember gradually becoming so annoyed about the fact that all the others were riding in the warm taxi, where as I had to run up the hill to Bolsterstone on my own to join them. My thoughts distracted me so much that the distance became a blur and I would arrive in Bolsterstone village all hot and bothered not remembering much about it.

I remember resorting to asking the teacher of the last lesson of the day if I may leave the class slightly early, even five minutes was helpful. This almost always meant having to explain my reasons for such a request. Some teachers were sympathetic but others weren't.

If I were allowed out of school early, I could arrive in Bolsterstone relatively fresh and happy, but if the teacher was unsympathetic it was hard going.

The extra mileage the taxi had to travel by the road was very important to me, as was any delay the taxi had along the way, giving me more time, and time was so important. I remember many occasions arriving in Bolsterstone Village Square at the last second; absolutely winded tumbling into Lewis Scholeys taxi exhausted.

I remember the times when Mr Vic Barlow was the driver, and when I had chased up the fields and into the village square to arrive at the very last minute only to be left behind as the Taxi School taxi disappeared down Yew Trees Lane. Without me!

Mr Vic Barlow. He was a full time driver employed by Lewis Scholey. Always very good with children, but he was apt to forget that I might be arriving in the village from the other school just a little late, maybe a couple of minutes, no more. But Vic would be ready to go as soon as the last pupil from Bolsterstone School was safely aboard, forgetting completely that I wasn't on board. If he remembered he would wait for me, no problem.

On those occasions when I had been left behind, I was faced with another even longer walk to get home from Bolsterstone to our farm. I had to walk along Heads lane past the cottage where my Grandad Dyson lived at Hungerhill across fields, and along muddy footpaths and cart tracks. Sometimes arriving home in complete darkness covered in mud from the muddy footpaths especially if I had tripped and fallen in a puddle along the way.

During the same difficult period another problem occurred which effected me socially as far as outside the classroom activities were concerned.

Once a week my class year of thirty or so juniors travelled to Sheffield with a Bus taking them for swimming lessons, at Hillsborough swimming Baths.

Once again I was denied what I considered to be normal, as I couldn't go with them, the reason being the swimming Bus always arrived back from Sheffield outside the school gates about ten minutes after Lewis Scholeys school taxi had departed on its way to Bolsterstone.

It all meant if I had gone with them to Sheffield, I would have been left with no alternative but to walk all the way home. Every time.

Consequently I never went even once with my fellow pupils to the Sheffield Baths. Even though in the beginning I wanted to go so I could be like the rest. Eventually as you may imagine I lost all my enthusiasm of wanting to learn how to swim.

After many weeks of letter writing arguing with the authorities my parents eventually extracted enough sense out of them which allowed me to travel all the way from home to the new school in Stocksbridge with the school Taxi. At last things were becoming what I considered to be normal.

If we go back a few weeks, to when I started to attend the new school in Stocksbridge, and to the day when our class was scheduled to use the big assembly hall for a sports lesson. We were sent off to the changing room with instructions to change into to our shorts and pumps for the lesson. All the other kids went back into the hall thus attired, but not me; I didn't have any shorts or pumps. I don't think I had ever seen footwear such as pumps before. However all was not lost for a pair of shorts were quickly found to fit me as were a pair of dark blue coloured pumps.

I never did have a pair of pumps of my own as my mother refused to buy me any, but I did prevail on her to buy me a pair of shorts, eventually she conceded by declaring they could be quite useful. It was the same with football boots.

I never had a pair of my own so when it was football training I had to make do with a pair from the cupboard in the changing room, no doubt they were someone else's cast off".

Because I lived in an isolated environment I continued to have problems with my education.

For when I was old enough, I managed to qualify and be selected to attend Barnsley technical college. However I could not take up the offer, for there was only one way for me to get there and that was to catch the Barnsley bus at Midhopestones. This meant I would have to walk the five miles or so each way every time I went, and I didn't fancy that at the time.

So I attended night school in Stocksbridge instead travelling by bicycle studying cabinet making and engineering.

Cabinet making! Because that was my favourite subject during the whole time I was a student at the Stocksbridge secondary school. When I had completed any examinations I always finished up top of the class. The tutor didn't particularly like that situation and he regularly demonstrated his - lets say jealousy - by subjecting the whole class to some difficult task and he gave me some of the most difficult ones to boot.

However, when I started to attend night school I had to choose between two completely different categories, one was Mechanical and the other was Electrical Engineering. I chose electrical because my forward thinking suggested that the promised mains electrical supply that would eventually come to our area could be more profitable in the long run.

I became interested in electrical engineering when I was quite young, I can remember equipping some of our beds in our house with little lights attached to the Head boards, powered by a double cell cycle battery. Using a small toggle switch and a small screw in type bulb. The idea worked it proved to be far superior to the candles we had used previously.

Later father bought a small petrol powered generator from the Club Inn Midhopestones; the generator became redundant when the village was connected to the mains supply.

After the mains were connected to the public house, the regular customers were able to enjoy their pints in relative peace. For the sound of the generator exhaust had been a feature for many years as it topped up the batteries to keep the bar room illuminated.

I remember well the day we collected the generator from the Club Inn with our tractor and trailer. I wasn't old enough to have a licence to drive the tractor on the road so father had to drive, and we had to be careful with the many glass accumulators for they were quite vulnerable to breakage besides being filled with acid and to boot they were very heavy.

Back at our farm just inside the coalhouse door, was a little room that had been used for years as a dog kennel. Father had already decided that it was the ideal place to house the new (to-us) generator.

So father turned the dogs out much to their annoyance and he constructed a concrete base to bolt the engine and dynamo down to the floor. Luckily the little room had a flat roof made of stone slabs; the space on top was normally piled up with all manner of rubbish. With all that cleared away the resulting space left plenty of room for the many glass batteries to be stored.

With the engine below and the batteries above it was certainly a very compact arrangement.

One of the most difficult parts of the job however was knocking a hole through the wall to allow the engine exhaust pipe and silencer to pass through to the outside. The wall was all of two foot thick so it took father hours of crashing and banging accompanied by intermittent bouts of swearing to eventually make a hole in the wall big enough for the exhaust pipe to go through.

At first we found the sound of the generator exhaust a little difficult to get used to, as usually when all the daytime activity of farm work ceased, all one had been able to hear in the evenings were the sounds of the night.

Not anymore, the only sound we could hear now was the sharp bark of the exhaust of the petrol engine as it constantly charged the storage batteries. Don't get me wrong, the engine didn't have to run all the time, but if we were using a lot of lights they would soon begin to fade as the batteries ran down. To elevate the problem we found it best to let the engine run especially whilst the house lights were being used.

It only took me a few weeks to wire some of the farm buildings to take advantage of the new (to us) phenomenon. The light intensity wasn't too good but it was better and safer than oil lights or storm lanterns.

Travelling to Stocksbridge by bicycle to continue my night school education had its own problems. Riding to the evening classes was easy for the going was almost all-downhill but returning home afterwards was a pain literally. I remember I always struggled with the bike on the return journey, especially when it was dark, as my only illumination was the twin cell cycle lights. Sometimes I had to resort to pushing where the going became too steep.

I remember the bicycle well, it was a black Gents Wigfalls Royal sit up and beg style machine that I had acquired for next to nothing. Heavy in comparison to some of my earlier home built lightweight machines.

One day I had read in a motorcycle magazine about the advantages of a new style engine attachment intended for cycles.

The 'bumf ' suggested it would revolutionise travelling by bicycle. So I wrote to the manufacturing company concerned asking for more information, and it did indeed sound interesting. The information even suggesting it might be just what I wanted or better still needed. Maybe that was the point when things started to take a turn for the better.

The attachment known as the 'Mini Moto' was powered by a tiny petrol engine. The assembly had to be affixed to the rear of the bike in a position similar to where a carrier normally fitted.

I began to beg of my parents to buy me one, and they eventually conceded to my request after I had repeatedly extolled the advantages that it would afford me.

I reminded them that by having one fitted to my bike would make it much easier for me to attend my evening classes.

When the Mini Moto arrived I found it was quite easy to fit, but after testing I was slightly disappointed when I discovered it wasn't as powerful as I had expected!

However it did save me considerable effort on the level and slight inclines. On the steeper hills it failed to impress me as I had to put quite a lot of effort into the pedals to help the little engine maintain any sort of speed.

Right from the start it had two speeds slow and slower still.

I suppose the fact that I had two dynamos fitted to provide satisfactory lighting didn't help matters. Down hill and on the level the lights were brilliant, uphill however the light intensity left a lot to be desired for they faded or went out completely.

I put up with the Wigfalls/Mini Moto means of transport whilst I saved from my meagre income of catching rabbits and grouse beating on the moors until I had saved enough to indulge in a proper motorcycle.

Later in the year I began travelling to Sheffield with the Wigfalls Royal engine powered machine with the sole intention of having a look in motorcycle shop windows to see what was on offer.

I returned home on one occasion armed with some literature that described the little BSA bantam 125cc machine as a 'popular runabout'. But I couldn't find one for sale at the time.

Whilst searching the motorcycle press I discovered 'Kings motorcycles' of Manchester had one advertised for a certain figure delivered, after gathering my meagre finances together I posted a suitable deposit to them, and my parents agreed to sign for the balance on HP.

The little bike was transported in the guard's van of a passenger train from Manchester to Deepcar railway station.

Kings had informed me earlier that before despatch all the fuel would have to be drained from the fuel tank because of the British rail fire rules.

So I carried half a gallon in a can on my back as I walked all the way from Garlic House to Deepcar to collect the bike.

The little BSA revolutionised my travelling. I know it was only a 123cc engine, but it travelled up and down the hills in and around our area without any problems whatsoever for quite a while before I converted it to a competition machine.

And that as they say is another story.

After about a year of having to mess about with the increasingly unpredictable second hand generator father had bought from the Club Inn Midhopestones. He finally announced he was going to buy a proper 240volt AC full blown generator, which didn't need any batteries, only the one to start it with.

As far as I can recall Delco Remy an American Company manufactured the equipment.

It loudly announced in its advertisement that it would run all the lights we needed on the farm and a television if we had one! And drive the milking machine vacuum pump much more efficiently than the petrol engine.

The generator father decided to invest in was the lesser (or cheaper) of the two on offer. Starting the engine on the one he ordered was by pressing a starting button secured to the equipment, whereas the deluxe version started automatically when a light switch was pressed anywhere in the system. Father reasoned in view of the extra cost it wasn't worth the luxury of buying the higher priced version, for the generator was going to be housed in the same building as the existing one anyway so starting it wouldn't be a problem.

Father only fear as far as I can recall was when he realised the engine would be running all the time we needed power. Of course it would have a more efficient silencer fitted than the one we were using at the time, and because it was a twin cylinder engine the noise emitted wouldn't be as pronounced as a single cylinder.

In consequence I had to rewire the farm yet again.
To do a thorough job I had to install an overhead yard crossing to supply the milking parlour and the building where the electric motor was to be installed to drive the milk pump.
I wired up all the haylofts and the corn chambers making the paraffin storm lamps almost redundant. After I had completed the rewire it was a pleasure to work in our farm buildings or in the house where I had fitted a couple of sockets for chance we obtained a better television at some later stage. And I fitted the luxury of an outside swan neck light over the house door to light up our way to the coal shed and the toilet.
It took me quite a while to complete the job but it was worth it. Because I was studying electrical engineering I had established an account with the London Wholesale Warehouse Queens road Peckham London SE15 to supply me as and when I needed electrical spares.
I have in my hand as I write a delivery note numbered A 6721 dated 16/11/54. It may be for some of the spares I was using at the time to rewire Garlic House.
Most of the heavier electrical fittings and rolls of wire were delivered to Deepcar railway station, from where I collected them with my little BSA motorbike. The postwomen delivered some of the lighter parcels. I can remember Mrs Poppleton who ran the Bolsterstone Post office one-day jokingly complaining about the extra parcels that they had to deliver now I had started with my part time electrical work.

Four

Garlic House farm

It was in the early spring of nineteen thirty-five when my father took over the tenancy of the 200 acre hill farm known as Garlic House Farm Ewden, Bolsterstone, Nr Sheffield.

The farm was clinging on grimly to a rain lashed hillside surrounded on three sides by the heather clad moorland of the Broomhead estate.

Father had previously arranged to have delivered the few head of cattle he had been able to buy to start his new life as a farmer, and they were to be delivered when he actually moved into the farm. On his first walk around the farm he was disappointed to find there wasn't a single gate hanging or otherwise between any of the stone gateposts separating the fields. So his first job was to arrange some make shift pole barriers to keep his small herd of cattle in the field he wanted them to stay in.

He had planned on mowing some of the fields to provide hay to feed the cattle during the coming winter months, but he soon discovered the fields were so poor hardly any grass grew at all, never mind good enough to mow for hay! Nonetheless he mowed every field that was accessible with his own horse plus a borrowed horse and mowing machine, (He always declared he had mowed every blade of grass he could find) and the resulting yield was a paltry ten cart loads of poor quality hay. He realised that the haul was nowhere near enough to feed his small herd of growing stock.

Father had kept on with his job at Samuel Fox and Co the steel makers of Stocksbridge where he'd worked for a number of years, working eight-hour shifts. His job entailed unloading pig iron by hand from railway trucks; his usual transport to work at that time was by motorbike and sidecar. However on some occasions especially in good weather, he preferred to walk to work instead passing on the way the extensive Oxley Park (twenty or more acres) recreational grounds owned and maintained by the local Stocksbridge council.

On one such occasion he'd noticed the long unmown grass in the park, noting that no one had attempted to mow it. Just what he wanted to make up the deficiency what was lacking at home on his farm.

So during that days shift at work he thought long and hard about what he had seen or more to the point what to do about it.

He made the decision to visit to the town hall as soon as he had finished work at 2 PM that same day to ask the management what they intended to do with the grass in the park.

After work father went to the town hall to make enquirers about the grass, and he was informed that something drastic had happened to the council' grass-mowing machine.

This had consequently delayed the workforce from cutting any grass anywhere in the Stocksbridge area, including Oxley Park.

Spurred on by this information my father quickly suggested he would do the job for free if he could have the resulting grass for nowt. The grounds-man' office was quickly contacted, and father' proposal was agreed to in principal, providing he made a good job of it!

So far so good! However as Oxley Park was quite some distance from Garlic House, father would have to borrow another horse (he only owned one horse, and mowers were two horse machines) and a mowing machine to do the job. So he went to see Albert Hague of Waldershague Hall farm Bolsterstone, (a farmer he had worked for when he was a teenage farm labourer), and to his delight Albert offered to lend him a horse and mower. When a suitable day arrived father rode his own work horse from Garlic House to Waldershague, hitched it and the borrowed horse to the mower, and travelled with the team all the way down from Bolsterstone to the park in Stocksbridge to mow the grass he so desperately needed.

Apparently he mowed all the grass in the park during one long session. Later when the hay was ready to haul he borrowed a dray from the same farmer, and using his own horse he hauled the entire crop back to Garlic House. This was achieved by riding his heavy cart horse and dray to the park each day where he un-harnessed the animal. Letting it loose whilst he completed his shift at the works.

After his shift finished at fox's he'd walk back up the hill to the Park, catch his horse attach it to the borrowed Dray and from then on it was a case of loading and hauling the hay all the way home. He did that every day until he had cleared the entire crop of good quality hay from Oxley Park. The distance in miles from Garlic House to the park was all of six miles or even more, and it wasn't the easiest road to travel with a dray and a load of hay.

It must have been very hard going for him but it saved his small herd of cows from going hungry during the following winter months, that was all that mattered to him at the time.

One day in the spring or early summer of 1940, father was going round the stock doing his daily routine of counting suckling cows with their calves and rearers when he discovered he was a couple of beasts short. He realised it was not unusual for young animals to go missing for a day or so, they would usually just turn up none the worse after some adventure somewhere, but on that occasion they didn't, as they were still missing the next day.

He let it go for another day before he became worried enough to make a better search with his dog only to find them both dead almost submerged in a swampy area in one of the heavily wooded areas towards the neighbouring farm of Nether House. Sadly he moved the rest of the cattle into a nearby secure area he had been hoping to mow for hay.

Later during the summer when he thought the ground was dryer he moved the stock back into the area but the same thing happened. Again he lost a couple of good strong heifers.

So he complained to the Broomhead Estate office, declaring the area was costing him stock he could ill afford to loose and more importantly what could they do about the situation!

Nothing happened for a while until it became common knowledge to everyone in the area that the farm further up our road known as Cottage farm was being broken up, and ceasing to operate as a working farm.

Fathers' ears picked up the information and he quickly contacted the Broomhead Estate office to put forward the suggestion. 'If Garlic House was to give up the fields nearer to Nether House farm (the one where he had lost the stock earlier) could the estate let him have some of the land coming available from Cottage farm which bordered our farm Garlic house, instead?'

Broomhead replied enthusiastically by suggesting he take all the land belonging to Cottage farm if he wanted it! But regrettably the estate would have to raise his rent accordingly in consequence.

Father briefly considered the idea but quickly rejected it, for the level of the rent was going to be too high, more than he considered it was worth, or could afford!

Eventually they came to a compromise where father selected the fields he wanted in exchange for the ones he didn't. Most importantly to father without any increase in the rent.

Broomhead hummed and arred for a while before finally agreeing to his practical suggestion. The exchange increased our farms acreage very slightly but the quality of the land was far better and as an added bonus he would be able to grow better crops such as cereal or arable whereas before most of the land was only fit for grass. And it was nearer home into the bargain.

I recall whilst I was of a young age having to milk cows by hand before going to school and again when I came home again in the evening, until father bought our first milking machine in 1947. Whilst I milked cows by hand a certain ritual had to be adhered to so both the cow and myself knew where we stood, so to speak. First thing to do was turn my flat cap around so the neb (peak) was to the back. Place my milking stool in the correct position on the floor by the side of the cow, making sure there was a single leg to the rear. Sit down on the stool and wedge my head in the hollow in the side of the cow - where the cows rear leg meets its belly- all the while talking quietly to the cow to settle it down, before placing the milking pail between my knees ready to start.

I mention above with a 'single stool leg to the rear'! In practical terms what this meant was if the cow proved to be restless and moving about, I was able to lean backwards to the left or to the right or forwards whilst I was still sat on the stool without actually falling off. All genuine milking stools had three legs especially made for that reason or purpose.

When I first started to help with the milking I was usually given an older more placid animal to milk but occasionally if I felt adventurous I would have a go at milking one of the Ayrshire's father kept in the top shed. I knew before I started that Ayrshire's were temperamental and they let it be known pretty early how temperamental they were, by trying a well placed kick before I was even prepared or ready.

Then of course everything could finish up in the gutter including the milk pail, milking stool and of course me. Then a row would be the result between father and me for letting it happen. Then another row between the cow and me, for not allowing me to settle first.

Father knew instinctively that I hadn't been fully concentrating on my work or daydreaming, (as he put it) and any lost milk running down the drain was a complete waste.

Nevertheless I still had to do my stint of helping with the milking before going to school each morning. So there was always a deadline to meet, that was when Lewis Scholey with his school taxi arrived at the farm gate. Most mornings I would be standing outside the gate ready and waiting.

However, if things had not gone to plan and we were late Lewis Scholey would come into our farmyard, to stick his head through the open top half of the milking shed door and loudly bellow, 'Hurry up, Hurry up, up, Hurry up. Then he'd quickly trot back to his car to wait for me.

He knew I would immediately abandon my milking job and dash into the house to quickly have a wash and change into my school clothes, rush out again into the taxi in double quick time, (no wonder I smelt of cows all day).

If we had family or friends visiting, the kids or even their parents nearly always wanted to watch us, as we milked the cows by hand. And I didn't especially like it! I became paranoid about visitors being around when it was milking time.

They would try all sorts of reasons why I should let them have a go at milking. I always refused or completely ignored all their pleas or request, as I knew very well if anyone other than father or me had even tried to mess about with a cow's udder a sound well placed kick would be a reward. I was only doing my work, but I'm sure they thought it was a spectacle, or I was a spectacle. I even thought I was probably a butt for their jokes.

On some occasions the kids would start to run around the parlour alarming the cows. I was always afraid the cow I was milking would eventually take exception and kick everything me included into the gutter, as some of the younger cows could and did regularly.

On such occasions father sometimes had to step in and clear the parlour of noisy kids or warn their parents about keeping control. Some of the younger new calved heifers were always difficult to milk at the best of times without added distractions.

In those early years when we milked the cows by hand most of the milk we produced was either to feed the calves or for use in the house for making butter or cream. In 1946 our farm became a registered milk producer and all the milk was then sold to the MMB (Milk Marketing Board).

A little joke may be in order here, the Milk marketing head office was at a place known as Thames Ditton and my father always insisted in referring to it as 'Thomas Ditton'.

Father had earlier in the year requested Broomhead estates to alter some of the buildings to conform to the rigorous standards required by the MMB, the

33

contract to alter the buildings was awarded to Bertram Shaw the estate builder from Bolsterstone.

Bertram finished the building alterations just in time for us to start at the date set by the MMB and to add to the excitement father had also invested in one of the new 'Fullwood milking machines'; this was also installed just in time. So it was a revolution at Garlic House for we not only had a new milking parlour but also a new milking machine as well. Could it get any better?

Father soon discovered that by using the new mechanical milking machine made the job so much easier and quicker he even bought more milking cows to add to his herd.

During that time most if not all of the milk went into the churn to be sold, and the money it raised was the main income for the farm.

Father had built a milk stand of stone with a huge flat stone slab on the top on to which we could just about fit four ten gallon milk churns to await collection.

The churns were placed there on the milk stand with appropriate labels attached.

The Labels listed the producers' name, the date, the farm name, and the total number of churns to be collected that day, with the total gallonage of the shipment.

The churns had to be there on the stand waiting for when the milk lorry came around to collect them at about 10 o'clock each morning including Sundays.

I can hear it even now 60 years later, as the big green Albion lorry laboured up Ewden Beck hill on its way from Broomhead home farm to our farm each day.

For more than a decade our milk was collected by the same lorry with the same two drivers who shared the driving over the entire period, one week it would be 'Little Bill', and the following week it would be 'Big Bill'! And vice versa.

Little Bill was as the term suggests was rather short in height but made up for that shortcoming by his width, added to that he was immensely strong. His way of dealing with full milk churns was to hoist the milk churn up onto his shoulder. Trot across to the lorry and drop it in the precise position he wanted amidst loud banging and clattering of all the other similar 100 or so milk churns already on board.

Whereas Big Bill who was much taller, had a huge belly sticking out front. He just bent his knees to grab the churn by its handles, perch it on his belly with his arms wrapped around the churn, then he'd waddle across to the lorry, and with a huge heave the churn would be installed exactly where he wanted it on the lorry. Two completely different characters achieving the same end result.

In the summer time and the sun was hot we had some difficulty keeping the milk cool before the lorry collected it. Father's method was to immerse the churns in the stone, cold water trough, until we could hear the collecting lorry grinding its way up our hill. Then he would pull them out of the water and trundle them across and lift them onto the stand just in time before the lorry arrived. In winter it was obviously different, I can remember the time when any churns standing on the stand waiting to be collected had there lids precariously perched on a column of solid frozen milk sticking out of the churn tops, but the quality of the milk was never effected.

Were we talking about stones?

At Garlic House farm the soil was so shallow, everytime we ploughed some of the fields new stones would come up, especially after 1947 when we used our new Ferguson tractor to plough the land.

The tractor plough went quite a bit deeper than the horse plough had done for centuries, in consequence before a crop could be planted or even cultivated ready for a crop to be planted, we had to pick off the stones by hand that had come to the surface.

A lot of them were small enough to be thrown onto the trailer to be hauled out of the field and used for repairing roadways or gateway entrances. But sometimes they were just tipped in a heap in a corner of a field for future use. On occasion I have known slabs as big as a table top sticking up in the field, these had to dragged away by chain hitched to the tractor so we could get on with preparing the field.

It could be, I suppose, the slab of stone on top of our milk stand came from one of our own fields! I remember ploughshares were sometimes a problem, the standard Ferguson ones were made of cast steel and would break so easy when challenged by a stone underground so father had to buy them by the score to keep things going.

Eventually he became wise to the problem and started to invest in better quality items, these had hardened tips to make them last longer. He found out it was a lot cheaper over a season.

The corn crops we grew at Garlic House were mostly for our own use. These were used as feed for the milking cows, or rearers. Oats, wheat, barley or rye cannot be fed to stock in its raw state - as harvested; it has to be milled, ground or rolled, or the grain will go straight through the animal, without being digested.

Father grew all these variations of cereal crops at some time or other. We had to transport our grain for milling by tractor and trailer to the nearest corn mill, which was in our case at Oxspring nr Penistone. The name of the millers at that time was Goldthorpes.

Goldthorpes corn mill in Oxspring was down a lane off the main Penistone to Wortley road near Penistone. I can remember all through the period that we transported our grain to Goldthorpes for milling, I would always find myself inside the shed where the steam engine used for driving the mill was housed; it stood down in a pit with the workings showing just above floor level.

It was an enormous and wonderful steam engine with its brass fittings gleaming and a flywheel that must have been ten foot tall at least. I remember standing there open-mouthed watching it as it drove the many shafts connected to the various operations of a working corn mill.

It was a noisy place with the flat drive belts flapping and clacking but the actual steam engine ran so quiet it was almost silent, just a small amount of hissing and slight puffing or so it seemed to me.

I remember we usually had to wait some time for the corn mill personnel to locate and get the appropriate comparable milled feed ready into a position where it could be bagged, weighed, and loaded onto whatever transport we had on the day, which was usually a tractor and trailer.

So I had to make sure I was ready to go and help when father shouted me.

However father had to buy in other feeding stuffs to supplement our own milled feed for the milk cows especially, such as 'Sugar beet pulp'; this came in huge hession bags. The Sugar beet inside was so light the supplier had to use huge bags to make up any-sort of weight. I remember they were difficult to carry especially through narrow doors and passageways, and they took up a lot of room in the buildings where it was stored.

The cows loved Sugar beet pulp, and the milk yield and quality improved whenever we used it, father always declared it was worth buying.

Another feeding product that the milk cows liked were known as 'Brewers grains' reputed to be the residue from the breweries in Sheffield. Brewer's grains didn't smell very nice but the cows loved some mixed in with their feed. However it wasn't always available, so we had to be careful how much we fed to the cows to make it last.

Another product we had to buy in was flaked maze, this was used sparingly for the livestock but more liberal when it was fed to the laying hens, it was reputed to make the egg yokes a more brighter yellow colour, just what the decerning housewife wanted at that time.

After much deliberation father eventually decided we must have our own corn mill, he plumped for a relatively new type of corn grinder known as a 'Hammer Mill'.

The company supplying the new mill not only delivered it but installed it as well in our 'Lathe'

(Stone barn). This was the stone barn with the tall double threshing doors that opened directly into the farmyard. A flat belt drove the new corn-grinding mill, so father had to go to Penistone, to buy a suitable belt from the agricultural agents in the cattle market. Taking careful note beforehand of how long the belt had to be to reach the drive pulley on the back of our Ferguson tractor, when it was parked just outside the barn door.

If the big double doors were closed when the mill was running the drive belt had to pass through the little access door so anyone wanting to go in or out of the building when the mill was running had to step over the flapping belt. Precarious I know, and awkward, sometimes downright dangerous especially if the visitor was a stranger.

If our visitor was a woman she had to hitch up her skirts first before stepping over the belt that ran through the barn doorway.

We soon found the standard hopper on the new Hammer mill was much too small! In actual fact the mill gobbled up grain so quickly that keeping the feeding hopper full became a pain, so we made another much bigger one. Eventually fabricating a wooden hopper which held enough grain to last half an hour or so. It worked a treat after we had ironed out a few initial teething problems. But the noise the Hammer mill made whilst it was running was unbelievable, it howled something terrible in fact it could be heard two or three fields away from the farm, no doubt it did a good job as the finished meal was quite acceptable to the cows.

Talking about noise! When everything was running there were the hammer mill, the milking machine vacuum pump, and the generator, so all in all Garlic House Farm had become very noisy. It was a good job it didn't go on all day!

At other times living at Garlic House was as tranquil as it always had been before the age of mechanical inventions took over.

My brother Lewis recently reminded me to look up my records of 1949. And they revealed an interesting fact, that 1949 was the year when we had problems with our water supply.

The year when the spring supplying the water to the stone water trough in the farmyard and the house became reduced to a trickle.

And when father went up to the top pasture field to check the water situation there, he discovered the spring feeding the trough there had dried up completely! This discovery made the situation serious for we relied on the top pasture water for the milk cows to get enough for their needs during the daytime whilst they were out grazing.

What were we going to do about it? That was the big question. Things were turning into something of a panic at Garlic House for the situation hadn't actually happened before certainly not whilst father had been the occupant of the farm anyway. Obviously the animals couldn't manage without water; especially the milk cows as they each drank gallons of water every day.

After much thinking father decided that we would have to move the barbed wire fence that normally kept our cows away from the bank of a small stream in a corner of our furthest field, this would allow the stock to drink straight from the stream.

But when we went to move the fence we discovered even that stream had been reduced to a mere trickle. So we dug a sump in the bed to allow enough of the slow running water to collect so the cows could have a proper drink.

Father even contemplated driving the stock down to the beck at the bottom of the hill each day to let them drink their fill in the main river. But the practicalities of such an operation would have meant it would have taken all day to complete the job, so the idea was shelved.

For the immediate future, at least. However, the situation took a turn for the worse when the house water tap ran dry! Then father had no alternative but to approach Uncle Jim Dyson the manager of Broomhead farm. To ask him if we could fill some milk churns from their water in the farmyard at Broomhead, to use in our house and wash up our dairy utensils.

He readily agreed to our request, but told us to be careful not to take too much at any one time, for even that supply was slowing down.

We knew the Broomhead water supply was piped from a souce quite some distance up the Broomhead moor, I also remember it tasted slightly of peat, but we didn't care what it tasted like so long as it was drinkable.

So every day we had to travel with the tractor and link box loaded with four 10-gallon milk churns to Broomhead to fetch water from their trough in the main yard, hauling it across Ewden beck to Garlic house. We didn't have any rain at all for many weeks or even months that year before a series of thunderstorms finally brought to an end the drought. As always happens in situations like that. Once it started to rain it didn't know when to stop! Fields soon became flooded and boggy, the beck was full and noisy, and we soon forgot that we had come through the driest summer recorded during the then recent history.

It had side effects of course for all the corn and root crops that year were so poor father even had to buy some in. There's a saying in farming circles relaying the legend 'Always have a Bay of hay spare in the barn as a reserve for the following year'.

Unfortunately during the following autumn and the winter there was hardly enough hay to feed the stock, never mind leaving a reserve.

Of course we had some lighter moments at Garlic House. One of them was for instance when a fellow who (I can't recall his name) when he came to see us always finished up parading around the farmyard with something perched on his chin. It could have been anything such as a pitchfork, hay rake, a calf bucket, yard broom or shovel.

If the item could be lifted onto his chin he could balance it there as he walked around the yard. If he tripped or stumbled on the uneven ground, he would stagger around amongst the loose stones until he regained his balance, it was very rare for him to loose whatever he had perched on his chin. His antics always made us all fall about laughing.

This brings to mind an unforgettable incident that happened one afternoon in summertime as I recall it was well before milking time when a youngish fellow rushed into our farmyard wanting to buy some milk. He had apparently parked his small car in the entrance to Ewden Wood just down the road from our farm. Just as his family was settling down to have a picnic, and feed their two-week-old baby boy; they found to their consternation they hadn't brought the babies milk with them. Understandably they panicked, quickly they remembered passing a farm on the way down the hill (ours) so the father ran up the hill to our farm with an urgent request for milk to feed the little one. My father explained to the fellow that all the spare milk had been used in the house that particular day and the cows were out grazing in fields quite some distance away.

The chap was desperate even suggesting substantial remuneration for any inconvenience if my father could fetch in a cow to extract some milk to satisfy his offspring's immediate needs.

However gathering a herd of cows and driving them back to the farm is one thing but persuading one cow on its own is quite another. Even with a dog!

Eventually agreeing to the desperate plea's of the fellow, father had great difficulty (As predicted) in rounding up and persuading one cow to come quietly to be brought home on its own, it took a long time before he reappeared driving the reluctant milk cow.

The cow knew it wasn't milking time so it was very indignant about being separated from the herd so there was quite a lot of bellowing involved.

The cow didn't take kindly to being milked at the wrong time of day either. Eventually the required amount was supplied to the by then desperately impatient father who thanked everyone profusely for the service tearing off at a rapid rate running back down Ewden Hill to feed his no doubt yelling infant.

Our family and the Bradley (their name) family became firm friends. We soon learned that Mr Bradley's mode of transport was an Austin 7 soft-top, and that they lived in small town called Middlestown located somewhere near the large industrial town of Wakefield Yorkshire.

This leads us on to another related incident.

This was during 1945 and George V1 the King and his daughter Elizabeth were due to come up from London to declare open the Ladybower Reservoir in Derbyshire. We had heard about the intended celebrations but we couldn't do anything about attending the spectacle, the location was too far away to walk, and we didn't have any suitable transport other than the tractor.

Anyway, Mr Bradley in his Austin 7 unexpectedly arrived at the farm gate early on the morning of the September celebrations declaring he was on his way to the Royal opening of the Ladybower reservoir, he asked my parents if he could take my brother Lewis and me with him.

Understandably we were both ecstatic about the idea, so we pleaded with our parents to let us go, eventually they said, yes we could. We both excitedly climbed into the back of the Austin 7 car to sit on the leather seats. My brother and me soon noticed how tiny the Austin 7 really was, for our experience of riding in motor cars at that time had been restricted to the ones Lewis Scholey came with to take us to School in the mornings. Even though the vehicles were quite variable they had one thing in common; they were all big and roomy.

Our regular taxi was usually a black wedding limousine I think it was a Daimler, and sometimes it had confetti scattered all over the interior, and smelt of perfume.

Another regular car was a huge black Austin with two rows of seats in the back, at other times Lewis would come to collect us with a shiny black Rolls Royce, or on a few occasions a Daimler hearse! Yes a hearse!

For Lewis Scholey's everyday business was Scholeys the undertaker of Deepcar. I suppose to make his cars work for a living they had to be used for the daily school run as well.

Anyway back to my story. Understandably the Austin 7 did seem very small in comparison. I remember quite well Mr Bradley driving along the road that passes by the Strines Inn.

The road in those days was quite bumpy (it probably still is) and I can remember very clearly my brother and me hitting our heads on the roof of the car, as we bounced and bumped along the road on our way to Ladybower. Maybe it was the framework? I'm not sure now because the car had what was called a soft-top. Anyway we both thought the whole trip hilarious we thoroughly enjoyed our day out with Mr Bradley, even though I cannot recall seeing the King whatsoever!

Relating to you that little snippet brings to mind an incident my brother Lewis reminded me about. Not related whatsoever to the above story just that it happened around the same period.

It was at the time when the mobile hen sheds had been dragged by the horse from one of the furthest fields to a location much nearer home, just across the road from our farm entrance.

Our hen houses had to be dragged, because they were on skids not like some others of that time that were on wheels.

Anyway mother always looked after the hens carrying the feed to them twice a day. I tried to help where I could no doubt sometimes being a nuisance rather than help. As usual we dropped the flaps on the sheds for the hens to come out to feed in the long troughs into which we had poured their feed. Out jumps the big red cockerel, as normal he glared around at everyone and everything. He was such a nuisance for he persisted in flying at mother or me almost everytime we went to feed them.

Well that day just as I walked away to have a look at the level of the spring water in the water trough the hens used, the big red cockerel ran up behind me and pecked me at the back of my leg behind my knee. I was furious. Apparently I chased that cockerel everywhere until I eventually caught it. I grabbed it by the neck and dragged it struggling and squawking across the field to the water trough and held its head under the water until it stopped struggling, then I released it.

But it was dead. Drowned, and I was glad. That cockerel had been warned by me many times about its behaviour and that day it both frightened me and made me so mad I finished it off.

However it wasn't wasted we had it for dinner.

It was a big bird and I was only eight years old, so when it was all fluffed up for a fight it was nearly as big as I was. The incident was the talking point in our house for months after that, relating the somewhat by then amusing episode of the time our Wilfred killed the big red cockerel.

Both my brother and me can remember the incident quite clearly. So you my readers all now know as well. The wound where the cockerel had pecked me behind my knee was very painful and it took many weeks before it finally healed.

And yet another story comes to mind, just as above during a similar period.

As we go through the stone barn 'Lathe' and into the fodder room, there's a flight of flat treaded wooden steps that take us up to the corn chamber above. One day the steps had been taken away to use somewhere else, and for some reason my brother Lewis and me wanted to urgently go up into the corn chamber.

I went up first clambering up the hay-rack on the right hand side then with a struggle I was able to grab the edges of the hole where the ladder normally fitted and then drag myself up into the chamber above.

I lay flat on the wooden chamber floor and reached down for my little brother to grab his hand to steady him as he struggled with the manoeuvre. He was almost up when my hand slipped; and down he went all the way to the stone flagged floor below landing on his head.

I was aghast and horrified, as he lay there crumpled up on the floor below. I rapidly retraced my actions to get down to his level, being careful not to fall myself, and to my relief Lewis was able to stand up and we both went to seek help from mother in the house.

Obviously mother was mad as she franticly wiped the blood off his head to make sure there was no permanent damage; I hovered in the background knowing when father heard the news I would be in for it. I remember surviving a more or less verbal beating. Both Lewis and I had to promise not to attempt such a foolhardy venture ever again!

In that same fodder room another incident on another occasion took place which I shall never forget. There is or more accurately was a row of pot bellied wooden corn tubs on the right hand side as one walked towards the flat steps I have just mentioned. In the tubs we kept such feeding stuffs as layers mash for the hens, calf nuts for the young rearers or flaked maze to mix with almost anything.

Anyway one day as I went to scoop some of the feed out of one of the barrels, I had to lean right down inside to be able to reach the small amount left in the bottom, and I was at a most vulnerable and critical position. In fact I was almost overbalancing and falling inside, when something bit my hand, I was shocked, I screamed I went berserk. It was a huge rat. I had always been afraid of rats for some reason but to be bitten by one when I was not in a position to defend myself was at the least totally unacceptable. I wouldn't ever put my hand inside a tub after that without first looking inside to make sure there was nothing in there waiting to attack me.

I can't stand rats even now 60 years later, even though I have caught them in traps I just don't like to be exposed to a rat.

Because our farm was situated in a tourist area, sometimes during summer months we had an influx of what one might call walkers or hikers, sometimes cyclists.

Many knocked on our house door asking for a drink of water.

If father was within hearing he always directed them to the stone water trough near the yard gate, perfectly good spring water always full to the top and clear as a bell to the very bottom.

A few of the assembled walkers took father at his word and knelt down on the base stone to have a long cold drink just like we always did.

But others, no they wanted a cup of water from the tap in the house even after we explained it was just the same water, it came from the same spring just directed by a pipe to the house instead of to the outside water trough.

Father would quickly get his hair off with them telling them in no uncertain terms

'If tha wants a sup er watter that bad get thessen darn like ivvry wun else and have a sup there's nowt wrong wi it its just cawed'. Some did as they were bid others didn't they would rather do without than have a drink at our water trough.

Another more serious incident happened one year. It was on a Sunday early in the spring maybe Easter time, just after we had had a delivery of Superphosphates.

Superphosphates are a fertiliser for the land. On one particular day it was lashing down with rain, and a bunch of hikers had taken shelter in the open fronted cart shed where the fertiliser was stacked. We didn't take any particular notice of them, but we knew they were there because of the noise they were making, but walkers or hikers didn't normally do any harm so father left them to it. But later in the day when they had gone and father was checking round to see if everything was in order he found someone had slashed a couple of the fertiliser bags open with something sharp allowing the contents to spill out onto the floor. What a mess!

Because the cart shed floor was made up of compacted dirt it was normally wet with damp and by the time father saw the damage the Superphosphates powder was already starting to become a sticky mess. It's a fact that if Superphosphates fertiliser is exposed to the slightest moisture it turns into what resembles highly toxic putty. Then it cannot be used in a shutter drill at all afterwards so it had to be spread on the land by shovel.

After that incident Father declared he was going to close up the cart shed to walkers so they couldn't use is as a refuge from the elements but I don't recall whether he ever did carry his threat out.

Earlier in this chapter I mentioned Garlic House Farm as clinging grimly to the hillside! This is not an empty statement or even jest. For when a team of ministry personnel came around one day to check the sea level bracket attached to one of the stone barn walls. We were told that our farm buildings were sliding down the hillside at the rate of an inch each time the bracket was checked. What he failed to tell us (and we never asked) however was how often was the level checked.

From that day we lived with the fear that one-day the farm would suddenly collapse, or suddenly gain momentum and finish up in the beck. But it never did! Not whilst I lived there anyway.

Five

Changing Times

Father was always proud of our horse drawn cart; for one thing no one else in the area had one like it. He always supposed it must have been a one off. I remember it proudly displayed a local maker's nameplate on the side. (But I cannot recall the name at the moment).

The cart in its original standard form did not carry a tremendous amount of anything at any one time but the design was faultless; it was constructed with concealed hinges underneath the main bodywork so the body could be raised (pushed up) by an attached pole. If the operation was done carefully the body could also be secured in the raised position allowing whatever was in/on the cart to slide or be dragged out of the back onto the ground.

To allow our single horse drawn cart to carry bigger loads of such crops of Hay or Straw we had to fit a purpose made wooden framework. This slotted onto the top of the cart body effectively making the load carrying area wider and longer. The assembly was secured to the cart body with nuts and bolts.

This was generally referred to as 'Shelving's'. To the shelving's framework we then attached gate like structures secured almost vertically one to the front and one to the rear measuring around five-foot tall and these were also secured with nuts and bolts.

These were known, as 'Gormers'. When we had fitted the Shelving's and Gormers to our original horse drawn cart it was capable of carrying good-sized loads of any loose crops we were harvesting.

The only problem with having the extra load carrying capacity was it made the cart unstable and rather top heavy. So we had to be careful when crossing areas where the ground was rutted or soft, and because our cart was only equipped with the standard tall narrow iron shod wheels they could/would easily sink into soft ground.

The consequence of the wheels sinking too far into soft ground especially on the lower side could be catastrophic, for the cart complete with its load could topple over causing all sorts of problems such as a broken cart, shafts, wheels or even injuring the horse.

I always found feeding the work horses a bit of a pain, their feed was all stored in the chamber above the stable. If it was my turn to do the chore, to save time I nearly always endeavoured to take a short cut via the horse's manger. By squeezing through a gap in the wooden hayrack at the front of the horse. From there I could clamber onto the top rail of the hayrack so I could reach up and raise the trap door that led into the chamber above, where all the feeding stuffs were stored. 'Jubilee', our black horse, was the mischievous one of our pair of horses. He would ignore me entirely until I had completed the first two manoeuvres, but as soon as I tried to climb up onto the top rail he would be there with his nose, pushing my foot off everytime I tried to pull myself up onto the rail.

This would happen a few times until in exasperation I would give him a sharp kick on the nose. Then he'd wait until I was standing on the rail, trying to lift the lid up far enough to squeeze through into the chamber above. Then once again he would push both my feet off the narrow rail with his nose resulting in me loosing my grip on the trap door lid and I would fall back down into the bottom of the hayrack.

I have fallen down into the hayrack so many times caused by that trick of Jubilees.

If I shouted at him to stop it he would completely ignore me and look the other way as if I wasn't there at all. It was so annoying.

Sometimes I would give it up as a bad job and go the long way round. This meant having to go through the stone barn, up the wide wooden steps and climb over a dividing wall inside the building, to get to the trap door over the horses' hayrack!

A simple task you would imagine! But the trouble it caused me you wouldn't believe.

The other horse 'Darling' was no trouble at all; she would stare over the dividing stall and roll her eyes as she watched Jubilee playing his games. Don't get me wrong it could have been quite funny, but if I wasn't in the mood or I was in a hurry, it was all a pain to say the least.

Muck (manure) hauling was usually carried out in the late autumn when the ground was still hard enough to allow the standard cart to be towed without the wheels sinking in too much or alternatively, during a hard frost in the winter months.

The first job when reaching the area where we were working was to remove the back door of the cart and hang it on hooks provided on the side.

Then pull out the metal securing bolt at the front so we could lift the hinged body to the height we wanted, and secure the lifting pole into its locking device. With the cart body tilted up, it was easy to drag the manure out of the back with a drag fork until there was a good (barrowful) sized pile on the ground.

A quick shout 'go on' for the horse to pull the cart for say 5 yards or so till the worker shouted 'woe' for the horse to stop. So another pile could be dragged out – and so on till the cart was empty. Then it was back to the farm, to fill the cart again with another load of manure.

Repeating the process again and again, until the field was completely dotted with the barrow sized piles of manure.

The next task was to spread the piles of manure by hand with a five-pronged muck fork effectively covering the complete field with a fairly thick coat of manure. It was very exhausting work spreading manure by hand but it had to be done. Father used to say to me-

'Tha noes it's a mans Job spreading muck'. But as I became bigger and stronger and father became older, eventually he had to amend that statement by admitting that it was more of young mans job... Gradually I became the main manure spreader on our farm, until my brother Lewis grew up then he became even more proficient at the job. But even so father still did his share.

When the manure had been spread evenly over the ground the field could either be ploughed for root crops such as swedes, kale, or potatoes. If it was grassland the horse drawn chain harrows came into use to work the manure down into the roots, it was all hard manual work but as I have said it had to be done.

'Where did all the manure come from'? You may well ask.

Well, the milk cows had to be cleaned out twice a day contributing to the stockpile; the horses had to be cleaned out every day. It was different for the calves and rearers it was usually a once or sometimes twice a year job to clear their sheds out or when the depth of the manure became too deep for comfort (for the stock) or us. So at certain times of the year we would be waiting for father to suddenly declare 'We'll have to clean yon shed art sooin tha nose afore muck gets too bloody deep'. From then on we knew we were in for a hard time!

It was a case of all hands on deck requiring two or more strong workers to clear (fork) the manure out of the shed into the yard. If it were a big shed it sometimes it had to be cleared in relays resulting in a huge pile of manure ready to be hauled into a suitable field.

After many hours of hard very physical work constantly forking the manure out as a team effort until we were suddenly rewarded as the stone floor became visible. That was the time to start relaxing a bit for we all knew the job was almost finished.

Next job was to give the floor a brush with the broom and spread new straw thickly around before letting the rearers back in. They always galloped around like loonies for a while cavorting around with their tails in the air until they became exhausted and quietened down.

Whilst our own on farm produced manure was the main fertiliser, we did have to buy in other somewhat more specialised soil conditioners.

One was crushed limestone.

Limestone was delivered by lorry from Sam Longstone' own quarry near the village of Eyam in Derbyshire. The huge lorry tipped the loose granulated limestone into a big pile, near to where we wanted it. As soon as the lorry had gone father would quickly make sure the pile was covered with a waterproof stack sheet. This served two purposes, the first was to stop the fine powder blowing about in the wind, and the second was to stop moisture getting to it before we could use it. If father hadn't covered the limestone up and it rained, the whole pile would quickly fuse together resembling rice pudding, making it virtually impossible to spread.

So as you can imagine it was a case of making it a priority to cart the limestone to where it was needed quickly in case it did rain. Once again it had to be done manually by filling the cart/trailer with shovels, and then setting the limestone out in small piles around the field ready to be spread by hand, similar I suppose to the manure we had used elsewhere.

When the hauling had been completed spreading usually started immediately, with all hands to the task, for if the limestone were allowed to stay in piles for too long the result would be burnt areas. And these were unsightly later where the roots had been damaged.

Another fertiliser we used at that time was 'Superphosphates'. This came in granulated powder form in very heavy bags.

To apply Superphosphates to the fields we always spread it by shovel direct from the cart or trailer onto the land and we wore gloves and a handkerchief or similar over our faces to protect against the burning sensation to the skin if the wind blew some into our face.

Yes, spreading Superphosphates was quite a hazardous job one I just did not enjoy doing.

There was another type of fertiliser known as 'Basic Slag' this was brought to the farm in bulk form by a high-sided lorry; it was tipped in a heap to be dealt with in a similar manner as the limestone. What the advantage was to the grass field or ploughed ground was I cannot recall, but it was hard work spreading it by hand, just as were all the others.

As I have mentioned before by 1947 father had bought our first tractor. The following year he decided we should have our own mechanical fertiliser spreader, as this would save us having to spread the more hazardous materials on the fields by hand.

So one-day father and I travelled the five or six miles on our tractor to the little village of Low Bradfield to collect a fertiliser spreader he had bought from a farm near to a public house known as the 'Hay Chatter'.

Neither father nor I had been to that farm before so the farmer Mr Len Shepherd had to show us where the drill was located then he left us to it, his parting words were

'When yer's gorrit art er t'shed, remember to shut dooer after yer'.

At first both father and me stared at the drill, for neither of us had seen a drill as wide as that before. The implement known, as a shutter drill was in a shed where it just fitted in, not sideways as you'd expect but long ways with one of the big iron spoked wheels towards the opening, the actual drill being almost 10 ft wide. The shed door opening was a mere 6-ft wide.

We scratched our heads in puzzlement, how had they got that drill in there? We asked one another. Had someone built the entrance smaller with the drill already inside we wondered.

But wondering wouldn't get the drill out so we had to give it a try.

We tried levering it with a fencing stake, but only succeeded in breaking the stake the actual drill didn't even budge; we tried lifting the drawbar to see if it would actually squeeze through the opening. There was no chance. Then father declared we would have to walk it through.

The walking idea was to move around one end of the drill as far as it would go

49

then do the same to the other end. Continuing the action again and again until gradually, very gradually we managed to edge the drill out of the opening to the outside.

We were so elated that we very nearly forgot to shut 'dooer' as Len the farmer had requested.

Now the fun started!

Mr Shepherd had had his lane and gates widened at some time to accommodate the bigger implements he had bought over the years. But we soon found out all the other roads around the village of low Bradfield were mostly still the width of horse drawn vehicles.

And towing the ten-foot wide implement home behind our tractor was a nightmare, for we had to negotiate five miles or so of very narrow roads all the way to Garlic House farm.

Along the way most of the roads had stone walls or steep banking on each side.

So I had to walk at the back ready to shout or holler for father to stop or slow down if the machinery was likely to get damaged, or direct father in a particularly slow corner or negotiate a awkward bit of roadway.

Eventually we arrived home with our prize and we were delighted to find it could be jiggled quite easily into the shed we had designated for its storage.

I'll explain here about why it was so important to park the drill indoors! Metal parts on fertiliser spreading equipment are notorious for corroding even if only slightly damp. So it was very important for the drill to be parked somewhere inside a building, in the dry and out of the elements when not in immediate use.

Of course all our field gateways at Garlic House were too narrow for the drill to go through, so we had to giggle it through each and every one before we could fill the drill with fertiliser. But once the drill was in the field it was a doddle, the job could be completed in no time at all.

The drill was so wide it only took a few times round a small field to complete the job, with the bigger fields it took longer of course but it was far better than spreading the compound by hand as we had done in the immediate past.

However we still had to protect ourselves against the corrosive elements whilst spreading such as ground limestone, Superphosphates or slag the same as we had when spreading it by hand. Windy days were one of the worst conditions; here we had to make sure any dust clouds raised blew away behind us rather than over us as we drove the tractor.

Tractor cabs hadn't been invented at that time so drivers sat in the open and vulnerable to all dust clouds raised in their wake.

On exceptionally windy days it was better to run with the wind without the drill operating, and turn around into the wind before re-engaging the spreading mechanism, as this made sure the wind blew the dust cloud away instead of over us.

On wet days we had to refrain from using the drill at all for everything would soon become a sticky mess, so it wasn't worth the hassle.

Alfie Reynolds a regular visitor to our farm was very practical helping father with difficult tasks, one of them was to convert the standard horse cart so it could be towed behind the Ferguson tractor. To do that he had to remove the two original shafts and replace them with a single draw bar.

Alfie had talked to father about replacing the big irons rimmed wheels, and use a pair of smaller rubber tyred wheels instead.

After making enquirers Alfie discovered the only ones that would fit had to come from a specific lorry and they were very difficult to find, and costly even from a scrap yard at that time. Just after the War. So the big wooden wheels were left in position on the cart, for the time being anyway.

However using the cart with the original big wheels caused a slight problem, we had of necessity to travel very slowly particularly on metalled roads or the cart would more than likely fall apart with the vibration. Horse drawn carts were only supposed to travel at horse speeds. IE Slow!

However once we were off the metalled road it didn't really matter how fast we travelled for the going was usually quite soft on the land.

It must have been a year or so later when Alfie Reynolds designed and made a proper two wheeled trailer to be towed behind our Ferguson tractor. It had rubber tyred wheels, it was good, very good in fact.

Earlier Samuel Wilson, the tractor dealers had tried to sell father one of the all new all steel-tipping trailers, especially made to use in conjunction with the Ferguson tractor.

Even though a tipping trailer would have been very nice to have, they were so expensive.

So father had to refuse all their efforts and any offers they came up with, by telling the salesman we'll have to manage with what we have for now thank you.

It was another couple of years before father invested in a new Ferguson corn drill. Again, this was another implement especially designed and used in conjunction with the Ferguson hydraulic system. It was a good buy, and did a first class job drilling seed for the next seasons cereal crops. But as was all equipment for tractors it was very expensive especially when it was only used maybe two full days a year.

When the corn drilling had been completed the implement was thoroughly greased, and the coulters oiled, and the machine was once again parked at the back of the cart shed until the following year. Then it would be brought out to do couple of day's work before disappearing back into the gloomy depths of the cart shed yet again. This happens to a lot to farm machinery nowadays, for implements have become so specialised many machines can only do one job and then another machine has to take over to do the next stage.

As I was writing the above it reminded me of the time when farm tractors and machinery became universally equipped with pneumatic tyres. And when the 'blown up tyre' brought with it a new problem. The dreaded puncture.

Punctures in farm tractor tyres were quite common in the early days for there were many things lying about in the grass waiting for the unsuspecting tractor driver to run over.

If a puncture occurred in a rear tyre, the restoration was usually beyond the average farmers abilities, for he didn't have the necessary tools to remove a rear tyre so a specialist had to be summoned to deal with the problem, especially if the tube was 'ballasted'.

One could expect to pay an arm and a leg for a specialist to come out to a farm such as ours in the back of beyond, to put the matter right.

Ballasted? Is the term used when a tube has been filled with a solution of salt and water the main propose being to give the wheel or wheels added weight to aid traction in boggy or slippy conditions. Using water as ballast was ideal but to take into account any freezing conditions in the winter months salt had to be added to the water to alleviate frozen and possibly split tyres as that would have meant even bigger bills.

However if the puncture was in the front wheel the complete wheel could be removed with relevant ease so a farmer with the necessary tools could tackle the job or a local garage using car tyre changing equipment could fix repairs easily.

I remember well the occasion when our Ferguson tractor suffered a puncture in a front tyre.

We were in the midst of hauling in the harvest; father had tried to pump it up with the Stirrup pump, and after hundreds of fruitless pumps he gave up in disgust and prepared to remove the wheel intending to try and repair it.

Whilst having a short breather after his exertions father espied the relatively new Ferguson corn drill standing outside the barn, still awaiting to be put away in storage, his gaze settled on the wheels. 'Mmm' he thought.

He went to have a closer look at the wheels on the drill and to his delight discovered they were similar and they might, - just might fit the tractor. In no time at all he had removed a corn drill wheel to compare.

He soon discovered the complete corn drill wheel wouldn't fit normally, but it would fit the wrong way round. That is to say inside out!

Anyway with the odd wheel now fitted to the tractor father completed the harvest without further mishap, albeit somewhat lopsided for the drill wheel was much fatter than the original tractor wheel. However that didn't matter at the time, all that mattered was for the wheel to go round.

Most of all we had to be somewhat careful when going through narrow gateways as the odd wheel made the tractor quite a bit wider than normal.

When the harvest was safely stored in the building, father had the punctured wheel repaired and replaced on the tractor where it belonged.

We had learnt a lot from that experience, as a puncture in the front wheel no longer caused the mayhem it had always caused in the past. All we had to do now was find where the corn drill was parked and borrow a wheel for the duration.

I recall vividly the occasions when any visitors came to the farm and saw the odd wheel on the tractor, they would always scoff, but who cared, we knew what we were doing and that's all that mattered!

Six

Vehicles

There were very few private vehicles in and around Ewden Beck during my early years, and the few vehicles that were around were predominantly military vehicles. The War had ended by the time my parents decided to indulge in a motor car. They finally bought our first family car in 1946, and it was by then almost ten years old. Father bought the Hillman Minx saloon from a distant family relation who lived in Stocksbridge paying £300: for it. I remember the figure well as father always insisted that he had paid over the odds for the vehicle.

He didn't particularly like the car, but as cars were scarce he was repeatedly told not to complain being reminded that he was lucky to have one anyway. Because of the constant shortage of money to pay for the running costs the Hillman only came out of the building where it was housed about twice a month, or when he wanted to take a bull calf or two to Penistone market to sell. To carry the calves he had to remove the rear seats, consequently the car always smelt of calves even after he had supposedly cleaned it out.

The 1938 Hillman Minx bore the registration number of EWB 9. Our family history records show that soon after the original owner bought the car the War years began, and private car ownership was actively discouraged. And petrol was rationed or in short supply consequently the Hillman spent most of its time shut away in a little lock up garage in Stocksbridge.

The original owner of the vehicle was a huge strong industrious person who had retired some years previously, and it was said he had pushed the Hillman car out of the garage every Sunday to give it a clean and polish. Unfortunately all the cleaning and polishing had a detrimental effect and the paintwork gradually changed colour from burgundy to orange, as the lighter coloured undercoat underneath began to show through.

So by the time father bought it, the colour was most definitely orange. It wasn't long after father bought the 'orange' coloured Hillman when every time father went out with it he came home complaining about the steering.

Declaring it was too stiff for his liking, insisting he could not steer it properly. He'd say 'Ahh can't steer yon bugger theeres definitely summat wrong wee it'.

Eventually father decided to do something about the steering, so he took the car to a Mr Morley of Bolsterstone garage for it to be attended to. However, when the car came back father still complained, this time he insisted the steering was too slack!

Father's complaint came after his first trip in the vehicle when apparently he had all his work cut out avoiding collisions with roadside walls and backing's. I was of course by that time 11 years old and old enough to be able to have a say in certain matters, so I voiced my opinion to be allowed to have a go in the offending motorcar 'supervised' of course. After a short trip I was able to confirm what father had said by declaring the steering was indeed too slack making the vehicle quite unstable! So the vehicle was once again confined to the shed, only taken out on market days or emergencies.

However after saying all that, father must have kept the tax and insurance up to date. For later the same year a Mr Dyson a tractor fitter from Sheffield, took my Mother, my brother Lewis and me to the seaside with the Hillman and he didn't complain about the steering at all.

How the trip came about was when George Dyson came one day to the farm to attend to a fault that had developed with our relatively new Ferguson tractor, and he mentioned to me that he and his wife were considering taking a trip to the seaside. During the ensuing conversation, I must have let a little snippet of information slip out to George that our car was no good, and I had bemoaned the fact that neither my brother nor me had any prospects of seeing the sea for the very first time in the foreseeable future at least.

Anyway George must have discussed what was said with my parents and the outcome was we were all taken to the seaside in our Hillman car later that year.

And we thoroughly enjoyed the experience.

Unfortunately, soon after that the Hillman car had to be sold to raise much needed funds for the farm it was quite a few years later before father bought another road going vehicle.

One of the earliest cars I can recollect in our area was a fairly large Austin 4 door saloon, with the registration number CWY 701. It belonged to Harry Ward the Broomhead Hall head gamekeeper. Harry Ward always parked the car outside our farm gate, not in front of the gate but just to one side so it didn't interfere with our work, and there it remained all day until he came back for it later.

My father always voiced the opinion that maybe Harry didn't trust himself to drive any further down the steep 1 in 4 Ewden beck hill, or whether the car wasn't up to the task, we were never quite sure. But Harry Ward never went any further down the hill than our farmyard gate with his Austin car. It was parked there all day almost every day so anyone who saw it regularly could have been excused for thinking it belonged to us at the farm, but it didn't.

Captain Reginald Wilson of Broomhead Hall had a big car of course; it was garaged in a specially heated building accessed by driving into the courtyard to the rear of the farmyard buildings. The car was a beautiful Rolls Royce always shiny and sparkling in its illustrious dark blue colour.

Broomhead Hall employed two chauffeurs to drive the master of the big house to wherever he required taking to whether it was day or night.

Jim Blyton was one of the chauffeurs; he doubled up as a valet to the Captain when the occasion demanded. The other was Arthur Senior. Both had to wear the appropriate uniform whilst driving the Rolls when Capt Reginald Wilson had business commitments in Sheffield to attend to or when he was the guest at other landowner' estates.

During the grouse-shooting season many examples of the Rolls Royce motorcar were to be seen bringing the Gentry for the day's sport. Another popular make of car used by the well off was of course the Bentley, in either saloon or what was known at the time as the station wagon. Quite a few of the Gentry appeared to like the station wagon style bodywork, maybe it was because of the extra space inside to house their gun dogs so they could keep them separate behind a grill of some sort. Other cars that brought the landed gentry to the grouse shooting days were the Lancia and the Lanchester all nice cars I'm sure, but obviously not as salubrious as the Rolls or the Bentley with an occasional Daimler.

Even so they were all just as highly polished and well looked after. I must say, all the years that I went on the moors as a grouse beater I cannot recall seeing a car used by the gentry showing any signs of neglect or of it being abused in any way. They were all immaculate!

Our nearest neighbour Spencer Steward of Ewden Lodge farm had a rather ancient black Vauxhall saloon; with a folding carrier rack affixed on the back, it could have been a De-Lux version I suppose because it ran on large sized wire-spoked road wheels.

On the front of the long bonnet was a round gauge with coloured segments that served as an indicator informing the driver of the level of the water temperature in the radiator.

Spencer sometimes carried a couple of bags of potatoes secured to the rack on the rear, taking them we presumed, somewhere to sell. We could hear the vehicle rather than see it as it rattled and banged about as it slowly travelled up his lane, in fact most of Spencer's access lane was only a cart track, so no wonder his car rattled and bounced about during it's progress.

Steward's lane as it was known to us, was sunken well below the surrounding fields and bordered with stone walls on both sides so we could only see the top of the car occasionally as it traversed the lane. In the summer time when the lane was dry a cloud of dust marked the progress of Spencer' car all the way up his lane, until the car emerged at the top where the lane joined up with the metalled Mortimer road. From then on we could see as well hear it as it gathered speed roaring up the hill usually amid a cloud of blue smoke. The smoke cloud followed the car all the way to the top of the hill before it disappeared over the skyline, out of our sight.

Vauxhall cars must have been quite popular amongst farmers at that time (1940's), for there was a similar vehicle owned by Gordon Shaw of Nook Farm Bolsterstone.

That particular Vauxhall car was used daily delivering milk to the Bolsterstone infants' school. On the rack at the back were two polished milk churns secured with straps, the churns were resplendent with highly polished brass taps for decanting the contents.

Every day Gordon drove the half mile from his farm up Morehall lane to Bolsterstone stopping outside the school gate to dispense milk from the churns into the huge enamelled jugs brought out either by the school cook Mrs Sampson, or the caretaker Mrs Cheetham. The jugs of milk were conveyed with extreme care and attention through the main door of the school through the middle of our classroom into the kitchen, for use later in the day.

Mrs Sampson was old, or so we thought, quite tall and plump. Whereas Mrs Cheetham was very short, thin and very bow legged, and quite often the butt of our schoolboy jokes. Both it must be said had rather sharp tongues so we the pupils kept our distance, except of course when they were dispensing beverages or dinners. Both the ladies lived quite near to each other in the row of houses across the road from the Castle Inn Bolsterstone.

From our vantage point in the school yard we could see them every day coming to work in the mornings usually during our first play time before lessons started.

With Mrs Sampson purposely striding across the Village Square, closely followed by Mrs Cheetham who rather shuffled along with her shoes knocking together with her knees sticking out at an ungainly angle.

One of the jokes banded about at that time declared Mrs Cheetham would never be able to catch a pig in a gennel. She must have known what we were saying but she never shouted at us or rebuked us for being cheeky, she just pursed her lips and carried on whatever she was doing.

Lorries were just as scarce as cars during and just after the War, there were a few but not many, I suppose they may have been expensive so only the better off businesses were able to afford them. Broomhead Hall Farm had a Morris commercial lorry; it was mostly used for hauling produce from the farm to Sheffield, such as swedes and potatoes. However when the shooting season came along in August each year, the lorry was cleaned up and used to transport people to and from the areas where the action was. Long bench type seats were secured along each side in the rear; these had a wooden rail attached along the back of the bench for the passengers to lean back on or hang onto when the ride became rough. At other times the lorry carried guns and ammunition for the Gentry during shooting days.

As soon as the first days shooting had been completed, the lorry was brought into use again, this time to take sealed baskets of dead birds to the railway station in Deepcar or Sheffield Central to catch the express train to the Capital City of London. The idea was to have grouse on the menu in the high class London restaurants for the evening meals especially on the 12th of August the traditional start of the grouse-shooting season! I always considered it to be more of an ego thing, for what difference does it make if one had grouse to eat on the twelfth or the following day?

It would have saved a lot of rushing around for sure.

Our groceries and farm feed supplier Henry Mitchell had a similar lorry that came all the way from Holmfirth, a small market town in West Yorkshire. It delivered groceries and farm feeding stuffs or seed potatoes, when they were in season. The representative from the shop called at the farm on a particular day once a fortnight to take our order. I remember that every time the lorry came to deliver stuff, I always had to have a look at the temperature gauge. To do that I had to climb up onto the front bumper of the lorry and stretch up to peer at it.
It had coloured segments showing in the glass face with a needle pointing to the state of the temperature at the time.

Henry Mitchell and sons had supplied groceries and farm feeding stuffs to most of the farms in our area, for all the years I lived at Garlic House.
And the Morris Commercial lorry never failed to turn up as I can recall. It was only in really bad weather such as in the winter months that it was even late.

Another Morris Commercial lorry in our area was the one belonging to Mr Bertram Shaw, the builder, who lived down Morehall lane a short distance from Bolsterstone School.
Bert as he commonly was referred to, had a yard in Bolsterstone village where he stored his building materials. The yard was just over the school wall across Heads lane opposite our School toilets. If it were playtime or midday when we were outside in the school yard, and someone had suggested something unusual or different was happening across the road. There would nearly always be a rush of kids, especially boys, to the boundary wall. Next thing there would be a line of bodies hanging on to the wall top by finger tips, all straining necks to stare across the road into Bertram Shaw's builders yard trying not to miss anything. From that somewhat privileged position we were sometimes able to witness Bert and his assistant Mr Pears loading sand or gravel with shovels on to the back of his lorry, we always thought they overloaded the poor thing. Indeed sometimes it was so low on its springs that we thought the tyres would burst dumping everything onto the road, before he even got to the place he was going to.

Badgers Transport of Sheffield was a company that owned a huge green Albion flat bed lorry.

It came every day to collect our milk from the stand outside our gate.

One distinctive feature I can remember about the Milk collection lorry was the whine. The noise we supposed came from its transmission. I suppose the driver would have been using the lorries lowest gear most of the time, for it was quite steep driving down long bank, and even steeper climbing up Ewden Beck hill to our farm.

Whether there was anything wrong with it I don't know. It was certainly a reliable lorry though, as it never failed to come every day including Sundays to collect our milk churns.

Wortley District Council also used a flat-bedded Albion lorry to carry out work in our area, and the transmission whined on that one as well. So we rightly or wrongly presumed it must have been a feature rather than a problem.

The council lorry was normally fitted with sideboards when used to collect sidings, or to bring materials to repair the roads with. But when we'd had say six inches or so of snow in the winter months, the same Albion lorry would come around with a snowplough on the front, with a couple of council workers standing in the back spreading grit on the road afterwards.

Yes, the Albion lorry was a tough machine, well up to all the varied work the Council workers asked it to do.

I think G C Knowles of Manchester road and Albert Jackson of Shay house lane Stocksbridge used Austin lorries. They were two of the best greengrocers in Stocksbridge and both came to our farm to collect produce to sell in their respective businesses.

Both the grocers used quite new green coloured lorries as I recall. And when they came to collect stuff from our farm they always reversed their vehicles into our farmyard so they could get as close as possible to the access door where we had stacked the prepared potatoes for them to collect. I also remember both the Knowles and Jackson drivers made a point of opening a couple of bags to have a look inside, before starting to load, just to check I supposed to see if what was inside, was what was supposed to be inside. If you see what I mean?

But father always said if anyone had pulled a fast one with either of the shop owners it would be the first and last time they did!

When everyone was satisfied, the 112lb bags of potatoes had to be carefully

manhandled through the small opening to someone outside then passed on again to someone else on the lorry to stack. It was always a difficult and heavy job. If it was a cold day the drivers covered the bags up straight away for protection. If swedes were part of the consignment they were never covered for they are much hardier than potatoes. Swedes could stand frost, no problem!
Not at all like potatoes, for once frost had got into them that was the end they would go black then rotten within a week.

Another service provider who came to our farm was Colin Marshall the coal merchant; he brought our coal with an Austin tipping lorry.
I can remember the numerous occasions when the driver had great difficulty getting to where we wanted the loose coal tipping. We always had our coal delivered loose (not bagged) for we had to shovel the coal through a small door into our coal storage place in the buildings after the lorry had gone. Sometimes the driver had to have many attempts before he could achieve his goal of getting as close as possible to where we wanted it tipping.

Last but not least we must not forget another very important lorry. The lorry that called at our farm every week belonging to the Sheffield Corporation Water works, it came to collect the outside earth closet toilet bin. I think that was yet another Austin, a specially prepared version.
For many years Jack Hague from Yew Trees farm Bolsterstone worked part time on that particularly smelly vehicle. It was Jack who always made his way from the lorry to collect our sometimes overfull dustbin type container from where it was housed at the far end of the coalhouse. Emptying it out into the back of the waiting vehicle before taking it back to where it belonged. To get there he had to pass where our cow dogs were housed and sometimes a commotion developed when the bin man and the dogs had an altercation.
When the lorry had moved away father would say I'd bet Jack was tempted to pour the contents of the bin on yon bloody dogs to shut the buggers up.
We all agreed with this sentiment, if it had been any of us carrying the bin we would have certainly been tempted to do just that. Whether it would have shut the dog up may be debatable.

Seven

Growing up

I was just about fifteen years old in 1951 when my father suddenly declared he had come up with a plan, and I wasn't to let slip or divulge this plan to anyone else!

The only bit of information that he would divulge about this 'Plan', as he called it, was that it would only involve him and me. And apparently we were going up Broomhead Moors to do something together at the very strange time of midnight, taking with us a couple of empty cow cake bags.

To say that to a fifteen year old boy was tantamount to a world secret. But even after a considerable ammount of questioning I couldn't gain any more information. So I fell into trying to guess what we were going to do, as the very idea of wandering around on Broomhead Moor in the night with cow cake bags sounded at least mysterious, daft or even downright suspicious. In actual fact I had almost hoped father had forgotten about the idea when he announced it was almost time to carry out 'His plan'!

Then one day he confided that we would be going up Broomhead Moor via the rough (bomb) road at the top of our hill to the old abandoned American Tank target practice Bunker so we should both put on warm clothing and wear our heavy boots.

That snippet of information fired my imagination still further, adding even more mystery to what father had in mind. Eventually on a particularly dark night off we went, and as planned we both had a couple of cow cake bags rolled up and tucked under our arms.

It was OK walking up the metalled Ewden Beck road in the pitch dark, but when we started trekking up the bomb road we stumbled over every little thing on the rough surface. Father had told me earlier that it would be out of bounds for either of us to carry a light.

There weren't any stars or moonlight that night so it seemed to take a long time before we eventually arrived at the old bunker, father searched around for some time in the heather and long grass before he eventually found what it was he was looking for.

It was a rusty steel rail! Yes a rusty old rail. And it was then that father finally admitted it was the rail that we had come to collect.

I was somewhat disgusted and voiced my opinion that we should both have been in bed not messing around miles from anywhere with an old rusty rail.

And when father told me we were going to carry it all the way back to Garlic House I was even more bemused for the rail was I suppose around twenty-foot long, and looked very heavy.

'How?' I asked,

'How what?' he grunted,

'Do we carry it?' I snorted,

'On our backs of course' father cheerfully announced.

Now I hear you ask what about the cow cake bags we had both carried with us from the farm? You may well ask! I was told to wrap both my hessian cow cake bags around the rusty rail about three foot from one end, then hoist the rail up onto my shoulder, father did the same with his end. The idea of the cow cake bags was to help stop the rough iron chaffing our shoulders causing bruising or other injury. Very thoughtful I'm sure, but it didn't make it any lighter.

Soon we were ready for the off on the long journey back home carrying the heavy rail, we staggered away (well I did) father was in the lead so wherever father went I had to follow.

We went what appeared to me to be a very long way round to get back to our farm keeping to the shade even though it was still pitch dark.

Eventually we arrived home absolutely buggered up; so I went straight to bed for a couple of hours before it were time to start the morning's milking.

The purloined rail was used for many years as an aid to building the bases of hay or straw stacks in the stack yard. You may ask was it worth the effort? My candid answer. 'Probably not'.

I can still recall workers on threshing days asking father when the stack had been completely dismantled and the rail came into view; I can almost repeat the question word for word -

'Where did you get that rail from Walter'? As far as I can remember father never gave the questioner a proper answer, but now that I have spilt the beans (as they say) everyone knows!

I still remember how my shoulders ached for weeks after carrying that rail from the American Tank target practice bunker to Garlic House Farm in the pitch dark all those years ago.

I left School on my fifteenth birthday 16th July 1951.
Actually the truth of the matter is father wouldn't let me go to school even a day later than my birthday, so I spent my birthday at home on the day I was fifteen. I wasn't even allowed to attend the final few days of the term, father said that was that, as far as school was concerned.
I didn't really argue the toss for it didn't bother me one way or the other, but I would have liked to have been able to attend the parties and school dances and frivolities that were always arranged for the leavers the end of a school term. Then about a week after I had 'left school' Mr Chadwick the school attendance inspector came to call. He caught me trying to hide in the barn, I remember he attempted to get me into his car with the excuse of taking me back to school with him, but father was not having any of it. Threatening to set the cow dogs on him if he didn't clear off. I remember Mr Chadwick shouting from his open car window as he drove away,
'I'm reporting this to the authorities', which he must have done, for the following week a policeman came to the farm with a summons-citing father as failing to send me to school for the remainder of the school term. Father was fined five shillings by the magistrate's court for his pains.
By that time I would have finished school anyway!

Father didn't or wouldn't pay me anything for working except my keep and clothes so any money I had at that time I had to earn from either grouse beating, helping with heather burning on the moors or catching rabbits to sell on our potato round in Stocksbridge.
Another exiting prospect about my being fifteen years old was that I was big and strong enough to make myself available to help on other farms in the area, especially on threshing days as there were always a need for extra help on those special days. My parents did not mind me doing the extra work so long as our own farm work was up to date and all done each morning before I went off to do whatever.
Although it wasn't every day or even every week when I could earn money, it was just occasionally. I wasn't afraid of work so almost anything manual was just up my street.

If you recall I mentioned threshing earlier!
Now another incident involving a corn stack comes to mind. I was helping with the threshing on a farm near high Bradfield either at Sam Saddington farm or his brother Percy'. I remember the farm quite well; it was down quite a long narrow lane nr Low Bradfield. Mr Saddington was a short very old man with a white beard that he always kept tucked into his belt. It was said the beard was long enough to trail on the floor, so he had to tuck it into his belt whilst he was working or he would be constantly tripping over it. I was working on top of the threshing box that particular day as the second man feeding loose sheaves into the drum.
As the corn stack gradually diminished I began to notice an old wooden building with a collapsed roof slowly coming into view. As the stack went lower the shed became more visible and I was able to see what the broken roof was resting on, it what I can only describe as the most fantastic looking motor car one could ever imagine.
The car was obviously American, huge and open topped with spiky fins and huge lights at the back. What could be seen of the car's original colour, was vivid cream with chocolate livery.
The collapsed debris had wrecked the soft-top and filled the vehicle full of rubbish from the fallen roof, some of the paintwork and the interior was covered in green lichen or mould.
The car had obviously been in the old shed for many years, and I would have loved to have been able to take a look under the long bonnet, I imagined the engine would have been a huge V8 or something of that order. But unfortunately for me by the time the corn stack had been finished and the base all cleared it was nearly dark, so I had to get on my bicycle and ride home sharpish to be in time for milking.
The next time I went to that farm for a days threshing I made it a priority to take a look in the area where I had seen the motorcar, but it had gone as had the broken down shed it had been parked in. Ohh well!

Now that I had reached the age of fifteen, I was by then deemed to be old enough to go with my Grandad Fred Dyson up the moor heather- burning. This essential job was usually done in January or February. It was necessary to burn off various sized patches of old long legged heather on the open

66

moorland, to allow new young heather to grow.

The tender shoots of new heather were needed for the little grouse chicks to feed on; for heather was the staple diet of grouse up on the open moorland. It obviously took a couple of years for the new heather to grow and become restablished after the burning process so it was an on going thing, patches or areas of heater was burnt every year when conditions allowed. The size of the patches varied sometimes a few acres or at other times it was clearing out a corner somewhere measuring a few hundred yards or so where everyone had to be very careful with any nearby forestry or woodland. Most of the burning however was high up on the top of the extensive moorland of Broomhead or the Strines moors. The gamekeepers knew exactly where it was necessary to burn because they knew where the grouse population preferred to nest.

They also knew where the local population of predators congregated, predators such as buzzards, hawks, foxes or any other wild birds or animals that preferred grouse chicks as a ready meal.

When the burning site was selected and the date set, that was the time for the relevant Gamekeeper to visit local farms in the bid to raise labour to help with the task. I was quite conversed on heather burning even though I hadn't done any, my Grandad Fred Dyson had answered so many of my questions about the subject. He knew I could reel off all the answers asked by the recruiting Broomhead head Gamekeeper Harry Ward.

The real reason I wanted to go heather burning was of course the money, I was always saving up for something and at that time it was to buy more cycles to restore and sell, to raise my funds even higher. The daily pay for heather burning was good considering the risks involved. Over the years that I helped with the task I only sustained slightly burnt clothes and a few blisters. Blisters are easily acquired on the moors especially whilst burning long legged heather.

As one could very easily trip over our own feet as they became entangled in the long stems of the old heather, and down you would go with hands outstretched straight into the hot burning heather. The wearing of gloves might have helped but it was generally frowned upon, for it was the general opinion amongst those that knew, that a burning glove can do more damage to hands than not having any on at all!

I helped with the burning on Broomhead, Midhopestones and Strines for a few years until something more interesting or rewarding came along.

When I was sixteen or so I enrolled to attend Stocksbridge technical college in the evenings studying electrical and cabinet making, both of those subjects attracted me at the time.

Using my best roadster cycle to get there and back a round trip I suppose of 10-11 miles using all the short cuts available to a cycle. So that activity took care of one or two evenings a week in consequence I didn't have much time to spare for anything else

Father one day declared to me if I wanted to carry on doing work for other people he wouldn't stand in my way but there was one condition and that was before I could leave our farm all our own work had to be up to date.

What he meant to say if he had anything ready for me to do, I would have to do it first.

It was about that time when I began to install electrical equipment in such places as deep litter houses, lambing sheds and crew yards were the requests from farmers in and around the locality. Fitting electrical equipment into porches, garden sheds and garages were other popular requests from private householders, it was very interesting work, easy in fact, easier than what it is nowadays with all the new regulations one has to adhere to when doing such work.

Much of my area covered Bolsterstone, Midhopestones, Bradfield, and sometimes beyond. It was all done by recommendation I never had to advertise my skills, and I had as much work as I could manage on my own.

By mentioning the word 'Hessian' earlier in this chapter, brings to mind one of the reluctant chores I remember having to do especially in the winter time evenings, it not only involved me but my brother Lewis for he had to do whatever he could to help with the task.

Mother collected everything to do with cloth, thick cloth, coloured cloth, such things as old jackets and long coats or even old hats, these she stored somewhere in the house

Then mother would - I'll not say make, but ask nicely, my brother or me to cut up some of the accumulated cloth into two inch by one inch strips, then again she separated the colours and stored them safely away again. Both my brother and me knew what was coming, for soon after that preliminary task was completed mother would bring out the rug- making machine. I say machine loosely here for it wasn't a machine at all. It was a free standing wooden frame with the two ends connected by a four foot long wooden cross member, all along the top edge of that cross member were hoops hammered in somewhat like a long row of fencing staples I suppose. Mother would buy

68

from somewhere a piece of Hessian made especially for the job and the size she wanted for a new rug; the Hessian was stretched across and along the length of the 'staples'! And with a special pegging devise we made cloth or rag rugs. It was as I recall mostly done in the winter months when some of the outdoor activities were curtailed because of the short days and long nights

Why do I describe it as a reluctant chore! I remember it well for it made my fingers sore after a while cutting up the cloth or even pegging the rugs afterwards. It took hours and hours of painstaking work to produce a suitable sized rug to fit in front of the fire or at the side of a bed. They were warm and hard wearing there was never any doubt about that. For I remember well how cold those stone flagged floors were in our house in the long winter months, especially in a house with no heating whatsoever except the heat given off by the black kitchen range with its open fire.

However the rugs didn't last long. They didn't have time to wear out; they just became soiled instead by the grubby coats and feet of the cow dogs and cats that managed to sneak into the house. They would always make a beeline for the rug on the flagstone floor in front of the black kitchen range.

If we wanted the rugs to last longer it was essential for the cats and dogs to be kept out of the house. And I can assure you it's quite a difficult job on a working farm especially in the winter when the kitchen was probably the warmest place in the house.

Eight

Moors

I was just 6 years old when my Grandad Fred Dyson finally conceded that I was old enough to accompany him up Broomhead Moors for the first time. During earlier grouse shooting seasons I had heard the guns popping all day somewhere up the Broomhead moors just across the Beck from our farm, and I wanted to see for myself what it was all about.

Fred Dyson was my mothers dad, he was what was known as an under gamekeeper on the Remington Wilson extensive Broomhead estate.

I remember excitedly sitting there in the back of the estate lorry amongst the other grouse beaters clutching my stick, which had a white flag, attached that my mother had so painstakingly prepared for me.

We were on our way to take part in the first drive of the day.

The lorry took us to the bottom of Dukes Drive Agden, where we disembarked to walk up the rough unmade road, leaving a person every 200 yds or so, they were told to wait there in their position until the starting time then carefully follow instructions.

Duke's Drive is a wide rough stony road that that runs on the skyline, forming the boundary between Broomhead and the adjoining Strines moors. After 2 miles or so Dukes drive peters out to become a footpath crossing a low lying swampy area, and from there it meanders up and over the skyline where it eventually leads down into the Derwent valley.

As you walk along the footpath through the swampy area.   Look to your right, you may still be able to see the remains of the underground bunker used as a control centre by the military, when that area of the moors was used to formulate a decoy 'Sheffield' during the middle period of the Second World War.

The extensive decoy light systems used in the operation were to try to confuse the German bomber pilots as to where exactly was Sheffield? Was the city of Sheffield where their plans said it was, or was it where the decoy lights suggested? It must have caused some confusion!

After the war had ended there were miles of electrical cables used in the exercise strewn around the moors the remains of which could still be seen sticking out of the peat bog areas.

Most of the black rubber electrical cables had lamp holders still attached; these were the remains of the thousands of lights that lit up a network during the early nineteen forties. The latticework was designed to mimic the streets of Sheffield. We were led to believe.

Whether the operation was worth the effort is debatable. For it became a well known fact that as soon as the operation came to an end and the decoy lights were finally switched off, the very next day/night Sheffield sustained one of its biggest hits by the German bombers of the whole war period. In later years when I was a regular grouse beater crossing the Strines moors in the very same area, the ground was littered with thousands of anti tank gun shells, some exploded, some not. We were told not to touch the unexploded ones for they might blow up and cause an injury even though they had been rusting away in the peat for some considerable time.

Back to my story.

I stood with my Grandad at our designated place at the side of a huge pyramid type stone cairn to wait. The only sounds that could be heard were the curlews, skylarks, and sheep bleating as they foraged the sparse grass amongst the heather, add to this the occasional cackle as the grouse moved around minding their own business.

Half an hour or so later we heard the faint sound of the starting gun go off to signal the start of the bottom drive, gradually the noise from the cackling grouse grew in intensity as the beaters came slowly up the moor disturbing the birds. Some flew directly towards us, the flankers! We waved our flags franticly to try and turn the grouse, towards where the Gents with their guns in the shooting butts were waiting. Some of the grouse turned others ignored us to live another day I suppose. I instinctively knew what to do as my Grandad had briefed me on such matters beforehand.

Fred Dyson was a rather large fellow with a bright red face with white whiskers and bristly moustache. He wore what was typical dress for Gamekeepers at that time. Heather coloured plus four suit and leggings, and boots especially made for Gamekeepers who worked on grouse moors. To a lay person those boots looked quite strange, for the toes were quite steeply curved up at the front intended to make it easier for the wearer to walk up and down steep bankings during their long days working on the moors. For headgear Fred wore a flat cap.

I mentioned leggings! The full-length type could be made of leather or from some form of felt or cloth, and there were shorter versions available similar to the ones regularly worn by the military known as Putties.
The main reason moorland workers wore leggings was to keep the bottom of their trousers from getting caught up (snagged) in the strong heather stalks or bracken growing on the moors.
Wherever he was working on the moors Fred Dyson was accompanied by his black Labrador dogs Jake and Don, and he always carried a twelve-bore twin barrelled shotgun,

----

Back to my first day grouse beating:
Grandad Dyson and I were what were known as flankers. Our job was in fact quite important in a way because when grouse have been disturbed they will usually fly directly to the area where they were hatched as chicks and brought up to being adult birds.   So many of the grouse that were being disturbed by the beaters from the Mortimer road drive instinctively flew towards the Strines moor straight over our heads. So as I have said our job as flankers was important because we had to try and turn them towards the waiting guns by waving our flags.
As the beaters from Mortimer road approached our positions we were able to join in walking up the moor waving our white flags shouting, whistling or even singing.   Gradually we approached the shooting Butts where the gentry were ensconced with their guns, trying there best to shoot the swiftly flying grouse.
Which is not easy I am told especially when it's foggy, raining, windy or even too sunny.
To me at six years old it was a terribly exiting; I had my miniature white flag on a stick taking an active part in a grown up sport?
I had of course heard the guns many times on grouse shooting days from our farm across the valley. We could hear them clearly banging away, especially when the wind was blowing in towards the farm, and now I was actually on the moor I could see for myself where the noise came from, as the gentry tried

73

their best to bring down the low flying grouse.

After the drive had finished, the beaters waited around until the gentry with their many assistants and gun dogs searched for and recovered most of the grouse that had been killed during that first drive. Then the beaters carried them down the footpath to the 'Cabin' to be laid out on the ground to be counted.

When all the collected grouse had been counted they were placed in wicker hampers, and loaded onto the sledge to be hauled down the track by the horse to the game-room just outside Broomhead Hall yard. Some of the days 'bag' were hung on the game rack. Others were carefully selected and packed into a different type of travelling basket to be loaded on to the estate lorry then taken to Deepcar railway station. From there they were despatched to London on the next express train destined for the posh restaurants to be listed on the game menu that same evening or at the latest the next day.

I must explain a few words here

'Drive' is the term used to describe the location or stretch of moorland that was walked over by the beaters waving a white flag attached to a long walking stick towards where the Butts are located.

'Beater'. A typical Beater! Especially the ones I knew and worked with on the local moors had of necessity to wear dark coloured old but tidy clothes. Not too heavy especially if it was a hot day but strong enough to withstand all the abuse of the clinging bracken, gorse bushes, and old grown heather. Including occasional river crossings and scrambling up or down steep banks that were encountered during the day's work.

'A brace' of course is two grouse. Grouse were always countered in brace'. For footwear, most beaters wore strong work boots with hobnailed soles.

Strong boots were essential, for the rigors of walking miles on the open moorland could ruin anything that wasn't strong enough for the job.

Some of the older beaters wore leggings, or putties. I didn't have either. So I had to tie the bottom of my trousers with strong string or binder band to stop them getting caught up in the heather and bracken.

The wellingtons we wore at home on the farm were no good on the moors for sharp spikes of gorse or heather would and could easily puncture the strongest wellingtons. So when the grouse season started we reverted to the trusty hob nailed boots and leggings.

We all had a long stick, most of us preferred one called a 'thumb stick' that is to say the stick had a V at the top to place our thumb through to stop our hand sliding down the stick as we climbed up the steep banks. The stick had to have a white flag securely attached at one end.

The stick was used for beating the heather to disturb hiding grouse, and the stick helped us to keep our balance as we walked across the rough moorland. 'The white flag' was used for waving at flying grouse to try and turn them to where we wanted them to go.

We all carried our lunch bag on our back, usually an ex army gas mask haversack and a rolled up waterproof plastic cape with a sling to hang it around our neck for if the weather suddenly changed during the long day on the moors.

'Butts' there are many locations of the shooting Butts and they are built roughly in line in-groups of nine especially on the Broomhead moor. The Butts are built from sods dug from the surrounding heather and peat, and built into a square or rounded formation, about five-foot high with a rough flat top most of the way round.

Each butt is provided with an entrance and a door (to keep the dogs in) with either a duck board floor or concreted, the final inside dimensions are somewhere around 5ft by 6 ft.

Sometimes the Gentry would have to be very patient for the drive to commence, sometimes having to sit on their shooting sticks whilst the loaders kept a sharp look out for the first birds (grouse) to fly over for them to shoot.

The occupants of each butt included a gun loader, sometimes two in a multi gun butt. For sometimes his wife or another family member could accompany the Gent who could also handle a gun. And there is always a limited amount of room available in a Butt, so naturally the more people there are inside the more difficult it is to operate a shot gun, as you can well imagine.

Everything happens fast when the birds come over, there is always a lot of dodging around ducking the swinging gun as the Gent hurries to sight his gun before pulling the trigger then quickly exchanging his empty hot gun for a freshly reloaded one.

At times there are arms frantically waving around trying to grab a newly loaded gun, or passing an empty gun back to the loader.

And it must be said, shot guns can get very hot when things are hectic (especially on a hot day) so the gentry and their loaders have to wear gloves or at least mittens during a busy shoot.

You probably notice that I have been referring to all the gun operators as men but that is not strictly true.

For there are many women who can shoot as good as men, and they can control a butt as good as men on a shooting day, and get good results.

'The Cabin' is a building located on the Broomhead moor, it is a long building somewhat similar to a bungalow built of stone with a blue slate roof situated about two miles up the big moor. It is divided into two parts one part is for the beaters with benches and tables for them to have their lunch (carried with them) and there is always an urn of fresh hot tea or bottles of ginger beer available.

If the older beaters wanted an alternative a few dozen bottles of beer were available provided by the estate, but they never lasted long before they had all gone.

The other half of the cabin is where the Gentry have their lunch. A trusted employee of the estate acting as a valet for the day usually manned this area. Jim Blyton was one of the Broomhead estate trusted employees; he had worked for the Broomhead estates for many years as a chauffeur with occasional valet duties so he was entrusted to control the Gents cabin on shooting days.

If the meeting had some important significance Jim had an assistant to help with all the extra work involved.

Jim will have been around all morning busy unpacking the lunch hampers containing the food for the Gentry; all of it especially brought up the Moor with the horse and sledge driven by a member of the staff from Broomhead farm.

The Gentry's lunch in the cabin was always a proper sit down affair especially fitting for the Ladies and Lords, Dukes, Earls, Colonels, Majors, Admirals and such ilk. In their part of the Cabin they had a polished table with a white table cloth, silver cutlery with polished chairs to sit down to have a banquet style lunch complete with wine, whisky, and cigars.

Many times over the years some member or other of the Gentry wasn't in a fit state after the lunch interval to be allowed to continue handling a gun, so they had to be content with being a spectator for the rest of the day.

But let's now go back to my first taste of grouse beating in 1942:

Whilst the Second World War was in progress grouse beating had to carry on, albeit in a more subdued manner to keep the grouse population down to an acceptable level. The reason why grouse had to be 'culled' was to keep the numbers down to an acceptable and manageable level as they are very susceptible to catch certain diseases, and some of the diseases can be so severe it could easily wipe out the entire stock on a moor. So the Broomhead estate continued to have grouse shooting days all through the war years whilst outside in the bigger world the hostilities continued.

However, it didn't effect me for I was far to young to be bothered by such things I was there for the experience and the excitement. And I experienced plenty of both on my first day on the moors with my Grandad Fred Dyson. The first drive I had witnessed and taken part in that day had been driven up Broomhead Moor from Mortimer Road.

In reality the first drive was an exercise thought up by the Broomhead gamekeepers. It was a move calculated to get the majority of the grouse that hadn't been shot during the earlier bottom drive to settle further up the moor, where they would be ready to be driven by the top drive down over the guns again!
The 'top drive' started on a sheep track right on the edge of the Broomhead boundary beyond Margery rock. From that elevated vantage point one could see the Derwent valley in Derbyshire on the one side and Midhopestones moor on the other.
The top drive swept all the way down the moor taking two hours or more to complete. When the grouse killed in the shoot had been collected it was time for lunch (as they called it) where most of the beaters and Gents had a break for an hour or so.
After the lunch break, it was the members of the top drive who were out of the cabin first. For they had to walk all the way back up the big moor using many well defined sheep tracks to the top boundary to get prepared for the next (top drive) later in the day.
Next the Mortimer road beaters came out of the cabin. They had to walk the mile or so long cart track back down to Mortimer road to take up their positions, to beat the bottom moor yet again, just as they had done earlier.
Then it was the turn of the Gentry to make an appearance. They walked or staggered their way back up to their respective Butts to get themselves ready for when the action started again.
Yes, the big moor shooting days were tiring for everyone involved, the beaters, and cabin staff, the sledge driver, gun loaders and Gentry. Not forgetting of course the gun dogs.

History books record that Broomhead moor had a remarkable day in the early part of the twentieth century. August the 27th 1913 to be exact.
It records that Broomhead Moor gained the World record for the number of grouse shot with 9 guns in one day as 2,843 birds. I do believe this record is still intact?
To record the occasion the Broomhead estate had presented all the

Gamekeepers, Fred Dyson included, with a large chiming clock and this was proudly displayed on Fred's sideboard in his living room for many years. On a brass plate affixed to the base was an inscription stating all the relevant facts.

Broomhead estates had six sets of Butts: - some of these were in regular use on the big days others were only used on the smaller days, I list them below in no particular order.

The main ones were of course up the big moor, as was Pike Low and Margery rock. Middle Moss was situated near Mortimer road. Barnside, and Long lane Butts were only used on little days. However, they all had one thing in common they were all on Broomhead property and used at some time during the shooting season.

The Butts on Barnside moor, for instance, were shaped more like a horseshoe without a proper floor or door and they were poorly maintained. The ones on the Long lane moor were made up from timber more like hides rather than Butts; even so they were well hidden behind a stand of tall trees.

The Butts on Pike Low and Margery rock were well maintained on a par I should say with the ones up by the lunch Cabin. They were all provided with duck board floors and a door to keep the dogs in. As for the ones on Middle Moss, they were as far as I can remember always waterlogged and boggy inside I don't think the Gentry especially the ladies liked those at all.

You will have noticed by now that I have been describing the grouse shooting days as 'big days', and 'little days'. The difference was not the length of the days but the locations.

Let's first look at the big days.

These were usually centred on the main Butts up the big moor where the cabin was situated.

Big day guests were made up of Lords, Dukes, Earls, Colonels, Admirals and their ladies.

Special guests sometimes included a Member of Parliament or the Royal family.

Whereas the little day guests who shot the Barnside, Long lane, and middle moss Butts, usually consisted of company Directors, Solicitors, or Doctors.

When a grouse shooting day was imminent. The Broomhead Gamekeepers would have had to thoroughly clear out the butts of spent cartridges, and accumulated rubbish including any empty wine or spirit bottles or the occasional broken shooting stick, all the rubbish was shovelled out of the Butt and buried deep in the surrounding peat.

Before leaving each Butt the gamekeepers were instructed to make sure the door (if fitted) still opened and closed satisfactorily and that it could be secured in the closed position.

If the floor was concrete or it had duck board it had to be swept with a broom so when the day arrived Captain Reginald Wilson could direct his guests, to their allotted Butt's with confidence.

An inspection of all the Butts to be used on the following day's shoot would have been conducted by the head Gamekeeper to make sure everything was OK.

If he noticed anything untoward it was woe betide the keeper whose patch it was on, or the one who had been directed to do the work.

Above I mentioned to there 'allotted Butt'.

On the morning of a big moor shoot, all the Gentry and their aids gathered in the Broomhead Hall yard. When everyone was accounted for, a hat was produced with nine numbered slips of paper inside. Each Gent or his helper plunged a hand into the hat to produce a slip showing the number of the Butt they were to occupy during the mornings shooting session. Later in the day during the lunch break the same thing happened. The idea was so that each and everyone had a fair chance at a good day's sport and it eliminated any idea of favouritism in allocating shooting positions.

Nelson Kaye, and his brother Leonard, were farmers from Windhill farm Stocksbridge. They were regular beaters on the Broomhead moors; they knew precisely where they were supposed to be, at the precise time they were supposed to be there. In fact the Kaye brothers were entrusted with the safe keeping and the operation of the starting gun, which they operated at the precise time to start the top drive. On a summers day the starting gun could be heard clearly by most of the beaters who were impatiently waiting ready to start on time. If for any reason the gun didn't work the beaters with watches were instructed to wave their flags straight up in the air making sure everyone was away on time,

Later when the Kaye brothers came into the Butts from the top drive with the rest of the beaters, one or both of them would have a bunch of white heather and they would offer to share some with the other beaters. It was quite normal in fact for most of the beaters to eventually have a sprig of white heather secured in the lapel of their jackets or the band of their hats or caps; it was a sign of good luck. Some even secured a small bunch to the front grill of their motorcar for the same reason. White heather was always scarce and difficult to find amongst the thousands of acres of purple heather, on the moors of the Broomhead estate. If there was any to be found it grew on the higher reaches of the moors where the Kaye brothers went whilst they were beating grouse.

According to local folklore in 1926 my Grandad Fred Dyson, was dragged over the coals for mistakenly shooting dead a very rare 'Pine Martin'. Some well-respected history books record the misdeed as being performed in long bank wood. That is not strictly true for the Pine Martin was actually killed in the rabbit warren. My mother (his daughter) was with him at the time so she would have first hand knowledge of the occasion and I'm sure my mothers account cannot be refuted.

A Pine Martin? Well it is in some ways it is somewhat similar to an overgrown ferret in appearance and by shooting it but more to the point reporting shooting it, was a big mistake for Fred Dyson. Pine Martins are or were at that time so rare they could have been a protected species. Anyway the Sheffield newspapers got to know about his misdeed, and then wags started to write to the papers saying Fred should be thrown in gaol or publicly flogged or even tarred and feathered for his disgraceful behaviour. Apparently it was quite some time before the press and publicity people allowed Fred to live down and resume his relatively tame Gamekeeper duties free from hindrance.

Myself I thought the following rendition was quite funny? It all happened sometime during the 1950', when the Broomhead estate bought a new Allan scythe. It was intended for the Gamekeepers to use in the summer months during the shooting season, when they traditionally cleared the many footpaths and walkways of bracken and ferns, especially for the Gentry to use as they crossed the open moorland whilst changing from one set of Butts to another. Anyway a couple of years later a young apprentice Gamekeeper was using the machine when he reported it missing. Apparently when he was mowing bracken the machine disappeared down a hole in the ground, it was never seen again despite all the Broomhead estate's efforts at digging with picks and spades looking for it. It was a mystery that was never solved!

An 'Allan scythe'? (For those of you who are not familiar with this excellent type of mowing machine) was powered by a single cylinder petrol engine. The machine had a cutting blade on the front, and the whole machine was mounted on large wheels with handles for the operator to guide it along as it cut the heavy vegetation down to ground level.

Absolutely ideal for what the Gamekeepers used it for.

Unfortunately the estate would not buy a replacement machine, so the Gamekeepers had to revert to mowing the access paths and walkways manually using the traditional scythes.

After that debacle many of the footpaths and short cuts became overgrown through disuse.

Occasionally a brown Hare or even two were included in the bag of grouse to be carried down to the collecting point at the end of a drive. For some reason the Gentry couldn't resist having a pot at a Hare. The Hare would have been scared or just minding its own business, but to the Gentry they were an easy target. I remember when I had to carry one down to the grouse collecting point I usually had to sling the Hare over my shoulder for they were so big I couldn't carry it without trailing it in the heather as I walked along.

I mentioned above 'brown hare' they were brown during the summer months, but when winter came along their entire coats would turn white. Pure white.

Later on in the year when I was helping with the heather burning during January – March and I saw a Hare they were perfectly white. It was quite easy to imagine when the moors were covered in snow, the wild Hare' would become more or less invisible. I suppose it was a kind of camouflage to protect them from their natural predators Fox's or even Hawks who were out looking for a appetising meal.

Nine

Snow

There is an old saying in the Yorkshire Pennines suggesting we had six months of winter and six months of bad weather, that sentiment could well be true, especially some years anyway. We expected a certain amount of snow to fall every winter, but even so some winters were more notable than others were. Take for example 1947.

The winter of 1947 was what one could call exceptional.   I was 10 years old at the time old enough to clearly remember everything, one of the most notable memories being that my brother and I did not go to school at all from January until after Easter that year, because of the snow.

It was the year when our farmyard was at least four-foot deep with snow. Father had to re-dig the walkways almost every morning for the animals to get to the water trough to drink.

Any new overnight snow had to be scraped from the established pathways down to the hard ice so the wheelbarrow could be used to barrow the manure from the sheds to the temporary tipping places dotted around the farmyard.

I recall the difficulties I had pushing the heavy barrow loads of manure along the slippy walkways. Our only wheelbarrow at the time had a wooden wheel with a narrow iron rim, and it would persist in digging in the soft snow/ice in the bottom of the walkways, getting into a wobble then finally toppling over dumping its load in the snow, in the wrong place!

I obviously wasn't strong enough to control it. It was hard work having to refill the barrow and start again.

It was the year when father took our milk churns by horse and sledge to Broomhead Hall farm, and from there both ours and the Broomhead farm milk was sledged to the co-operative dairy in Stocksbridge. It was so cold sometimes the churns had a column of frozen milk standing up above the neck of the churns with the lid perched on top.

The chore of transporting milk by sledge to the dairy went on for weeks as our normal milk collecting lorry could not get anywhere near our farm, or any other of the dairy farms in the area. Eventually Wortley Council workers made the Bolsterstone to Wigtwizzle road passable with the help of a caterpillar tractor and blade; from then on the bottom gate of Broomhead Hall Park, became a communal churn collection point for most of the milk producers around the area.

But even so it was several weeks before the big Albion milk lorry was able to get into the farmyard at Broomhead Hall. But of course we still had to take the milk from Garlic House to Broomhead to be collected, as the road to our farm was still covered in ice and deep snowdrifts. It was many weeks later before a thaw came to clear the roads enough to bring some resemblance of normality to the area.

Sometimes whilst my father and the Broomhead farm worker were away taking the milk to the dairy I would walk across the valley to the Hall especially to have a ride back home on the sledge. On one memorable occasion my Uncle Jim informed me that there was a large parcel waiting for me in the tack room!

'For me, are you sure'? I queried! I knew I wasn't expecting a parcel from anyone. But I went as directed into the tack room to have a look, and there was no mistaking the name on the label, it said, To. Messer's Wilfred and Lewis Couldwell, Garlic House Farm Ewden. C/o Broomhead Hall farm, Bolsterstone. So Uncle Jim was right it was for me and of course my brother.

I continued to stare at it until one of the Broomhead farm cowhands Tommy Cockayne came into the tack room to declare.

'Cummon lad, oppen it so's we can all see whot' tha's gorrin in theer' so I did. The parcel contained a brand new sledge/ toboggan, with iron runners, and a wooden top; it was very tall so it had loads of clearance, and to me it looked absolutely wonderful.

It came complete with a towing rope already attached. I was astounded and overwhelmed, but who could have sent it?

Between us we searched for a note amongst the feverishly ripped brown paper wrapping. Eventually we discovered a note from Uncle Steve Draycott of Queens road Sheffield, saying he had made it himself especially for my

84

brother and me.

When father arrived back from the milk run and I showed him the toboggan I could tell he was just as delighted as I was, especially when he saw who had sent it.

To transport our prize home we tied it behind the horse sledge and it was towed carefully back home. It lasted for years giving my brother and me absolutely loads of pleasure.

The new sledge proved to be especially handy when we had to collect our fortnightly delivery of essential groceries from Midhope. Father had a long-standing arrangement with the owner of the Carpenters shop in Midhopestones. The arrangement was if a new fall of snow prevented Henry Mitchell' lorry making it up the hill from Midhope towards our farm, the driver could leave our grocery delivery with them at the shop, and we would collect them from there ourselves.

Everytime we had a new snowfall the new toboggan had to be brought into use to carry feed to the laying hens, who were housed in their 'Hen oyles' a couple of fields away from the farm.

The hens had to be fed twice a day just like any of the other livestock on the farm.

We had to laboriously prepare and mix the feed for the hens fresh each morning, usually it consisted of potatoes previously boiled in the 'Sett pot' in the back kitchen, these were mixed with layers mash and flaked maze.

The concoction was still warm even after we had sledged the buckets across the fields to where the hens were housed. The mixture was poured into the long feeding troughs outside the 'Hen oyles'. (Hen houses). When we let all the pop hole flaps down for the Hens to come out, it was literally an uproar of squawking hens as they all tried to squeeze through the single holes at the same time. Once outside they immediately grabbed a large piece of the stuff and ran off somewhere to gobble it.

Above I have been mentioning a 'Sett pot' if you are wondering what that could be?

A Sett pot was a round shaped cast iron container somewhat similar in shape to a large upside down policeman's helmet, it held I suppose around 20 gallons of liquid. The container was built into a brick framework in our back kitchen with provision for a coal or wood fire underneath, with a chimney above to take the smoke and fumes away.

Its main purpose was to boil the water for washing days, pig killing days, and cooking the small potatoes for feeding the pigs or hens during the winter months.

During the difficult winter of 1947 Mother continued to make bread and cakes, and it was only because of my parent's foresight that they had bought in sufficient flour to last through such a bad winter, and I suppose they were glad they had.

But we had to have more than bread and cakes so father on his trips to the dairy with the milk sledge would collect some other essential groceries from the shop in Bolsterstone; this included fresh yeast for the baking. But there was always a difficulty associated with bringing things back with a horse sledge. Because of the ruts and rough surfaces traversed during the milk runs the actual sledge would occasionally overturn, spilling everything far and wide.

Father eventually found the safest place to carry anything was inside an empty milk churn. Suitably padded of course as he explained, unless the churn fell off the sledge and the lid came off, things would be still be safe inside when he arrived back home, if somewhat mixed together. But that didn't matter at the time.

I recall a period when the paraffin tank almost ran dry. Paraffin was essential; it was the fuel we used in the lamps for the house and the storm lamps we used in the buildings, however all was not lost as father was able to borrow some from Broomhead, most of the other none essential things we could do without. Such as fresh meat, or vegetables.

Luckily Colin Marshall the coal merchant from Stocksbridge had delivered coal for the fires earlier in the year, so that commodity wasn't a problem. We had enough hay and straw stored indoors so that didn't cause problems either, however I remember it was very difficult getting to the swede/turnip clamp to dig some out for the stock. The milk cows would tackle frozen swede crunching them whole, but the young stock had to have theirs put through the pulping machine, and I can tell you that was hard work pulping frozen turnips.

Mucking the buildings out was one of our biggest problems, so was keeping the ice on the stone water trough in the yard broken for the cows to drink. Chopping straw with the chaff cutter for the horses was also hard work. The chaff-cutting machine was housed in a chamber inside one of the stone buildings, and the snow that blew under the slates formed some very substantial drifts on everything indoors. The snow piled up in the corn and hay chambers so it was unavoidable some days for the straw/hay to become mixed with snow when it was fed to the stock.

The kale in the field had to stay where it was, in the field, for there was no way we could get at it with six foot drifts of snow across the gateways. So the cows had to do without that luxury.

Yes there's no doubt about it the winter of 1947 was very difficult!

At that time another incident occurred this time it happened to our neighbour Spencer Steward from Ewden Lodge farm. He had decided for some reason he would have to walk to Stocksbridge for something, he urgently needed.

He remembered to be careful as he crossed the newly dug walkway at the top of his lane but must have misjudged the location of the cutting further up the hill and he fell down into it.

The only indication that something was amiss was when the lorry driver from Henry Mitchell who had left his lorry at Midhope was walking -read struggling- through the snow on his way to our farm with some essential much needed groceries in a cardboard box on his shoulder.

He explained later that the first time he thought something wasn't quite right was when he saw Spencer's dog running around in circles whining, then he noticed a hole in the surface of the fresh snow. Being observant the driver drew closer to have a look down the hole to be confronted by Spencer from Ewden Lodge farm staring up at him obviously suffering from the effects and early stages of hypothermia.

Spencer had fallen though the soft snow some time earlier disappearing from view and had been unable to get out. Eventually he had weakened so much he had given up the struggle. The deliveryman could not do anything there and then to help on his own so he shouted down to Spencer hang on I'll go and get some help. He dropped his box of groceries so he could move quicker down the hill to our farm to get father.

It was some time later when equipped with suitable shovels the delivery driver and my father eventually arrived back on the scene to find Spencer completely covered over the only indications of the exact location was the cardboard box still sitting on the top of a new snow drift.

It was a race against time digging Spencer out of the soft snow. They carried him almost unconscious down the hill to the nearest house Cottage Farm where Mrs Blyton administered some revival liquid such as whiskey and hot tea; this was administered to the rescuers as well. After a period of recovery Spencer Steward suffered no lasting after effects but the incident could easily have proved fatal!

Yet another notable experience occurred during this trying period.
A small holder farmer from Greenmoor by the name of Harry Taylor, had just killed a pig for us in our stone barn and was almost ready to cut it up when suddenly the conversation turned to how bad it was snowing outside the barn door. Harry was so worried he suddenly declared
'I'd better tek mi car to top er thill afoor it gets so bloody bad a carnt gerrit up'. So he did.
The car skidded around a lot, but Harry just managed to drive his car to the top of Ewden hill. Where he parked it on what he thought was the heather moorland at the side of the road, he returned to our farm on foot to finish cutting up the pig.
Later after he had finished we waved him goodbye as he left carrying his customary prized piece of pig mother had given him to take home to his wife, enough to make them both a tasty meal.
Then we heard he hadn't been able to find his car later that day, and, thinking someone had stolen it, he had walked to Midhopestones to catch a bus to Stocksbridge arriving home at his own farm very late that evening.
A number of weeks later someone mentioned to father that he had just seen an abandoned car parked on the moorland amid the remnants of the snow at the top of Ewden Hill, we just assumed someone had skidded off the road and abandoned the vehicle.
It was a few weeks later still before father noticed the car for himself, and the car did indeed look similar to the one Harry Taylor used to drive, so he sent word to Harry to come and have a look.
When Harry Taylor came to have a look for himself he was both surprised and delighted.
The only adverse effect was of course a flat battery. There was a note attached to the car requesting that the owner report to the police station to explain why it was parked there in the first place!

Eventually the snows of 1947 melted. I recall we all found it difficult to walk on the boggy surfaces exposed after all those weeks of slipping and sliding around. Everything was a mess; the farmyard was a quagmire with all the manure we had been unable to store in its proper place. It took weeks for everything to recover, to become normal again.

We could hear the river down at the bottom of Ewden beck quite clearly as it roared down the beck towards Broomhead reservoir. We could see the water cascading down the steep hillside across the valley from our farm past the druids' circle, as it tumbled down from the Broomhead moors in huge brown torrents mixed with peat and soil after the thaw.

As I said earlier we expected snow every winter. But 1947 was exceptional.

Almost every year I looked forward to snow for me to continue with a skill I had learned from Grandad Dyson. It was no good in any other conditions; it had to be newly fallen snow. Not just anywhere either but round the edge of fields or woodland it all depends where they took me.

What am I on about? Animal tracks in new snow!

When I was around ten years old I couldn't wait to finish my chores for the morning to get togged up for the cold and rush of to where I knew the tracks would be they're waiting for me to eagerly examine. The signs were at their best in the early mornings but as I had numerous jobs to do first it was more like late mornings before I was able to arrive on the scene.

If the sun were shining some of the tracks would be difficult to read for the edges sometimes became obscure by the sun melting the snow where it had been disturbed.

I remember selecting certain animal tracks and following them wherever they went, it wasn't difficult but I had to stick to it or I'd loose the track amongst the all the others.

I said animal! Birds also made good tracks especially the bigger ones such as crows or magpie or even pheasant all made distinctive tracks as they foraged for food amongst the new fall of snow.

However it was the animal tracks that interested me, the ones I liked to follow were the Fox or Badger for they were quite distinctive.

The most difficult one was the cat or squirrel. I knew all the bigger animals were looking for something more substantial for a meal. Like a rabbit or a hare. I would come across an area where some sort of fight had taken place, a place with blood on the snows surface or a pile of feathers where a pheasant, partridge or grouse had been taken unawares and killed by a predator.

Occasionally I would see where a bird had been attacked, but with no obvious tracks around where its attacker had stalked it. In such cases the obvious conclusion was it must have been a kite or harrier which had dived on the unfortunate smaller bird snatching it up to fly away and kill it somewhere else.

Rabbit tracks were interesting, the foot pattern was always the same, I could tell whether it was just idling along or travelling at speed just by looking at the distance between the footprints. Whereas a fox left the same track whether it was idling along or trotting. A cat was also quite distinctive showing a pattern that didn't vary much.

Whereas the badger just lumbered along mostly taking his time but if he did run the pattern changed completely.

With birds it was somewhat different they never hurried just meandered aimlessly along walking or hopping along just minding there own business. In some cases not even caring where they were going, for there were many tracks that showed where they had struggled to get over a wall to continue their journey.

If they had taken a little time and looked a little further there was maybe either a gate or a gap in the wall for them to get through without any problems whatsoever. If I were lucky I could follow a track back to where the animal had started. And I would make a mental note for future reference especially if it was a rabbit burrow as I was always on the lookout for a place to set a trap or snare to contribute to my catch that I took to sell to the housewives in Stocksbridge or Deepcar. Thus furthering my monetary income.

Ten

Sundays and Occasions

Sundays mean different things to different people but to my parents Sundays weren't much different to the other six days of the week. Garlic House Farm where we lived was perched precariously on a hillside above Ewden Beck, crowded on three sides by windswept open moorland. Where the cows, calves, hens or the work horses didn't know Sunday' were different for they either wanted milking, feeding or cleaning out just like any other day of the week.

But to my brother Lewis and I the seventh day of the week was a day of excitement and trepidation. It was much too far for us to walk to Sunday school like some of our friends especially in the winter months, so we had to be content with the regular weekly visit by our Grandad Fred Dyson, one of the Broomhead gamekeepers.

I can recall both of us excitedly watching the well-known stretchers of footpath he used as he came on his regular Sunday visits. And from our respective vantage points we competed with each other as to who would be the first to see Fred with his favourite black Labrador gun dog Jake making their way across the fields heading for our house. That was the exciting bit. But we both knew that as soon as he reached our house, the trepidation bit would begin.

When Grandad Dyson finally arrived at our farm, he always very carefully placed his shotgun out of sight behind a stone pillar in the cart shed, and instructed Jake his dog to guard it with the word 'stay'! Fred would then come into our house and greet mother with a hug. Then he'd grab either my brother or me and drag us over to the big arm chair where he would sit down, perch each of us on his knee and scrub his long sharp white whiskers on our face. We both received the same treatment and our faces burned for hours long after he had gone home.

He must have thought it was an affectionate greeting but I didn't like it one bit, neither did my brother Lewis. When we were small we accepted it as normal, as I grew bigger, older and wiser. I devised different ways of escaping the treatment. Such as the times I hid under the big table in the living room behind the Sunday velvet tablecloth that reached almost to the floor.

It worked for a while until I was discovered and unceremoniously dragged out to be given the whiskers treatment.

Sometimes Uncle Jim (mothers brother) also chose Sunday's to call at our house and he was even worse, for he insisted in having one of us on each knee to give us the whisker treatment despite our and mothers protests.

When I tried my latest ruse of hiding under the table Uncle Jim was even quicker at discovering my whereabouts. I remember trying all ways to avoid his groping hands as they searched for me beneath the table. I suppose it may seem funny to someone else, but to me it was a case of avoiding the inevitable as long as I could, for I knew what the end result would be.

I even tried hanging on to the table leg which proved useless as he was so strong I always had to let go to save upsetting the table. The longer I managed to avoid Uncle Jim the less time I had to endure the agony for I knew he had to be home for his dinner at a certain time - prompt.

He would suddenly shout

'Ahve got the little bugger, cum art a theer will tha'. His big searching hand would have found my ankle. It would suddenly tighten its grip as I was unceremoniously dragged out from under the table straight onto his knee where he performed what he considered to be his affectionate greeting. I couldn't win.

Before I forget I must relate to you here, about the time when Grandad Dyson came to our farm one particular Sunday morning as normal, he left as usual to walk home to where he lived at Hungerhill cottage Bolsterstone, to be in time for his Sunday dinner. After arriving home he went into the scullery intending to put his gun back into the rack where he normally kept it with the others, when he suddenly discovered he hadn't got it with him, or for that matter his dog Jake, for the dog was also missing. Fred was of course upset and quite perplexed about the whole thing.

His wife, Celia, my Grandma Dyson, later found her husband sitting on the bench outside the house with his head in his hands. She asked Fred what was the matter? He explained that it was the first time he had ever left his gun and dog anywhere all the years he had been a gamekeeper.

And that was the first time ever Grandad Dyson came to Garlic house farm twice the same day. The first time was as normal the second was to collect his gun and his dog Jake who was still sitting in our cart shed guarding the double-barrelled shot gun for his master.

The shotgun was of course still propped behind the stone pillar, exactly where he had left it.

My brother Lewis and I were surprised when our Grandad Fred Dyson walked into our yard for the second time that Sunday. We knew or thought we knew we had seen him go home earlier so the second visit was unexpected. After he had explained to mother what had happened earlier, she gave him a drink of something strong before he went home yet again. This time with his faithful dog-Jake following, and his 12 bore shotgun under his arm.

I remember birthdays; they were slightly different especially if there weren't any crops waiting to be harvested. Father quite rightly did treat each of our birthdays differently. We had of course to do the morning chores, such as milking and feeding round, but once that had been done the rest of the day was our own.

Until later in the day when milking time came round again and the never ending feeding of the stock. My own birthday was in July so I was always in a better position than say my brother Lewis, for his birthday is in October. And October is the month when most of the livestock are indoors for the winter months; consequently there was more work to do in the mornings before he could enjoy his birthday. Christmas day was treated in a similar manner; one of the biggest drawbacks of having Christmas day in December was the weather.

There could be mountains of snow around during that time of the year so Christmas day could be spent toiling around the yard feeding the stock doing the chores until late in the day in fact some times there wasn't much time at all to have a rest. We just had enough time to have a short respite in between to have a traditional Christmas dinner before it was back to work again doing all the same things again finishing the day exhausted and ready for bed.

Speaking of Christmas brings to mind the time when our traditional Christmas dinner escaped.

We didn't keep turkeys or ducks or even geese at Garlic House, but we had plenty of hens and a few cockerels around the place so our normal Christmas dinner was usually the choice between a fat hen and a big cockerel.

One particular year we had an abundance of big cockerels, so a week or so beforehand all the suitable birds had been rounded up and secured indoors to be fed extra rations, to finish them off.

On Christmas Eve father selected the one we intended having for the following days dinner.

Everything was going to plan, so far so good as one might say, father caught the one he had selected and pulled its neck out.

After it had stopped fluttering he handed it to mother, she congratulated him on his selection and took it into the house and placed it on the chopping board. With the specially sharpened big knife normally used for slicing ham or bacon rashers she chopped of the cockerel's head intending to immerse the bird in boiling water ready for plucking.

Suddenly there was a flurry of wings and the supposedly dead bird jumped down off the table, ran out of the house door and down the steps into the farmyard where it ran around like a head less chicken, but in this case it was a headless cockerel!

Mother shrieked 'Walter the dinners escaped', and it had. I remember watching as it ran around the yard until it fell over this time for good. Then the situation turned into a time of hilarious laughing, mother had to dry her eyes on her pinny before collecting the cockerel again to take it back into the house to continue preparation for the following days dinner.

The day the Christmas dinner escaped was a laughing matter for many years afterwards.

Then of course was the time our Christmas cake was spoilt, literally. I can't really say that I remember the incident personally for I was only one year old at the time.

But I remember it as if I was there by listening to local folk law and the fact it was serious at the time. It was mid December 1937 and my mother had finished preparing the Christmas cake and she had just placed it in the oven beside the specially stoked fire in our black kitchen range to bake. However the cake hadn't been in very long, when a bedraggled party of hikers came and knocked on our farmhouse door. They implored on mother to look after a distressed girl member of their group, whilst the rest of them went back up the Broomhead moors with a search party to recover the body of another girl.

94

It was the body of a girl who had died during the night, in a snowstorm high up near Margery rock!

Mother quickly bade the shivering distraught girl remove her soaked clothes to be dried, and not thinking she opened the oven door for more heat to help dry the girls sodden clothes, that action effectively ruined that years Christmas cake.

The incident of the dead hiker caused quite a stir in the area for a long time as the police and ambulance service had been called to the scene. The Remington Wilson family of Broomhead hall were involved because it had happened on their Moor. The verdict of the magistrates at the subsequent inquest declared that the hikers should have known better than to go up Broomhead Moor in the middle of winter, now they had a suffered the consequences.

One of the social highlights of our year was when my mother, my brother Lewis and I went to join up with the Whitsuntide Parade which started in Bolsterstone village. It was the only time of the year when we were bought new clothes. Such as a pair of trousers or a jacket or even a new pair of boots, initially to show off at the parade but the new items were in effect intended to be used for school so they had to last a long time.

We walked from Garlic House to Bolsterstone dressed up in our new clothes doing our best to avoid the mud and puddles to keep our new items clean especially our shoes or boots. We had to hurry to get to the village early to join the assembly behind the banner. When everyone was ready we followed the banner all the way down to Deepcar, where we joined up with other banner carrying groups.

From there began the long walk up Manchester road towards Stocksbridge. Opposite the town hall in Stocksbridge we turned left to toil up the very steep clock tower hill to eventually join many more groups in what was known as the Wragg sports field. In there we sang songs en- mass to the delightful music of the Stocksbridge works brass band. After some much-needed refreshments there were organised sports activities, and these lasted for the rest of the day. Whitsun was always a long day. I enjoyed it, as did all of us, and by the time we arrived back home to our farm, we were all happy and absolutely exhausted.

I always looked forward to Sundays! When the milking had been completed and all the associated chores finished such as cleaning out the milking shed, all the kit washed up, and the churns were on the stand waiting to collected. If it was summer time the cows had been taken to their new pasture or if it were winter all the stock had been fed round.

First thing after breakfast I went to check my snares or traps. Next probably once a month I would ride over to Trevor Cottons with my bicycle to see what was happening at his place. If he were also free we would sometimes go for a ride around the lanes for a couple of hours in the Bradfield area.

This brings to mind the occasion when we were messing around with our bicycles trying to go as fast as we could, or dared, down the steep Strines hill, careering around the sharp right handed corner on the bridge at the bottom.

We were both quite fast, and we were getting faster each time we tried. However the biggest problem was pushing our bikes back up the hill after each attempt. Pushing our bikes up the hill took us a quarter of an hour every time but the actual run down only took a couple of minutes to complete.

We persisted until after we had completed around six runs each when I ran wide on the exit landing with a loud splash in the left-hand roadside ditch just over the bridge, falling rather heavily as I recall. I struggled out absolutely covered in sludge, and all Trevor could do was laugh. He couldn't or wouldn't stop so in disgust I decided I'd had enough and I was going home, so we abandoned our messing around after that, and both of us rode home rather subdued.

Both Trevor and I continued with our mutual friendship when we progressed to motorbikes, doing more or less the same as we did with pushbikes careering err riding around the country lanes in and around what is now the Peak Park. We could ride much faster of course;

I rode a BSA 125cc. Trevor had a rather dilapidated BSA 250 rigid of some indeterminate year. We didn't go all that far away from our respective homes as it was only a bit of fun.

My close encounters with muddy ditches were played out (again) when I ran off the road into an ochre filled ditch somewhere near Low Bradfield. And Trevor laughed so much I finished up going home disgusted (again)!

It was only a few weeks after that debacle when another notable experience occurred.

I had been to Sheffield with the little BSA when it suddenly stopped as I was going up the hill from Hillsborough towards the little village of Bradfield.

The engine just backfired and stopped. No amount of jumping on the kick-starter could persuade it to start again. The bike had stopped on the outskirts of a built up area, and I didn't want to leave my bike in that locality to go and look for assistance, so I decided to push the silent machine. It was easy at first but as I became tired the bike somehow became heavier so eventually I could not push it any further. I was exhausted wet through with sweat and absolutely fed up.

I espied a little thicket of timber at the side of the road so I pushed the bike into it and continued my walk towards home without it. When I reached High Bradfield I decided to call in at a farm where my father knew the farmer, I knocked on the farm house door intending to see if they could do me a little favour and ring Broomhead hall.

When the farmer's wife saw my distress she dragged me indoors to have a refreshing drink so I could relate my predicament in more detail.
When she discovered the facts, she rang the housekeeper at Broomhead, to see if a message could be passed on to my parents at Garlic House. Informing them of my whereabouts and sometime later father arrived on the scene with the tractor and link box to recover both the broken down bike and me.
What was wrong with the bike you may ask? The contact breaker points had closed up in the ignition system, so there was no spark at the spark plug, when that was fixed it was just fine.
Other than that little hiccup that little bike served me well firstly as a road bike and shortly afterwards as a competition bike! Converting the BSA to competition bike was the absolute beginning of my long career of riding off road with all kinds of machinery.

It all started like this.
I was on my way home one evening after visiting Trevor Cotton; I remember it well it was early in the summer month of September 1952. I had ridden down long bank hill and was just about to ride over the Ewden Beck Bridge when a big motorbike suddenly appeared from the roadside ferns, it roared up the hill I had just descended, leaving behind a trail of mud. I stared wide-eyed, after a quick decision my bike was propped against the bridge wall whilst I went to investigate. The tracks left by the bike were easy to follow leading me to an area where whoever it was had been riding through a muddy ditch alongside the riverbank, and in doing so had stirred everything up. I was so exited I wanted to know more, so I rode the rest of the way home vowing to

find out all there was to know about the bike and rider I had just seen roaring away from the scene.
And the rest as they say, is another story!

Eleven

Ewden wood

Just down the hill from Garlic House is an extensive area of deciduous woodland bordering Broomhead moors in its upper reaches and Broomhead reservoir on its lower levels, known as Ewden Wood. All of it owned by the Broomhead estate. Drystone boundary walls of our lower fields effectively separating some of it from our land.

The woodland is exceptionally wild and beautiful especially in springtime when the blue bells are in bloom with wild garlic growing in profusion under the huge mature beech trees.

Running through the entire length of the wooded area runs a wide shallow bolder strewn river known as Ewden Beck

Passing through some of the wooded area is Mortimer Road, where a single arched stone bridge spans the Beck! The bridge (Ewden bridge) was at one time quite narrow intended for horse traffic only until it was reconstructed in the early 1950's making it slightly wider for motorised vehicles to pass over more easily.

Half a mile or so down the river from the Mortimer Road Bridge was (I say was because it may have gone by now) the precarious footbridge Fred Dyson my Grandad declared he crossed each morning on his way to Broomhead Hall to start his daily game keeping duties. All the time I remember it the Bridge was so decayed I never attempted to try and cross it, it didn't look safe. There were strong stone pillars at both ends and in the middle these supported the remains of the original 12" wide plank that formed the base for pedestrians to walk across. The Bridge had lost both its handrails at sometime in the past. It really did look precarious.

As you may imagine every time I saw it I reasoned if Fred actually used the Old Bridge like he professed he did, he must have been very brave. But I always suspected he crossed the river somewhere else to avoid the Bridge altogether anyway.

I shall always remember it was under that Particular Bridge where saw a water rat. It was swimming around a swirling pool of frothy water after a storm, directly underneath.

A mile or so up the river from the Mortimer Road Bridge is another narrow footbridge which locals refer to as the 'Wire Bridge'!

The Wire Bridge is I suppose, similar in construction to the one further down the river the one I mentioned earlier, the one that was in terminal decay. But here the similarity ends for up to the recent past the 'Wire Bridge' has been kept in relatively good repair. It had been used regularly by the Broomhead gamekeepers and the Gentry to cross the river with their assistants and dogs, on their way to the shooting butts, up on the Margery rock moor.

Slightly down river from the wire bridge, is a large area of multicoloured rhododendrons covering I suppose about two acres, very attractive and resplendent when they were in bloom.

However over the years they had spread further up the banks on the one side into the surrounding woodland, and on the other side into the heather clad moorland. I remember well the occasions when I would try to scramble through the middle of the tangled rhododendrons.

As I struggled I imagined it to be a rain forest in some far of land where I would have had to carry a machete to chop my way through. But it all belonged to the Broomhead estates so I didn't dare bring anything with me to damage the estate property. But there wasn't any harm in imagining.

Sometimes I could have done with a chopper of some sort for it was certainly a struggle trying to scramble through the middle. I would finally emerge bedraggled, scratched and wet through for the river ran under the branches and I couldn't avoid occasionally falling in the water as I endeavoured to reach my goal the 'Wire Bridge'.

As I became older when I had nothing particularly better to do, and I was feeling adventurous I would sometimes walk or trot down to the bottom of Ewden hill, and take my shoes and socks off to have a mess around in the river near the bridge. On other occasions I would try and walk in the water up the river amongst the slippy boulders to see how far I could get without actually having to come out of the water. Or again at other times I would endeavour to follow the path alongside the river to see how far I could get without getting my feet wet.

These fun and games might seem daft to some, but one of the reasons was further up the river the pathway quite often disappeared completely because

100

of the regular landslides in the area.

It meant I had to change from one side of the river to the other regularly to maintain progress up-river, unless of course I scrambled up the bank and over the top of the land slip with the added risk of falling down the landslide myself.

I preferred to keep crossing the river using the round slippery boulders as stepping stones quickly jumping from one to another on my way across, where sometimes the water was deep enough to swim in, but as I couldn't swim I had to be careful.

As you may well imagine on some of those occasions I was able to make good progress towards my destination (Wire Bridge) without getting wet, on other occasions I wouldn't get far before I'd slip off a rock and fall in the water.

So sometimes before I even started on my 'adventure' I made a pledge with my self-declaring to abort the idea as soon as I fell in. To keep this promise meant in fact on some occasions I would be back home quite early. Because I had fallen in! Or on the other hand I would be late home if things had gone to plan when I had made my destination it all depended on conditions and circumstances of the day.

You will have noticed I'm sure, that I keep mentioning the Wire Bridge?

Well, above the Wire Bridge the landscape became more or less just heather and bracken on both sides and the river became quite narrow in fact higher up still more the river became just a moorland stream. To me the interesting part of the river and any adventurous trips I made into the area always ended at the 'Wire Bridge'.

When my brother Lewis and I were quite young we had been warned to keep away from the area of Ewden Wood known as the 'ochre swamp'. The ochre swamp was an area of evil smelling orange coloured Jung, it was reputed to be bottomless, so we were told not to venture into it or we might just disappear, and be lost for good.

Both of us took the warning seriously as we didn't want to disappear for good, but we couldn't resist standing as close as we dared to look with wonder at the bright coloured ooze wondering what would actually happen if we did fall in?

Incidentally, here is a little snippet I learned about ochre. Yellow or orange ochre apparently had been used for centuries in the distant past, to dye wool in the clothing trade.

Nearby was the very small area where white bluebells grew. And every year my brother and I went into the wood to gather some to take them home for mother to display in the house. All the while pointedly avoiding the ochre area.

Well up the banking across on the moorland side of the river, was the area known as the 'the druid's circle'. This was supposed to be very ancient, to me it just looked like a circular sheep path with a few stones littered around amid the bilberry bushes and purple heather. I roughly measured across the circle one day, and I came to conclusion it was 30ft or so across.

Every year on certain dates druids could be seen shambling around the circle in their brown coloured hooded clothes. They looked as if they may have been chanting something but we couldn't hear what it was for it was just too far away.

However if the wind was blowing in our direction we could just about hear some of the mumbling sounds they were making as we listened from our farmyard.

They always came by bus as we could see it parked over the other side of the moor in a small lay-by near to the Broomhead Hall drive.

We at the farm didn't understand what the druids were doing, to us they were just wandering aimlessly around in a circle. It was just something different from our normal routine, and because it was happening so close to our farm almost on our doorstep (so to speak) even though it was across the valley, it couldn't be ignored completely.

Let's get back into Ewden Wood

Ewden Wood was where I had my den or even den's where I could hide in the undergrowth to be on my own without the hassle of the everyday rush. A place where I could be on my own, to contemplate. Whilst I was maintaining a suitable den Broomhead estates who owned the wood decided to fell some of the bigger trees in certain areas putting a somewhat temporary stop to me and my brothers capers, for a while at least. Soon a mobile home was established in our bottom pasture field and with it came two woodcutters one I can recall his name as Billy Jimmy but the other one's name I don't remember. They brought loads of equipment with them mostly hand tools and a huge caterpillar tractor complete with a scraper blade attached to the front.

Their hand tools consisted of crosscuts big and small. Axes of various sizes, and a pedal operated grindstone, to sharpen their equipment with. There were stacks of wedges and sledgehammers of various sizes and sundry other materials.

All of these were kept in a shed that was always secured by a huge padlock when they weren't around. Billy jimmy and his workmate couldn't be any closer to their work for they only had to cross the road from where they lived in their cabin to enter the woodland. Guarding the entrance to the wood at that time was a broken down rickety wooden gate no one had cared about for many years.

As soon as the two workmen started felling the wood what was left of the old entrance gate was lifted off its hinges, and carelessly thrown to one side, eventually becoming completely smashed.

As were both stone gates posts and the dry stone walls surrounding the entrance.

It was all done to allow the big caterpillar tractor with its wide blade to push a new roadway through the wood.

The new roadway was driven through the woodland all the way from the Mortimer Road entrance to a large flat low lying area below the old derelict Holt farm, best part of a mile into the wood I suppose. Undergrowth and large amounts of earth were pushed aside with the blade to make a clearing big and level enough to store the newly felled timber in huge stacks ready for transportation.

The caterpillar made the roadway wide enough to allow long timber lorries to travel along and down to the clearing to load up with timber. For many months we could hear the machines or personnel working in the wood. It could be the sound of axes clunking as they worked on the trees, on other occasions we could hear the sound of the caterpillar tractor moving around or the loud whining of the winch on the three-legged gantry doing its heavy lifting work loading the lorries with timber.

Some people regarded the new road as an eyesore, and they voiced their opinion whenever an opportunity arose, especially when the woodcutters had left the area, but it didn't take long for the roadway to become overgrown through lack of use. If anyone went there now and they didn't know precisely where the road had been located, they wouldn't be able to find it.

Ewden Wood had always been a private wood belonging to the Broomhead estates, where visitors were discouraged even though there weren't any signs saying as much, in the early days especially. If one of the Broomhead gamekeepers caught anyone in the confines of the wood they would be deemed to be trespassing. Further to that statement they were all tarred with the same brush and deemed to be poachers. On such occasions the Gamekeepers were empowered to confiscate all their poaching kit, if they had any, then escort them back to the road to be sent on their way with the warning not to come back for it was all private property.

Many times over the years my brother Lewis or I were discovered hiding in our respective dens by Grandad Dyson (we never had a communal den) by either of his two Labrador dogs 'Jake', or 'Don'.
My brother and I had thought that no one could possibly discover us for we had constructed our dens so carefully they weren't visible at all to anyone searching for us. But we hadn't taken into consideration the skills of Fred' black Labrador gun dogs.
When either of the dogs found us in our hideouts they just stood there staring at us with tail straight out, never barking just standing there quite still waiting until Fred came to find out what had been discovered.
When Fred turned up he would smile and say 'Ahh I've caught you little buggers agean'.

Another incident concerning Ewden Wood comes to mind. It was when I was sitting around the campfire one evening, with the woodcutters, chattering to Billy Jimmy and his workmate. When I suppose I must have become a nuisance, for they suddenly told me to clear off, but I wouldn't go! So Billy fetched one of their biggest axes and chased me all the way across the five-acre bottom field, over the stile in the bottom corner, and along the footpath belonging to Nether House Farm, but he wasn't quick enough, as I out ran him.
I always wondered what he would have done, if he had caught me! I was twelve years old at the time so I could run as fast as anyone, faster than Billy Jimmy anyway, especially as he was shouting, swearing, and brandishing the huge axe. I never went near the woodcutters after that, I always regarded the incident as serious. If they didn't want me to go and talk to them anymore it was their loss anyway.
Not long after that incident, the woodcutters completed their work and the caterpillar tractor, the cabin and the storage hut were all taken away, but they had left a very unsightly entrance into the wood. So it wasn't long before someone started to tip piles of building materials and spoil just inside the

104

entrance making the area even more unsightly.

No one saw or knew whom it was doing it but it was very unsporting of them to spoil the countryside with such rubbish.

After complaints a pair of new stone gateposts were erected, and the stone walls that had been so rudely demolished were rebuilt. A few weeks later a new wooden gate was installed.

The wooden gate swung on new hinges, to secure it in the closed position it had a shiny chain and padlock. Not that we could try it, we didn't even know who had control of the keys to the gate, for we never asked.

Before we move on to another chapter I must relate to you the story of how the gate to our bottom field was widened, the one just down the road from Garlic House.

To get through the gateway into the field with anything from the metalled roadway was always very difficult; the gateway had been made in one of the steepest parts of Ewden Beck hill. It was at least 1 in 4 or even steeper in that position.

The lower side had been built up over the years to make the way into the field slightly leveller installing a traditional stone gatepost on the lower side. On the other side the left side stood a large oak tree that had been used for many years as a pivot point to swing the gate on.

I suppose when the gateway was first introduced in that position the oak tree would only be a sapling so there would have been plenty of room for a horse and cart to get through.

As the tree grew fatter the entrance to the field became narrower until it became very difficult to get anything into the field at all, especially when we bought a tractor with its bigger implements.

Obviously we wanted to get into the field to do some work so father decided he had to do something about it. He looked at the right hand stone gatepost to see if that would move.

No it wouldn't! As luck would have it, as father was studying what to do, the manager of the woodcutters who were felling Ewden Wood came to visit his workers. So father asked him what he thought about the problem? The manager suggested they could cut the tree down (for a fee) to about five foot high, cut the stump down the middle, then take half of it away thus widening the gateway by about 3 foot. Father had no other option but agree, so he told the manager to carry on and do the work.

I remember when they had completed the job another gate had to be found to fit the wider opening.   The finished job allowed the gate to be opened sufficiently for our tractor and trailer to pass through without hindrance. Lovely job.   And I do believe it's still like that now!

During 1952 the year I was sixteen years old, Elliott Bros finally finished restoring the bridge over the river at the bottom of our hill.
The old bridge had started to deteriorate during the war years, when the American military used to bring heavy vehicles and machinery over it to get to there testing ground up above our farm.

The original structure just wasn't designed for such treatment.   The original was constructed for use by horse drawn vehicles, and horse riders.   It's a wonder the bridge didn't just collapse completely with the extra weight of motorised traffic.
Eventually Wortley District Council declared the bridge to be unsafe and put a weight limit order on it until it could be restored.
When the new bridge was finally finished the civil engineers Elliott Brothers had made a good job of the restoration, the road was wider allowing wider vehicles to cross easier, and the parapet walls on either side were much stronger.

Nowadays, when I go anywhere near the entrance to Ewden Wood, I drive very slowly remembering those times, many years ago, when my brother and I roamed the wood freely as if it were our own.
Sometimes I even stop to have a look over the gate at the entrance to Ewden Wood to have a look what it looks like nowadays, what I see is woodland just waiting for someone to come along and build a den somewhere, just to contemplate and plan!
Grandad Dyson has long since passed away so has his dogs.   I suppose the new Gamekeepers on the Broomhead estate might not be as tolerant as Fred was all those years ago.
As I move further down the hill and stop on Ewden Bridge to have a look over the coping wall at the river below, I remember all the fun I had messing around in the water.
Would I do it now?   Probably not, would I do it all if my time came round again?

106

Most definitely yes! They were enjoyable carefree days. It is now 60 years on as I write these words but even the thought of Ewden Wood brings on a nostalgic turn.

Twelve

Broomhead Hall

My brother and I were absolutely ecstatic when the Wilson family who lived across the beck at Broomhead Hall, gave us our first little horse. It was rather old but it was very good, except for a small gash in the side of its neck. Mother stitched it up assuring us that it didn't hurt the little horse all that much. It didn't eat anything as far as I knew, and it was clean around the house.

I rode that little horse for hours and hours until something more interesting came along.

But I shall never forget that little rocking horse the children from Broomhead Hall had sent us to play with. We all knew it was a cast - off but we didn't care it was absolutely fantastic. My brother tried to ride it but it was too big for him so I rode it for both of us.

A few weeks later the Wilson family sent us a huge fort or castle that had soldiers and riders on horseback made from lead and painted in fabulous colours. Neither my brother nor I had ever seen anything like that before. It was a source of enjoyment for both of us for a long time.

Captain Reginald Wilson's wife was living in London at that time so we never saw her or any of the children when they were small. They were at least teenagers before I remember them properly. Reginald and Harry the two boys, Caroline the girl the youngest one.

Garlic House Farm where I was born, was part of the Broomhead Hall estate not too far from Bolsterstone village near Sheffield Yorkshire. Our everyday lives were in a way controlled by the big house. It was where the sole telephone was in the immediate area, where we could go to ring for such specialists as the Vet, or the Doctor. For sometimes things happen on a farm which require professional services. If we couldn't use the telephone at Broomhead, the other alternative was to walk all the way to Midhopestones to use the public telephone box on the main Manchester-Sheffield main road.

The Broomhead hall that I remember when I was young was built in 1831 it was just one of a long list of buildings using the same site. Records show that Broomhead Hall had been restored or altered many times over the years, and the famously historical Wilson family had lived in the various versions for centuries.

.

But things had changed dramatically just after the Second World War, when the then owner Captain Reginald Wilson moved out of the big house into a smaller property. Apparently Captain Reginald had been living in the hall on his own for quite some years, but the house must have been so expensive to maintain he had finally had to move out into what was in effect an extended part of the housekeeper's residence.

It was rumoured that the military had taken over the Hall to billet officers and military personnel at one period during the latter part of the war, I suppose that may have helped the Captain to make his decision to move out.

I recall one evening in the late summer of 1946 when Roger the chauffeurs son, and I were playing around outside the Hall, he beckoned me to follow him around to the front of the house where the big games room windows looked out over the lawns. Roger went to a tall narrow window curled his fingers under it and lifted the bottom sash up; he quickly clambered through the small gap dragging me with him over the sill and into a large room. And I can confirm that there was certainly no one living in the house then.

We didn't stay long, just long enough for Roger to show me the huge staircase; it was so wide you could have driven a horse and carriage up. I didn't know about the unsecured window before, but Roger obviously did, anyway he only lived around the corner in the other yard so he would be expected to know.

Before I go any further with this story I must tell you about a tree, a special tree. This special tree grew quite some distance (maybe a ¼ of a mile or so) down the big park towards the bottom gates. At the time there was a small brass plaque affixed to the protective railings, describing in detail how an arrow shot with a long bow from the library window of Broomhead Hall had landed in that particular place. Apparently the feat had impressed everyone so much at the time that a sapling had been planted to record the effort.

110

And there was a huge stone sundial dated 1688 propped against the wall just around the corner from the main Hall entrance. Many times over the years when I had been playing around the Hall with Roger Senior, and we had lost track of time, we had tried in vain to decipher what the sundial suggested, it always defeated us, so we had to guess?

Immediately after the Second World War, many prisoners were still held in captivity in Britain. Most of them were put out to work on farms as labourers, at the end of the hostilities they were given the choice by the British Government to stay on in this country if they so wished to continue working on the farm of their choice. Alternatively they could be repatriated back to their country of origin.

A couple of the German agricultural workers who had been working at Broomhead home farm for quite some time decided to stay, their names were Bruno and Teo. Everyone knew them by those names, when they heard of the government's decision they pleaded with my Uncle Jim the Broomhead estate farm manager, to be allowed to continue working on the farm.

As there weren't any houses or accommodation available in the immediate locality, it was decided to allow them to live in the big house Broomhead Hall, as it was empty at the time.

Bert Shaw the estate builder was instructed to rudimentary convert two of the rooms on the second floor for their use. Bert made one of the huge rooms into a living room and the other into a bedroom. For toilet and washing facilities they had to use the ones in the tack room in the farm buildings such as they were. The ones in the Hall had been disconnected or weren't working.

They both lived in those converted rooms in the Hall in complete harmony for several years before they were finally obliged to return to their own country on government orders.

One of them, I think it was 'Bruno', was a qualified watch repairer before the hostilities, soon after coming to live in our area he was repairing timepieces for local people in his spare time.

I remember it being said that when they both went back to Germany when the Broomhead staff were clearing the rooms they had been occupying, hundreds of watches and clocks were found, most of them in a dismantled state. Apparently Bruno knew how to repair watches and clocks but he couldn't obtain the bits he needed to put them back together again.

We also had a couple of German workers brought by army lorry to work on our farm during that same period just after the War had ended. However in our case it was only when we were busy and needed extra labour. They were dropped off quite early in the mornings and collected later in the day to be taken back to where they were housed in a detainee camp somewhere.

They didn't have any security guards with them or anything like that they were trusted to behave themselves whilst they were out working, as it were. I suppose if they were reported as being anything but, they would have had their privileges cut or reduced.

I remember one year, it was a Friday evening, and we were hauling the corn from the six-acre field below Cottage farm with the horse and cart when the lorry came to collect our German helpers.

Of course when they had gone our labour force was considerably reduced and because I was only ten years old I could only do certain things. Obviously my efforts weren't enough for father continually complained about the loss of our helpers thinking I suppose we wouldn't see them again until the following Monday morning.

Imagine our surprise when the next morning, the Saturday, when one of our regular German helpers walked into our farmyard all smiles and courteous as usual.

Father went out into the road to look for the lorry to sign his ticket, but no our friendly German had walked. He had apparently broken out of his confinement camp in the middle of the night and made his way on foot to our farm.

He'd been walking most of the night from where the camp was situated to continue helping us with the harvest. Later that day when the crop of corn was all safe and dry in our stack yard our friendly German prisoner left us to walk back to camp where he would have had to break back in again. It appeared that no one was the wiser, for he turned up on the Monday morning with the lorry as usual reporting he'd had no problems whatsoever.

He had risked his privileges for us, and we appreciated it.

Back to Broomhead Hall. In the 1950's - the drawing room inside the house was used to store farm produce where grain was tipped onto the bare stone flagged floor. Apparently the reason why the hall was being utilised in that way was because the farm had run out of storage space.

So inside the Hall was the only place left available where it was dry enough to store grain. I can see it now the oats, barley, and wheat in huge piles on the drawing room floor. It didn't look right to me. Later the grain had to be bagged up to be carried around to the other side of the farm buildings, where it went through the farm milling process to be fed to the dairy herd.

By that time the huge wide carved oak staircase in the entrance hall had been removed; it had been sold and transported to America!

Later still sometime in the 1970's— the complete Broomhead Hall was dismantled stone by stone and transported to America...

If for any reason you are travelling along Mortimer road towards Bradfield and you look to your left just before the main drive to where the big house used to be, partially hidden in the trees you will be able to see a three-sided tall stone structure. It is in fact the remains of an open-air tennis or squash court. Many years ago it had a paved floor and the inside walls were rendered and painted matt black, to at least twenty foot or even higher. There wasn't ever a roof on it as far as I can remember so I suppose it must have been built like that.

There was never a wall on the end looking towards the main driveway and the greenhouses as far as I can recall. To anyone looking at it from the road it just appeared to be a ruined building where the roof had fallen in.

However sometime in the late nineteen sixties the estate fitted a tin roof and installed a gated front, so it could be used as a crew yard to house cattle.

Broomhead Hall Farm was one of the very first farms in the area to make and use silage to feed the animals. The silage Pit was constructed on a level area near to the ornamental fishing lake using old railway sleepers for the sidewalls. Initially it had to make do with a dirt floor.

The silage pit always seemed to have steam rising from it everytime I walked past it, and the sickly smell of molasses pervaded the air especially in the early days.

At that time silage making in this country at least was in its infancy, and the smell was unique to any one who walked by. Broomhead utilised two additives in their bid to make first class silage, these were molasses and aniseed. They were added to the green silage as it was brought to the pit before it was rolled. Both the additives came in huge tins and had the consistency of black treacle. Molasses that gives that sweet sickly smell to silage, but cows, like any other

113

animal cannot resist the attraction of aniseed.

You could smell it in and around the entire Broomhead farm and buildings, not an unpleasant smell, but I suppose it could be if one was exposed to it all of the time.

Broomhead Home Farm was also the first farm in our area to keep laying hens in battery cages.

As one walks through the archway leading into the big farmyard, to your left is the tack room and to the right is where the farm working horses were stabled.

If you go through a door on your right and up a flight of stone steps you are led directly into two large rooms, one directly over the tack room and the other over the stables. Those two rooms was where my Uncle Jim the farm manger had installed hundreds of new battery cages to keep the estate laying hens in.

When he showed me the set up one day, my first thought was what a smelly and stuffy environment. Maybe the Broomhead estates were trying to produce more eggs by keeping the hens in the cages, but I wasn't convinced.

But saying that my brother and I later bought some battery cages ourselves to keep some of our laying hens in. But as far as I can remember it didn't make any difference whether the hens were kept inside in cages, or ran free outside, they still produced about the same amount of eggs.

There was only one advantage with keeping hens in cages as far as I could see, and that was they were safe from marauding foxes.

Talking of foxes brings to mind the occasion when one morning mother and I went to feed the hens; we had to walk through a couple of fields carrying the feed in buckets to where they were housed.

When we arrived at the first hen house (hen oyle), we were shocked to find the complete side of the wooden shed wrecked. Most of the boards had been ripped off and scattered around on the ground, needless to say there wasn't a single hen left alive. Instead there was a mass of feathers and carcasses strewn around the area. The remainder of the half dozen or so hen houses hadn't been touched. Obviously we couldn't do anything at that time, so we carried on and let the hens out of the other sheds feeding them in the long troughs.

114

The very next day Grandad Dyson called to see us at the farm on one of his frequent visits, and mother mentioned to him the incident with the wrecked shed. He went to have a look, after a while he came back to declare 'That's not a bloody fox, he said, 'it's a badger what's dun that'. We always knew a fox would usually grab a hen and run. Or if a fox actually did get inside a hen house it normally just kills all the hens by biting their heads off, it doesn't wreck the shed, that's not normal for a fox!

After Grandad's diagnosis father decided to tow (with the horse) the remaining wooden hen houses nearer to home, he reckoned to be on the safe side.
It might just be an isolated case or it could be the case of a badger going mad, he wasn't going to risk having another shed wrecked.
It never happened again as far as I can recall.
The incident just came as a reminder to make sure the pop holes were closed well before dark if possible each and every day, as a deterrent against marauding foxes or Badger's for we hadn't forgotten the incident of the wrecked shed.
I remember if it wasn't quite dark enough I sometimes had to wait (where the hens couldn't see me) for the last one to scrabble up the ladder into the shed before I rushed in to close the flap.
I knew very well if the hens even suspected I was watching they wouldn't have gone inside. If there was just one left outside and I was in a hurry, first I had to make sure and close all the pop holes before giving chase to try and catch an indignant squawking hen.
After the badger incident, Grandad Dyson made it one of his priorities to walk around our fields occasionally in the area where the hen shed had been damaged.
He was on the look out for a mad badger.

I visited Broomhead Hall farm for many reasons over the years; initially I suppose it was when the school taxi collected me, from the age of five years old. Then my friendship with Roger Senior the chauffeur's son developed and I visited him to play around the big house and gardens.
Another reason was my Uncle Jim Dyson was the farm Bailiff his job was to control the entire farm with the every day working and the staff who worked there. And later I helped with the corn threshing days in the big barns.
Another reason for visiting was the telephone, for Broomhead had the only telephone installed in our area. When I was old enough I was the one to run,

walk or ride my cycle to the housekeepers cottage to ask if we could make a phone call to someone it could have been the doctors, vets, or the MMB. All this meant I saw the Broomhead head gardener Mr Poppleton quite often as I travelled past his main entrance door which opened straight onto the main drive to the farm.

Mr Poppleton was an extremely busy person for he had numerous greenhouses to look after and a very large walled garden surrounded by a ten-foot high brick wall.

When I got to know and became friendly with Mr Poppleton he showed me round his domain and I was intrigued when he proudly showed me his exotic fruit area.

And from that day I wanted to have a taste of a peach and a grape.

I didn't want to ask the gardener if I could have one to taste for everyone knew he was very protective of his various charges. So later Roger and me planned a scrump some for us mission!

We, or should I say I, had thought it would involve having to climb over that ten foot wall somewhere but on the day Roger led me to a damaged area where the remaining wall was low enough for us to easily climb over. I remember we collected a small number of peaches and grapes, not many just a few for we had to eat them whilst we waited for one of the under gardeners to move far enough away so we could make our escape. Our mission was quite successful, my curiosity was satisfied. As for the peach' and grapes they were absolutely delicious. So over the years we made various repeat visits when the fruit were in season. We were never discovered or apprehended during our undercover exploits so we were well satisfied.

Thirteen

Police

During the early 1940' until the war ended a motorcycle mounted police officer became a regular visitor to our farm, we knew him as 'Bobby Wilby' whether that was his real name we never knew? I remember when father asked where he came from he declared he was stationed in the mill town of Wakefield West Yorkshire

I can see him now as if it was only yesterday. Bobby Wilby riding his Triumph motorcycle down Ewden Beck hill, slowing down slightly to turn into the wide entrance of our farm gate where he stopped to step off his bike.

Everytime he came he always parked his machine on its centre stand, to make sure it was safe to leave he'd wobble the bike a bit with one hand on the handlebars and the other on the seat.

When he was satisfied he would carefully pull off his gauntlets and goggles before removing his helmet, pushing his goggles and gloves inside the helmet he'd place it upside down on the bike seat.   That ritual out of the way he would make his way through the small service gate into our farmyard and stalk along the uneven flagstones towards our farmhouse door.

To me at the age of six or so everything he did seemed to be in slow motion! Bobby Wilby was I should say thirty years old, a tall thin imposing figure dressed in his immaculate dark blue police uniform.

Bobby Wilby wore shiny black boots with long black leggings, and he scared my brother Lewis and me so much, we often went into hiding, until we thought it was safe enough to make our reappearance.

I suppose one of the reasons he scared us so much could be blamed on our parents. It was quite normal in those days to say to a youngster who had been particularly naughty, the words

'A policeman will come and take you away for that'!

Subsequently everytime a policeman came into our farmyard we would recall the impending threat promptly 'disappearing'. Only reappearing when we felt the threat had passed.

In the beginning our parents had often mused privately as to why a police officer should come all the way from Wakefield on what were by then regular visits; one of their favourite conclusions was because he must be a spy. Not a foreign spy, but a spy for the ministry.
He did finally own up one day, when my father asked him outright what was the reason for his regular visits to our area.
He readily admitted that one of his responsibilities was to check out all outlying farms on his patch in the Pennines as directed by the chief constable on behalf of the Ministry of Food. The Ministry of Food had the right at that time to search all the buildings and farm houses looking for any thing what wasn't supposed to be there. Anything that was either rationed or licensed! What one could call --contraband I suppose.
Obviously father didn't have anything on display that he wasn't supposed to have. Such as the cwt bag of sugar, hidden in the upstairs wardrobe. The even bigger bag of white flour, that was stashed behind the round table in the spare bedroom or for that matter the bags of cow cake hidden in the straw stack in the barn. The policeman would have surely noticed them, especially if they were anywhere obvious. The fact that Bobby Wilby may have wanted to look around more closely always hung over my parents conscience, so everytime he appeared they would both be on tender hooks wondering all the time when or where he may want to look on this latest visit.
However when he did actually have a look around, which incidentally was rare, he conducted his 'search' in a half-hearted manner, it always turned out to be a quick cursory look, nothing detailed or orderly. If he noticed anything 'not quite right' he never actually said or even suggested that he had, as far as I can remember.
What really interested Bobby Wilby were the sides of bacon and hams hanging up to dry on the hooks in the ceiling of our living room!
I remember quite well every time he came to call mother always made him a pot of tea with a slice of cake. He would sit at the table slowly munching his way through the slab of cake sipping his tea whilst staring at the hams and sides of bacon hanging just above his head.
Make no mistake my parents knew what he was thinking.
Eventually he would say

118

'That's a nice side of bacon Mrs Couldwell'! My mother would nod in assent, and then father would venture
'Would you like a piece Mr Wilby'?
'Oh yes please' would be his over quick response. Bobby Wilby must have learned from somewhere that we had killed a pig quite recently, so he had planned his visit accordingly. He would also have known we always killed a pig just before Christmas each year.

So father would cut off a nice sized slab off the bacon, and if he had hidden something he particularly did not want the policeman to notice or see, he would cut off a slice of ham to go with it.
Mother would then carefully wrap the plunder in brown paper for Mr Wilby to take to his motorcycle where he would place it carefully in the large black box affixed to the luggage rack on the rear of the bike, and then the box was securely locked with a padlock.
I recall on one occasion when I had raised enough courage to be more inquisitive I followed him back to his bike with the sole intention of having a look in that black box to see what he really kept in there? Only to be angrily shooed away by Mr Wilby before I even had the chance to look inside at all!
Soon after that, we began to think he was a blackmailer, and in his black box he kept all his ill-gotten gains. We imagined if Bobby Wilby was given stuff at all the farms he visited, he must have lived like a lord, or they all did back at the police station in Wakefield. For even during one day only he could have collected enough plunder to feed everyone at the Wakefield Police headquarters. Or so we surmised.
Anyway he never turned down the offer of goodies at our farm as I recall.

Then there was the occasion when the police from our local police station at Deepcar came to call at Garlic House; it was when an alleged escaped robber was on the loose. So they said. But as far as I can recall we never saw him. Numerous police officers came and carefully searched all the properties around our area including our farm buildings then we heard they had declared the exercise to be a complete waste of time, eventually they went away. So peace and tranquillity once again returned to the area. However a week or so later a stranger knocked on our farmhouse door to ask mother if she could spare a crust and a drink of water. The very next day the Police were at our door again asking if we had seen such a fellow? Which we obviously had! Next they came around with books full of what they described as mug shots, and Mother who had dealt with the stranger at the door was asked to look carefully at every picture in the book to see if his face was featured in it. But no it wasn't! Much to my disappointment.

On another occasion we were all subjected to being finger printed, which I thought was a huge breeze! We were told something had been stolen somewhere and the culprit could be hiding in our area and the police needed everyone's fingerprints to find out 'who done it' we were assured that our fingerprints would be destroyed later when the culprit was finally apprehended.

It was quite some time later before the suspect was caught and placed where he belonged in gaol, whether they carried out their promise and destroyed all our fingerprints, I've no idea.

Another such occasion was when my brother Lewis went on an errand to Cottage farm, about half a mile further up our hill. He knocked on the door to be confronted by a stranger who told him to push off and go away, which he did, so Lewis returned home to tell our mother. The next day we learned that someone had broken into the house and stolen all the stored shotguns belonging to Broomhead hall. That as you may well imagine caused quite a stir and a police presence in our area with many officers milling around for days.

But I can't recall whether anyone was apprehended for the misdeed.

Jim Blyton and his family lived at Cottage farm; Jim was for many years one of the two chauffeurs who worked for Captain Reginald Henry Remington Wilson of Broomhead hall. For some reason or other Mr Blyton had been keeping custody of the shotguns in his house though we at the farm didn't know it at the time!

My brother Lewis was lucky not to have seen or even said anything untoward for he could have been in great danger of being hauled into the house and something terrible happening to him at the hands of the burglar or burglars.

In the early days we didn't usually see many police officers around our area, our nearest police station being in Deepcar about 8 miles or so away, so we didn't actually expect a bobby to walk all the way from Deepcar to our area for any old thing. It wasn't until after the war that some of the beat patrol constables were issued with the so-called noddy bikes, which were of course the Velocette twin cylinder, 149cc LE. Those motorcycles were water-cooled and very quiet in operation, ideal one would have thought for the police to get around with.

Occasionally one of these did come past our farm, what they were looking we were never quite sure. Obviously they came to visit us at Garlic House when it was time to renew our shotgun licence or the dog licence, or to enquire if we had seen someone they were looking for who had committed a misdemeanour.

Later still when patrol cars became popular one of them would occasionally roar past our farm what they were chasing? We had no idea.

It was different though for my Grandad Fred Dyson, he had regular contact with the Deepcar police station occasions such as when he caught poachers on the Broomhead estate.

Local folk law has it that on one memorial occasion Fred had apprehended two poachers with all the gear such as ferrets, dogs, and guns somewhere on the extensive Broomhead estate. The tale goes he confiscated all their kit and marched them all the way to the police station to have them charged with the offence of stealing game or rabbits without lawful permission from Captain Reginald Wilson. It was all before my time so I don't know whether it was true or not, but Fred Dyson wasn't a chap to be trifled with even when I knew him, so maybe it was true.

August 12th is traditionally the start of the shooting season so a police patrol car could be seen circulating our area when grouse shooting days were in progress.

On those days there were many loaders and gamekeepers carrying guns around on the public roads and many more spare guns were stored in the cars the Gentry had brought with them.

I know most of them were in gun cases but they were still there to be seen. I suppose the police would have been issued with a list of dates beforehand by the Broomhead estate so that the police could keep an eye on the meeting, so hopefully nothing would go wrong on the actual day.

Grandad Dyson told me once, that when grouse shooting was in progress, which entailed using Mortimer road, the police had the power to direct traffic from Midhopestones through Stocksbridge and Bolsterstone via Wigtwizzle. Bringing them back onto Mortimer road beyond the shooting area, this diversion would then miss all the roads where the grouse shooting activity was in progress.

The only traffic allowed in the area was of course the cars of the Gentry, the gamekeepers and beaters. I suppose it made sure no unwanted members of the public infiltrated the area.

With all the loose guns and ammunition lying about, it was always a good idea to have a police presence. I don't know whether the estate had to pay anything for the service but I'm sure it would have been money well spent, especially for the visiting Gamekeepers.

They could be assured all the guns would be accountable when they came to collect them at the end of the days shoot to take back to their own estates.

We did have the occasional constable call at the farm investigating some of the bikes we had promised to store for someone unfortunate who had had an accident lower down our hill on the Saturday or Sunday. These were usually cycles, but saying that we did have to store the occasional motorcycle.

I suppose it was an evidence collecting exercise for them, always wanting to know what we knew of the accident. Mostly it was not a lot, but sometimes we had been given the name or address of the owner of a machine which lay in a mangled heap either in a disused pig sty or loose box at the bottom of Garlic House farm yard.

I recall on one occasion when the remains of a sports bike lay in the pigs' sty and the policeman had asked father to bring it outside for him to have a look at!

Father looked at the bobby and declared

'Tha'l have to fetch it art thesen if tha wants to have a look, ahv'e showed thee where it is naa ahv'e got some work to doo'

Father could tell the bobby didn't like the smell of the pigsty even though it had been empty for a while, obviously the constable didn't want to get his hands or his boots dirty.

So father' rather blunt rebuff meant the constable had no alternative but to go inside and have a look at the bike himself, as he wasn't going to get anymore help from father on that occasion!

I was there behind them both listening. Then I could hear the constable snuffling and snorting all the time he was in the sty.

As there wasn't a light in the pig's sty it was quite dark inside. But the constable didn't even try to drag out the mangled bike he was supposed to be investigating, for within a couple of minutes he was back out again pulling faces of disgust.

Father had by then gone to get on with his work, so the constable glowered at me instead, as if it was my fault? After wiping his hands carefully on a handkerchief he pulled his note book out of his pocket to scribble a few words before slamming the pig sty door shut and stamping off to his noddy bike, most definitely in a foul mood!

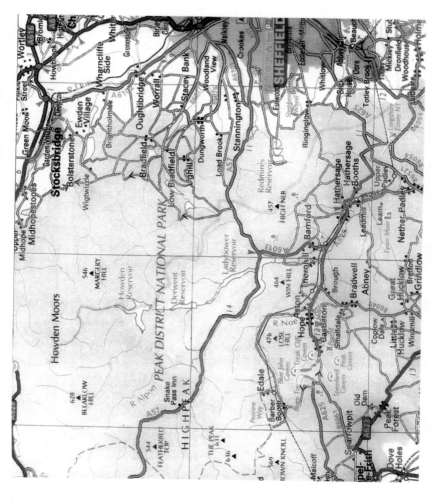

Chapter 4 - My father, my brother Lewis and me driving the tractor whilst hay making, c1952

Chapter 4 – My father (centre, in black coat & flat cap) and a group of local farmers on a day out at the Ferguson tractor works in Coventry

Chapter 6 - The first motorcar we had at Garlic house, a 1938 Hillman minx Reg No. EWB 9

Chapter 8 - The shooting cabin on the Broomhead 'big moor'

Chapter 8 - Hungerhill Cottage, Bolsterstone, where my grandfather, Fred Dyson, the Broomhead Gamekeeper lived all his life

Chapter 8 - An old picture showing Broomhead rabbit warren after it had been prepared by the estate gamekeepers for a culling day

Chapter 8 - A typical grouse-shooting butt, as built and used in the later part of the 19th century on the Broomhead moors

Chapter 9 - An excellent picture showing Ewden Beck caught in the throes of winter

Chapter 12 - Broomhead Hall, c1900. The one I remember before it was demolished and taken to America

Chapter 12 - The big sundial, dated 1688, permanently propped against the Broomhead Hall wall, on a corner near to the main entrance

These are the two 'Take Off' stones, along Mortimer Road.
One can be seen near the Strines Inn, the other at the top of Sheephouse Hill

Fourteen

Local Characters

I must begin this chapter with the local squire who lived at the big house Broomhead Hall, the owner of all he surveyed, literally, not just in a manner of speaking. He owned all of the farms and houses in our area and beyond. His title Captain Reginald Henry Remington Wilson or RHRW as he was known locally. After the Second World War, he could be seen regularly walking along Mortimer road with his walking stick. A tall slender very erect figure, he always wore a plus four suite, a deerstalker hat, and he always had a couple of gun dogs trotting by his heal. If he saw me anywhere in the mornings his greeting would be,

'Ha good morning Wilfred', to that I would always touch my cap and reply 'Good morning sir' for I had been schooled to address him in that manner. As long as we kept the farm tidy, paid the rent on time, didn't touch his pheasants or grouse father never had any trouble whatsoever from RHRW?

I think I have mentioned elsewhere that the Captain had moved into an annex of the housekeeper's cottage during the war years. Where he lived on his own most of the time looked after by his housekeeper Mrs Caddick.

Mrs Caddick was a nice straight-laced older lady who lived together in the housekeeper's cottage with her daughter Molly the maid. Molly was a very slim shy girl slightly older than I was.

If I was sent to Broomhead on any errand involving having to knock on the housekeepers door, invariably Molly would open it, and before I had time to ask her anything she would turn and loudly yell into the house from the open doorway.

'Mother there's Wilfred at the door!!!', then she would promptly disappear. I would have to wait outside on the doorstep until her mother Mrs Caddick came to see what I wanted.

Which was usually the request if I may use the telephone.

The black telephone sat on a small table in the hallway, I'm sure it frightened me most of the times I used it.   It was one of those upright things with a separate earpiece hanging on the side.   To use it one had to unhook the earpiece stick it at the side of ones ear then whirl the attached handle a few times all the while listening for a voice to say 'Number please?'

I always had the number written on a slip of paper, I would duly recite my number then I had to listen carefully for the voice to say 'Just a moment please I will try to connect you'.

After some clicking and buzzing the voice would say 'You are through now!' then I was able to deliver the message my parents had written down on the slip of paper.

Even though I knew the procedure I often came unstuck, so if I started to flounder or stutter Mrs Caddick would take over and finish the message for me.

There were two chauffeurs employed at Broomhead Hall, Mr Jim Blyton who lived further up the road from us at Cottage farm. He went to work on a small Royal Enfield motorcycle every day. The other chauffeur was Arthur Senior, he lived in a chalet type house on the very edge of the parkland; in fact most of the house overlooked the entrance to the farmyard.

The two chauffeurs shared the duties of driving the beautiful Rolls Royce motor car housed in the two-car garage near the Hall. They had of course other duties such as driving the estate lorry occasionally fetching and taking things for the farm, so they were always busy.

The Head gardener Mr Poppleton had a huge task on his hands, for he grew all the vegetables and fruits that were required by the housekeeper and the special occasions when the captain had guests to entertain.   Mr Poppleton had quite a lot of greenhouses to attend to on both sides of the main drive to the house; the ones inside the high walled area grew peaches and exotic fruits whereas the long greenhouse across the drive were always full of tomatoes when in season.

Unfortunately Mr Poppleton (I have forgotten his first name) came to a nasty end one hot summers day when he mistakably took a swig from a bottle which said lemonade on the label, but in fact contained weed killer. He died there in the potting shed when I was I suppose around ten years old.

I remember walking past the potting shed door the same day, at the time I thought it was strange why there was a policeman guarding the door until I went home later to be told what had happened. The post – mortem courts verdict was accidental death, caused by accidentally drinking weed killer by mistake. I remember we were told to always look twice at what was said to be in such containers as lemonade bottles, and if it looked at all suspicious pour the contents out onto the ground, not to drink it!

Mr Poppleton's job was taken over by the under gardener Tommy Downing who lived on a small holding on the road known locally as Cowell flats, nr High Bradfield.

Tommy Downing was a very short, wide red-faced quiet sort of person. He had worked in the Broomhead gardens for such a long time he knew all there was to know about the set up so there were no problems when he took over, I can't really remember whether the estate took on another under gardener when Tommy moved up in status.

My mothers brother Jim Dyson was for many years the farm Manager (Bailiff) controlling the farm and the staff who worked there. He lived with his wife (Anise) and family in an estate cottage in the little hamlet of Wigtwizzle.

At that time the estate kept a sizeable milking herd which required two or three regular cow men with another couple of casual workers to help during the busy feeding times, then they became tractor drivers when their yard duties had been concluded.

Now we can move on to the Gamekeepers. Harry Ward was the head keeper, my Grandad Fred Dyson was the under keeper, Herbert Hemsley and another two or three other keepers were employed to control the extensive grouse moors owned by the Broomhead Estate.

Harry Ward lived in the house known as Barnside lodge situated along the road to upper Midhope. It was a big house built in an isolated location at the side of Barnside moor surrounded by multicoloured rhododendrons that looked beautiful when they were in bloom.

Fred Dyson lived at Hungerhill Cottage Bolsterstone another Broomhead estate house where many of the previous estate gamekeepers had lived over the years. I went to Hungerhill cottage quite often with my mother; we had to pass the cottage on our way to Bolsterstone whenever we needed any extra groceries from the village shop.

So it was easy and pleasant to call and see Grandma Dyson.

I remember quite well Fred Dyson always kept some ferrets in the old house at the bottom of his yard; some were his own others were ones he had confiscated from poachers. And he would regularly show them to me describing how they were gentle creatures even if they looked vicious. I didn't particularly like ferrets at all they always looked nasty and ready to bite at any time so I usually kept my distance on our visits to the old house and the ferret cages.

However, on one occasion when Grandad wasn't around, I went into the old house on my own to have a look at the so-called gentle ferrets! Somewhat reluctantly I poked my finger through the wire door grill to attract their attention. I wasn't quick enough as one bounded across and promptly bit my finger, that scared me so much I never ever so much as touched a ferret after that, it put me off them for good!

There were numerous farms on the Broomhead estate some of them outside our area the ones listed below are quite local and where I knew them personally both socially and work orientated.

Our farm Garlic House was just one on the extensive Broomhead estate where my father Walter Couldwell had farmed since the early nineteen thirties.

Our nearest neighbour Spencer Steward farmed Ewden Lodge and had done so for an equally long time.

Over the skyline from us was Barnside Farm where Frank Hague had farmed for many years.

His neighbour Wilby Seddon farmed Barnside Cote and was probably the oldest working farmer in our area.

From our farmyard we could see Saltsprings Farm where Tommy Cockayne lived. He didn't do much with his few acres for he worked full time as a cowman at Broomhead. Lower down the hillside we could just see Nether House Farm, where Harry Brammer lived. He didn't farm his land either he let it out for pasture, he also worked for the estate employed as a part time Thatcher.

To me Harry Brammer was always very old; he was short and wide with a long beard that he tucked into his belt as he worked. Unfortunately he came to a sticky end as I remember for he allegedly fell to his death from a haystack he was thatching. He did work on other farms in the area to supplement his income as I remember, including thatching some of ours.

We mustn't forget Mrs Sampson or Elsie Wainwright the two post women who shared the task of delivering the post to us almost everyday. They didn't live in the area, they both lived in Bolsterstone village, but as they visited us almost everyday bringing the post. In effect we saw them even more regularly than our neighbours.

They walked all the way from Bolsterstone almost every day whatever the weather delivering the letters and small parcels. Every day was a challenge for them for they would sometimes arrive in our yard wet through; wind blown or almost solid if the day was cold and frosty. And they braved mountains of snow to deliver our post in the most difficult conditions during the winter months.

Another character who came into the area through work or other commitments was Ernest Hague, otherwise known as 'Midnight'. He acquired that unlikely name by overstaying his welcome, usually after a day's work, on farms in our area.

To elaborate the story –

After completing the work he had been engaged to help with, Ernest would stay and help the farmer with his final chores of the day and then stay for his tea, and then his supper.

Never showing any signs of going home, all the while talking endlessly with the farmer and his wife, until the farmers wife couldn't stand it no longer, she finally had to declare she was going to bed. This left the husband and Ernest to continue with whatever was the subject under discussion. Later still the farmer declared he was also going to bed and he would have to say to Ernest,

'Well ahh don't know about thee lad, but arr'm off to bed, if tha stoppin much longer thall afta lock up thesen afoor tha go's wom'.

Fortunately Ernest was never around the next morning and the house was always locked up as had been requested. How long Ernest stayed there after midnight no one could say for sure, but he acquired the name 'Midnight' quite quickly, and it stuck.

The name going with him wherever he went.

Continuing on now.

Deepcar, a somewhat smaller town near to Stocksbridge, boasted the best, not one of the best but 'The Best' fish and chip shop in and around the Stocksbridge area. Like all chip shops, when it came to the end of the working day when it was time to shut up shop, there could be either a few fish or a pile of chips left over that had not been sold, whatever they did with them normally I don't know. But on an average of once a week 'Midnight' would turn up just before shutting time, sidle into the shop and declare

'I'll hav all yov got left int pans to tek wom wi mi'.

He carried with him a holdall especially for the purpose; sometimes there was such a load he had difficulty carrying them on his moped. Apparently he took the lot home, gorged himself, and the next morning fed the rest to the chickens. Whether he got a discount for buying bulk no one discovered. But there again it would be well after midnight before he would have finished his solitary feast.

Over the years Midnight had become quite a colourful local character in the Bolsterstone village area so any exploits he was involved with soon became common knowledge and the following rendition was one of them. Which my brother Lewis declares to be quite true?

To set the scene the following incident happened one afternoon by the side of the little narrow lane known as Heads Lane Bolsterstone.

When two elderly gentlemen were having an animated conversation, one of the two had a stick and was laboriously drawing something in the dust, by the side of the lane to illustrate whatever they were discussing. When suddenly a motorcar could be heard coming along the narrow lane, So they dutifully stood to one side to let it go by.

Instead the car stopped, and the passenger side front window was lowered and a smart suited gent popped his head out to ask,

'I say my good fellow's, could you please tell me the whereabouts of'', at that point he broke off to consult a sheaf of papers he had attached to his clipboard. When he was satisfied he popped his head out again ' Mmm yes, a Mr Ernest Hague of Waldershague Farm?'

Hearing the name Ernest Hague mentioned, the two elderly gents looked at one another with puzzled expressions for a moment before enquiring of the suited gent in the car,

'Whom did you say'?

'Ah' said the gent in the car; he flicked the pages of the paperwork on his clipboard again before saying 'Err sorry, a Mr Ernest Hague'.

Both of the elderly gents stood up straight to whisper -

'He must mean Midnight' they quickly bent down towards the window to inform the suited gent,

'You will find him over in there'! So without further ado the fellow opened his door to step out of the car to have a look for himself.

What he saw was clearly a graveyard, and as he did not see anything moving he rather hastily got back into his car, slammed the door shut and scribbled something on his clipboard adjacent to the name he was still indicating with his finger. Before closing his window he politely raised his hat to the two gentlemen bidding them goodday, and turning to his driver he instructed him to drive away and they were gone.

'Something we said?' enquired one or the other; both shrugged their shoulders and continued with their illustrated conversation.

It transpired later that the two suited gentlemen in the motorcar were officials of some description from Sheffield. This information had been gleaned from the landlord of the village pub 'Castle Inn' where they had started their search earlier that day. It was later presumed that the fellow who looked over the wall must have come to the conclusion that Ernest Hague was deceased and he was one of the inmates amongst the many buried in the church yard.

But Ernest Hague was busy; he had almost finished a new grave he had dug that was needed for a funeral the next day.

And at the precise time when the suited gent had looked over the wall Ernest had been having a snack sitting at the bottom of the new hole he had produced that very day.

Whether the above story is true or not I couldn't possibly say!

Another character was the roadman Benny Windle.

Benny Windle was the roadman employed by the Wortley District Council to keep the roadsides in our area tidy. Such as cleaning out the drains and gutters along the road sides, and keeping the docks, nettles and thistles in control or building up any gaps in the dry stone walls the council owned, his stretch (length) was from Midhopestones to Broomhead drive.

Benny would time his day precisely to perfection when he was working on Mortimer Road, arriving at our gate dead on twelve o'clock. His dinnertime! Benny never sponged for food he always brought his own; this was packed nice and neat in his 'snap box'. At precisely twelve he would knock on our farmhouse door to ask my Mother if she could please make him a pot of tea to go with his snap. Mother always asked him into the house so he would be comfortable having his break. If I was in the house I knew what to expect I would settle down to sit quite close to Benny and watch him intently as he opened his tin box to extract whatever he had brought with him for his lunch. Then the fun would start, as far as I was concerned anyway.

Benny must have had false teeth, and they clicked loudly as he ate his sandwiches. He also ground his teeth so loud everyone could hear. It was all so very amusing to me.

All the time I was watching I always managed to keep a straight face, as for Benny he never looked at me all the time he ate his lunch, even though I watched him most of the time.

He just stared into the distance as if I wasn't even there until finally his box was empty and he got up thanked my mother for his tea and left. I know now

I must have appeared rude but I didn't know did I.

Mother admonished me many times about my habit of watching Benny eat, but I still did it, it was so entertaining and spellbinding I found it hard not to watch.

Benny never complained or said anything; he may even have enjoyed me watching him!

When Benny retired his son took over the job but he wasn't half as much fun, he was less tolerant, his teeth didn't click and if I stared at him he called me names. So I left him alone to enjoy his sandwiches, he obviously didn't want my company.

Mr Thorpe the bank manager from Penistone would come calling occasionally. He was very tall and wore an immaculate business suite; his visits were to see what stock father had to substantiate his modest overdraft.

He would request that father would be so kind as to take him around the buildings so he could take note of any stock we had. And sometimes he even wanted to look around the fields presumably to check the crops we were growing, all the while he would be scribbling notes in a little notebook he carried.

When he had completed his 'survey'? He donned another hat (in a manner of speaking) to become a salesman. Mr Thorpe was also the area representative for a fertiliser supplier; and it was at this point of Mr Thorpe's visit when suddenly my father acquired the upper hand.

Mr Thorpe did his best to get a bigger order, whereas father did his best to order the minimum knowing it cost money. It was funny really, for the person who controlled the money father didn't have was trying his best to make him spend more on fertiliser.

Eventually Mr Thorpe and father would go into the house for a cup of tea and a slice of cake then after a suitable chat, Mr Thorpe would doff his cap to mother and drive off in his car.

Another character was Fred Chantry, the threshing machine operator. He did not live in our local area but he spent quite a lot of time on the farms with his threshing kit.

He was a very boisterous person always very noisy. Whatever he said or did was noisy and when it was our turn to have the threshing done Fred would always arrive very early in the mornings not that it bothered us unduly but he expected us to be ready when he was ready!

On a working farm that's not always possible for all farms have their own routine and to deviate from it too much can cause problems especially with milking cows.

Anyway, Fred would turn up bright and early to get his kit the threshing box and the tractor that powered it ready. He did this with much banging and swearing; eventually he would be ready. Ready for his breakfast that is. He always expected his breakfast in the house whatever farm he was threshing at. So with his breakfast inside him he was more than ready for the off and if all the men weren't there to start the job he would rant something awful.

Once the threshing was underway he had to attend to his tractor, threshing box, straw bailer and oversee all the other operations going on at a frantic pace throughout the day.

We were always glad when Fred Chantry and his threshing kit pulled out of our yard to go somewhere else, but we couldn't do the job ourselves so we had to put up with his tantrums.

Percy Bush the National Farmers union (NFU) representative from Sheffield called at our farm quite often to attend to NFU business or to take orders for Ormond's animal medicine.

Percy Bush was a large red faced chap and one of his pet hates was for people to call him by his first name Percy. How he hated that name. Perc was OK, but he preferred Mr Bush especially when he was being addressed by anyone younger than himself

Percy Bush was in a way similar to Mr Thorpe the Bank manager for Percy also had two hats, one was of course the NFU representative, and the other the rep for the Osmond veterinary medicine company.

It depended what business Percy had come to our farm to discuss with father, which hat he had on that day. If it was just NFU business the visit could be some technical point about the latest problems within the farming industry, and what if anything the NFU members could do about resolving it.

On the other hand when he became the Ormond's rep he had to listen to father, either taking an order or complaint about some medication not being up to expectations. Percy Bush did well doing either job he always did them to his best ability. Percy's talents didn't stop there either for he had a third hat as well for he also ran a grocery shop in Hillsborough on the main Sheffield road. Not that we went there for anything, it was far too difficult to get there and back when we didn't have the necessary transport.

We had a regular visit to the farm by employees of Henry Mitchell and sons. They had a grocery and provision business in the small mill town of Holmfirth and supplied us with groceries for the house and feeding stuff for the animals outside.

One of them was Selwyn the representative he came on the same day every other week as a regular routine to take our order. An industrious and likeable fellow rather small and sallow but he did his job well. The lorry driver who brought the order was also a character; he was a large fellow always covered in flour dust. He always stopped at the house door before coming in to slap at his clothes trying to get rid of some, whilst his assistant busied himself on the back of the lorry. The driver methodically unpacked the ordered items placing each item on the kitchen table carefully ticking each item off on his delivery sheet. Nothing escaped the delivery mans attention.

He did the same with the outside farm order whether it was for cow cake, rearing nuts, laying pellets or layers mash for the hens, he ticked it off on his sheet as each item was carefully unloaded from the lorry by his assistant. So there was no mistake what we had ordered was what he had delivered!

When Selwyn came for a new order exactly a fortnight later, a copy of the previous bill was produced and scrutinised then he totalled up the account taking into account any missing items not delivered. Soon a final invoice was produced which father paid.

Then and only then could any new order be concentrated upon! Every new item ordered he entered on the new order sheet in his duplicate book for the next day's delivery.

In my what I call 'Historical records'. I have several copies of those delivery notes; most of them dated during the 1950'. The items are crossed off where they were correctly delivered, if something was wrong or missing it has a different mark against the item to signify maybe a shortfall or the item wasn't available.

All the ones I have in my records have a gummed receipt attached to signify that it had been paid in full.

Mothers brother my Uncle Jim Dyson was for many years the farm bailiff at

Broomhead Home Farm. But according to some supposedly knowledgeable historians Uncle Jim was a gamekeeper on the Broomhead estates. Wrong! In actual fact Uncle Jim Dyson hated gamekeepers, and anything associated with them, even though his own father was a gamekeeper. He regarded the Broomhead estate gamekeepers as pests, always wanting this or wanting that!
For instance the gamekeepers didn't actually have such a thing as a tractor, so if they wanted one to shift something difficult or heavy they dreaded asking Jim Dyson if they could borrow one.
My Uncle Jim was renowned for inventing excuses as to why the gamekeepers couldn't borrow something he was in control of. He would always loudly declare,
'Watts up wi yer Land Rover an trailer use thet'. He would continue to rant about those pesky gamekeepers long after they had gone away usually without acquiring the thing they wanted to borrow!
As far as he was concerned the Land Rover was good enough it was supposed to be an all round working vehicle, what did the gamekeepers want such a thing as a tractor for anyway?

He couldn't see why he should allow one of his prized tractors or trailers to be abused by the gamekeepers they weren't tractor drivers.
If they suggested he allow a driver to be supplied as well, he more or less went berserk.
Sometimes as a last resort they went to see the master of the big house to ask nicely if it were possible to borrow a machine of some sort, if the master agreed to their request my uncle had to reluctantly comply. He didn't like it but he had to comply with the Masters wish.

Another character or characters who came into our area pretty regularly was the blacksmith Fred Taylor and his son from Penistone. Initially during the nineteen thirties my father rode our carthorses to Penistone for Fred to attend to, enduring the long ride there and back because it had to be done.
Sometime in the middle of the nineteen forties Fred Taylor acquired a battered van in which they carried a 'Portable hearth' so they could shoe horses on the farms.   Fred Taylor was a rather rounded not too tall red faced fellow who shouted and hollered quite a lot as I recall.
The son part of the family business was extremely strong and would bend bars of thick steel to demonstrate to anyone showing any doubt as to his ability.

135

He had acquired the unlikely nick name of 'Putty' I don't recall what his proper name was we just knew him as Putty Taylor.

They came around occasionally to our farm to check and correct any faults that had developed with the horses' feet/shoes. They still ran the forge in Penistone so if we wanted anything making, bending or welding Fred Taylor's Blacksmith shop in Penistone was the place to go.

Last but not least I must mention one of our neighbouring farmers Spencer Steward and his wife Alice. Spencer Steward farmed Ewden Lodge Farm, our nearest neighbour.

When I was nine years old in 1945 an older cousin of mine Bernard Dyson, Uncle Jim's son from the little hamlet of Wigtwizzle nr Bolsterstone gave me his rather ancient Ariel motorbike.

Old but in working order. Bernard was going into the armed forces for a long spell of duties one of them was to become a guard at Buckingham Palace. I remember the day he showed me his immaculate Bearskin he had been issued with to wear when he was on guard duty at the Palace. He even allowed me to try it on.

Cousin Bernard had earlier declared to anyone listening, that if he were still interested in motorbikes when he came home again out of the army, he would probably want a newer machine anyway. He knew I was mad keen on motorbikes so he wanted to give the Ariel to me. My mother didn't like the idea, but father said he didn't mind as long as I was careful. I recall my mother having a long rather loud row with Uncle Jim about the motorbike but it didn't make any difference, the bike was duly delivered to Garlic House the week before my cousin went away. When I had mastered the art of actually starting the heavy machine I soon mastered the art of careering around one of our rough fields known as the bracken field. A field situated at the far end of our farm. Unfortunately it was also only a couple of fields from Spencer Steward's Farm Ewden Lodge. On one occasion I had taken off the silencer, or it had fallen off. I can't remember which, and Spencer Stewards wife Alice must have taken exception to the ensuing noise for when I stopped for a rest I could hear her screeching at Spencer to go and sort me out and put a stop to all that racket! As she unsportingly called it.

On another occasion she even succeeded in persuading Spencer (who was a quiet somewhat sour man) to go across to our farm to ask or tell my father if he could/would make me stop.

I remember eventually replacing the silencer to satisfy all and sundry. But I still careered around that same field.

I can still hear Alice' high pitched voice screeching '**Spencer!!!** Go and do something about Wilfred'. Then '**Spencer!!!** **Do you hear me,** go and tell Wilfred to stop that racket'. In response I probably made even more noise. But I can't really remember now can I!

Fifteen

Dry stone walls

In and around the Ewden beck area, most if not all the stone that had been used to build the field walls was grit stone. Over the centuries the stone has turned black through exposure to the fallout and elements blowing from the industrial towns of Stocksbridge and Sheffield.

So it is only when the stone is actually split open, that the true colour becomes evident. The majority of the stone used in building field walls around the area would of necessity also to have been quarried locally. Primarily I suppose because most if not all the transporting would have been by horse and cart or heavy wagon. And some of the locations where they needed the stone must have caused the wagon operators quite a headache, for most of the walls were built in such isolated locations it must have been extremely difficult for them to transport the heavy stone to the site.

I was only just out of the pram as it were, when I began to help father with what he termed the never-ending job of building up gaps in dry stone walls. My job was finding all the little stones to fill up the middle of the wall father were repairing. Father would frequently say,

'If tha dunt kep middle full tha noes, it'll fall darn agean'. And he was right. It was a well-known fact by keeping the middle full bound the wall together. If the middle was left empty and loose, the wall would more than likely collapse quite a lot sooner rather than later.

It was only after experiencing the consequences of trapped fingers and scraped hands that I heeded fathers warning about being careful when dealing with the heavy rough stones, in effect I quickly learned to handle heavy stones with respect or with the greatest of care.

Father always blamed stray sheep for damaging our stone walls, and any new gaps that appeared would bring on a bout of 'Those bloody sheep agean'.

He would loudly declare that most of the gaps were definitely caused by sheep that ran loose on the open Broomhead moorland, and he would quickly move on to a full rant about the owners of the sheep and what should be done about them. All the stray sheep as far as we knew came into our area from the Derwent valley where the farmers were known as Shepherds. The sheep had a free run of the moorland all the way from Derbyshire into the area where we lived in the Yorkshire Pennines.

During summertime father ran a big bunch of strong cattle in a fifty-acre field situated quite some distance from our other ground. The single somewhat isolated fifty-acre field was right on the edge of the Broomhead moors, in fact it was virtually surrounded by moorland.

So it was quite a normal thing for one of us late on a summers evening, to climb up as high as we dared up the stone slated coalhouse roof whilst clutching a pair of field glasses. From that elevated vantagepoint we could see with the aid of the glasses, most of the fifty-acre, from there we would try to count the stock. This action would normally save us quite a long walk, and father always said it was always good to know what was happening up there in the big field before we settled down for the evening.

We could usually count the full compliment of scattered cattle by swinging the glasses around the large field with its humps and hollows, bracken and bull rushes. Sometimes however we noticed there were unwelcome visitors on the way about to wreck havoc. These visitors came in the form of sheep and sometimes we were just in time to observe the remains of a bunch of sheep coming over the skyline at a run, and we knew we were in for a load of trouble.

As we watched through the glasses we knew instinctively there would always be one in the bunch that started the problem –a trouble maker- intent on jumping up onto our boundary wall and off again. Not always the way one expected either, for sometimes the sheep would jump back into the moorland where it had come from in the first instance, and then have another go.

Whilst the sheep was perched precariously on the wall presumably deciding what to do we could actually see through our magnified glasses, the stones falling off the wall helped by the scrabbling feet of the sheep.

When anyone asked father what he thought about sheep. Almost without exception the reply would have been they were thick, stupid and absolutely gormless. Well, most of them had all those attributes and more, for what

140

should be added is 'clever', they are very clever, clever at the art of tricking people and dogs. I'm sure the sheep knew very well, if they continued to jump around on the wall they would soon have a gap big enough for them all to clamber over, and they did. Through the field glasses we could actually see the gap growing bigger as many more scrabbling feet attacked the wall.
However for us watching the worst bit was to come when our cattle noticed the antics of the sheep. We could see them through the glasses as they slowly wandered across to take a closer look at the new interesting situation. It only took a minute or two for a headstrong bullock to have a go at the new gap in the wall, if he was successful all the others quickly followed.
Soon all our stock would be in someone else's field, whether the grass was greener or not?
The action of the bigger animals further scattered more stones around making the gap so big we had to do something quickly.
The fifty-acre field I am describing was well over a mile from our farm, so when it got to the stage where our cattle had escaped the situation needed some urgent attention.
For if we left them wandering around in someone else's ground until the next morning they could and more than likely done a lot of damage.
We were now faced with quite a brisk walk with a stick and a dog or two to do something about it. The first job was to find and round up the missing stock. Next was to try to get them back over the broken wall into our own field.
That's easier said than done, for sometimes we had to make the gap bigger, wider, or even lower before the beasts would allow the dog to drive them back over the wall.
Some of you may say why not use the gate? That's a good question really but in our case it was quite difficult or impossible to use the gate for one thing the stock could be in an area or field where there wasn't a suitable way out, without doing further damage. And there was only one gate to our field anyway and that was in the lower area, whereas the sheep nearly always targeted the top area of the field.
In practical terms we always found it was much easier to drive the cattle back over the gap which they had helped to form. After the stock had been returned to the field where they were supposed to be, and the sheep had been dogged back up the moor. We found it better or easier to cobble up the gap to make it secure for the night, and then return the next day to build the wall up properly in the daylight.

There were other reasons of course why stone walls fell down. Sometimes this was due to the shift in the land assisted by the high winds we had in the area.

Some of the walls were built on such steep hillsides that a wall could be up to eight foot high on the lower side and only five on the other.

It only needed the lower side of the wall to move around with erosion assisted by the wind and rain for a new gap to suddenly appear in a wall, sometime quite a long stretch of wall could go down all at one go. Of course the wall always fell down hill! Scattering the stones far and wide. When we came to rebuild the wall it was always difficult finding the stones amongst all the vegetation, especially the toppers. Toppers were the most important stones to find first and be placed on one side so they weren't used by mistake in the general building of the wall.

The next job was to start the bottom with a secure base by using the bigger heavy stones to make a strong building platform then continue on and up.

Some of the stones could be very long and heavy these were placed across the wall effectively binding the two sides together. It made for a more stable wall anyway. It was always preferable or good idea for at least two people to work together; when building up lets say extensive long awkward gaps. As more than likely all the stones would be on the lower side so workers had to change places regularly to ease the work load. If there was only one person doing the work it could be more than just difficult especially if both sides of the wall needed to be 'tidy'. A lone worker would have to be constantly changing sides 'to be on the right side,' as it were. Yes building up a big gap was time consuming, took a long time and was very tiring.

There is a saying in Yorkshire 'Once you have picked up a stone never put it down again unless you put it on the wall'. As there's always a place for it to fit if you look hard enough!

Sometimes it can be difficult to join your new work into the existing surrounding stonework, if the original wall was badly misshapen we sometimes had to pull down more of the original and rebuild it to make a satisfactory and lasting job.

To finish off the wall the toppers had to be replaced. If the wall was on the farm boundary the face of the topper was always towards our own land, that is to say with the back towards the neighbour's ground. In our area all toppers sat on the wall standing upright side by side. In some other areas I have seen quite different configurations, some where there is an upright topper then a flat stone in between before another upright sat on the wall. But it was never a common sight, especially in our area, as far as I know?

142

Then of course there are areas where the building stone is anything but flat, in consequence the walls constructed with the rough shaped stone can be rather unstable the local name for such a wall is in fact 'Cobbled'.

Cobbled walls built with rounded stones were mostly found higher up around the fields bordering the moors. Re building cobbled dry stone walls with rounded stones was rather difficult to say the least with all the effort of trying to get the rounded shape stones to fit together and sit stable.

There was definitely an art to building cobbled stone walls.

Lets go back again to the continuing problem of staying sheep, to the time when suddenly out of the blue someone came up with a brilliant idea. The idea was to erect wooden stakes spaced out about ten foot or so apart along the length of a stone wall.

The new stakes had to be standing proud of the wall top by about a foot. The idea was to string to these stakes a single strand of barbed wire near the top, so when the job was completed the wire was about ten inches above the wall toppers? It was a brilliant idea and it worked.

It worked like this, when the sheep attempted to jump onto the wall it hit the wire. The taut barbed wire threw the sheep violently back to where it came from; usually the suitably discouraged sheep would hopefully give up the whole idea and go elsewhere. If it were persistent and tried a second time the same thing would happen again. More than likely the sheep would have by then got the message.

Soon similar ideas were seen in such areas as the Derbyshire high peak and Yorkshire dales and beyond. Some areas used two strands of barbed wire, but this was thought to be expensive and wasn't any more successful than one strand anyway. When father adopted the idea our moorland boundary walls lasted much longer, it saved us hours of looking for stray stock and having to 'dog sheep'.

Dogging sheep! A term used for rounding up stray sheep by farm dogs, to quickly get them off land they weren't supposed to be on, and then drive them as a bunch to where we thought they had come from.

I recall vividly the many times father had dogged bunches of sheep up over the skyline above Spencer Stewards farm driving them back into Derbyshire, within hours they would be back again. I can even recall father penning a persistent bunch up in a building to summons the owner to come and fetch them and take them back to his farm in Derbyshire. He came with a cattle truck to collect them and took them all the way home before releasing them on his own land, but believe it or not those same sheep were back in our area the following day.

By road the farmer would have had to travel all of twelve miles each way. Obviously it wasn't as far across country for the sheep to be back so quick. I can't recall what happened after that but I know the situation was absolutely infuriating.

Why dog sheep out of ones field you may ask? Well, sometimes the field could have a crop such as corn, kale, swedes, or mowing grass growing maybe some on the point of being harvested. No self-respecting farmer takes kindly to someone else's sheep flattening or ravaging his or her crops.

Because our farm Garlic House was located in a tourist area. We had the occasional spate of wall toppers being pushed off on the higher field walls, especially along the roadside. Invariably the stones would roll down the steep fields coming to rest in the long grass. We had of course to clear these stones before any work could be done such as chain harrowing or ploughing the field ready for a new crop. It was a form of 'Vandalism'; it did not just happen to us, for it was quite prevalent in the Pennines and the high peak district of Derbyshire. It didn't happen all of the time either; it was like an outbreak of a decease that once it had started it could quickly spread to other areas. Many times we have actually seen them doing it. If father were around and he could get within shouting distance he would soundly berate them and try to make them collect the stones and return them back on the walls, but we couldn't be on the look out all of the time.

It was unnecessary vandalism caused by a small minority of visitors to the countryside that consequently tarred all of them with the same brush.

It spoilt many boundary walls for years, for many of the lost stones couldn't be found easily especially in the woodland areas, I'm sure if they had been told by their leaders not to do such silly things they wouldn't have done it.

It was a case of being ignorant of what they were doing I suppose.

Moving on again to when my brother Lewis had to look for work outside the farm, to supplement his own income. He started to work with another farmer's son, John Walker from Upper-Midhopestones. They managed to secure a contract rebuilding the many dry stone walls that had been pulled down or bulldozed to one side to make way for the installation of a 18" Sahara

144

gas pipe line in 1965 which passed through the area.

The work had not long been completed and all the surroundings cleared up nice and tidy when four years later 1969 to be exact, yet another pipe line came through on almost the same ground this time it was British gas!

Some of their good recently finished work was unceremoniously bulldozed to one side meaning they had to do it all again. Of course in effect they were paid twice but if things had been planned better the people responsible could have laid both pipelines at the same time but there you are.

The actual restoration of the miles of stone walls Lewis and John worked on at the time was very hard but rewarding work (They were paid by the completed yard).

But the one inherent drawback that could not have been foreseen however was the weather; for they had a time scale to work to and they had to work in all weathers to complete the task in time.

If one looks around the Yorkshire Pennines, the Yorkshire Dales and the high Peak district of Derbyshire there are absolutely miles and miles of dry stone walls that are now full of gaps. These were perfectly good sound walls at one time that have fallen down through lack of maintenance. There must have been a reason to build them in the first place all that time ago.

Some are built up almost vertical hillsides, over the top and down the other side, sometimes crossing rivers in the lower areas to carry on towards there destination.

I always wondered what purpose did they serve, were they guarding something for the landlord? Or dividing something from someone else? I suppose we shall never know or find out for sure as all the constructors have long since departed from the scene of they're labour.

Back once again to the farm.

If one stand's outside Garlic House Farm, and looks to the north that is to say almost directly up Mortimer road towards the skyline, you will be able to see our boundary wall right on the skyline at the top of the top fields. That wall in effect separates our top fields from Willie Hague's land just over the other side at Barnside Farm. If you look closer still you can see the many dividing walls of the various top fields, and where they join up with that top field boundary wall.

At the end of each of those intersections there are stone steps built into the walls to allow walkers to climb over them on their way along the official footpath that runs along the top. Just by each of these steps there are square holes built into the wall made by standing two slabs of stone upright with another across the top. There is even one in the wall where the footpath comes out into Mortimer road.

These 'holes' are big enough to allow sheep, dogs or even children to crawl through. What was the purpose of these openings? One wouldn't have thought the constructors of that bygone age would have considered dogs or kids, so we are left with sheep!

If it were sheep the constructors were catering for. It would seem that the animals could have been free to wander wherever they wanted just by passing through the holes connecting the fields or even onto the road/track, unless of course the land owner blocked the relevant 'Hole' in the wall to stop them doing so.

So lets now look at the wall in one of the lower fields of Garlic House there is another hole of similar construction in a wall that separates the bottom field from our neighbours Nether House Farm. Does this mean sheep in those far of days could wander between farms as well? Obviously we weren't around when those walls were built to ask the constructors what the idea was. So the answer remains guess work.

Back again to the stone walls

After father had bought our first tractor in 1947. Any new equipment he bought after that date was of course intended to fit the tractor, so the equipment was nearly always too wide to go through most of the original narrow gateways dotted around Garlic House. All the original field gateways were designed for horse drawn implements, so it was a case of necessity that we had over a period of time to widen most of the gateways.

I remember it was a task that was easier said than done especially on our farm for almost every gateway had a pair of solid stone gateposts one each side of the gate, and each of them weighed an estimated ton. Literally!

Fortunately we only had to move one of them at each location to achieve the desired width, and that was enough. First of all father had to select which of the two stone posts was the easier to move or should I say looked to be the easiest to move, for neither of the two would be what one might say 'Easy' anyway.

Then a section of the adjoining dry stone wall behind the selected gatepost had to be pulled down carefully stacking the stones on one side. From then on it was a case of digging around and down all round the stone post, until the

146

bottom could be established. And sometimes the part hidden below ground level could be just as big as the bit sticking out of it! Whilst all the work was in progress we had to keep a keen watch on the balance of the gatepost, or the whole thing could fall over. All this work as you can imagine needed two people at least to try to keep things safe. So with the aid of long crow bars and a sort of rocking motion the very heavy gatepost had to be gradually 'Persuaded' by hand into the desired position, where it was wedged securely so it could be left temporarily while the next operation could be undertaken. This was to find a suitable gate for the new opening, Sometimes we had to borrow a gate from somewhere else, so with the new suitable sized gate temporary in position the stone post could be sighted for accuracy to make sure it wasn't twisted or leaning. Then the spoil could be replaced around the stone gatepost tampered down with something heavy to make the job was secure.

Re building the dry stone wall behind the newly positioned gatepost was next, making a tidy job to match the surrounding original wall.

Sometimes father thought it would be a good idea if the gates were made to swing by adding hooks to the gatepost and irons attached to the gate itself. There were various methods used to fix hooks to the stone gateposts, we used a hammer and cold chisel to make the necessary holes in the stone post in the correct place deep enough for ragged edged hooks to fit nice and snug.

To secure the hooks into the stone post we used molten lead. To start the operation father had to light a small fire in a safe position to melt a small amount of lead in a 'Kettle or ladle', whilst this was going on I searched around looking for some soft clay to make a cup to affix to the stone post. When the lead was declared ready the ladle was lifted off the fire with some pincers, and quickly poured into the clay cup to guide the molten lead into and around the hook in the post.

The remains of the clay cup were quickly pulled off revealing the rough quickly setting lead this had to be tidied up with the aid of a ball peen hammer into a nice rounded finish.

Another method of affixing gate hooks to stone gateposts was having steel straps made to clamp the hook to the post. These could only be made by a Blacksmith and each one had to be accurately measured so it would fit, another snag was because the stone posts were rough each of the straps would only fit in one place. But I must agree, if the job was done correctly it was an equally good way of doing the same job. Even if it was somewhat unsightly. Of course all the hard work involved with hanging and making gates swing, was only appreciated when we came to use them.

All the heavy manual labour we had expended when we moved the stone gateposts during the 1950' soon became redundant. For when the wide combine harvesters became popular the gateposts had to be moved again.

In fact some of the openings had to be made so wide they needed two gates to close each opening, with each gate swinging from its own post. When closed the gates were secured in the middle by a special device that dropped over both gate ends keeping them in the closed position.

Moving the heavy stone gateposts by then had of course become much easier, for someone had invented a tractor attachment on the rear hydraulics known as a back/actor.

These were expensive machines operated mostly by agricultural contractors, and they made the job look easy. But saying that even much better machines started to appear, these were self-contained machines generally known as JCB' then the job really became a doddle.

Actually all earth moving jobs became a doddle as the contractors used these machines to there full advantage.

But because the contractors charged an arm and a leg for their services only the better off farmers could afford the contractors to do the work for them.

Soon the better off farmers acquired their own JCB', buying used machines cast off' from contractors as they came on the market. Nowadays JCB type machines can be found on most farms anywhere around the country.

No more pick and shovel that we used in those earlier years or using a wheel barrow or horse and cart to clear away the spoil, now it's a JCB with a dumper truck or trailer to shift the stuff ten times faster. How farming has speeded up with the bigger machines. Bigger tractors, Bigger trailers, Bigger mowers and balers or hay making machinery.

Now a field can be started and cleared in no time at all. Gone are the times when one could have ones lunch from a basket behind a haycock while the horse had a bag of oats to chomp on.

Where a little snooze may have been in order, if we had been in the field all day and the weather was settled. Relatively speaking, there was no hurry in those days. Now it's all rush and gallop as if there is no tomorrow. Is anybody better off by all the rush? I would say probably not!

148

Sixteen

Cycles and motorcycles

My first wheeled bike, well trike if you like, was a cast off from the Wilson family of Broomhead Hall, my Uncle Jim Dyson brought it with him one Sunday morning when he came on one of his regular visits to see my mother, his sister.

It had solid tyres all round as was normal at that time. It was intended for both my brother Lewis and me, but Lewis couldn't ride it, he was too little, so I had to do all the riding for both of us.

That wasn't a problem for I was well up to that, he was allowed to join in the activity by pushing me around if he so wished.

At first I was restricted as to where I could ride in safety, along the paving outside the house door, I remember being regularly being told that I would wear grooves in the paving stones with all the riding I did up and down the restricted area.

However one day I lost control completely and the bike with me still on board clattered down the short flight of stone steps and we landed upside down in the muddy farmyard. Unperturbed and with the help of my brother we dragged the bike back up the steps onto the paved area only to be confronted by mother, who demanded an explanation as to how we had both got into such a grubby state. Apparently I must have enjoyed my unplanned trip down the steps for later I was 'caught' time and time again riding down them, and sometimes I was actually in control of the bike. However, my parents took a dim view of such activity for they thought it was a dangerous act, so a barrier (A yard broom) was placed across the top of the steps to stop me, this effectively prevented me from continuing my rather enjoyable trips down into the yard.

Unfortunately by placing the barrier across to stop me also made it very awkward for anyone else wanting to use the steps, so the idea was soon abandoned and I was able to resume my frequent trips down the steps again without restrictions especially when no one was watching.

Unfortunately, the frame on the trike was not man enough to withstand my aggressive riding style, and soon a crack developed in the framework just behind the steering head, eventually the front of the bike parted company from the rear bringing my riding to a disappointedly early halt.

However all was not completely lost, and it may have been the beginning of my early aspirations as a mechanical fitter, as I studied the two separate halves.

Earlier that same week I had noticed my father throwing out of a building the remains of a large barrel, one that had been used to store layers mash in for the hens. It had fallen apart through damp and old age resulting in a pile of curved oak timbers (known as staves) some of them were 3 inches or more wide!   I had studied the pile of redundant staves for some time thinking of how I could utilise them to repair the broken bike.   Somehow (my parents told me later) I had managed to make a hole in one of the wider staves, big enough for me to attach it to the front part of the broken bike.

And again somehow I had managed to separate the axle and wheels from the remainder of the broken bike. I had begged father to let me have a few big staples the type he used when he was fencing. Using the staples and the aid of a large stone I had nailed the axle to the other end of the wooden 'stave'. With the wheels refitted I had a three-wheeled 'contraption' or new style trike. It could be pushed along the flat ground or up hill so I could ride it back down again. My idea worked! I was mobile again that was all that mattered.

It was somewhat similar to a scooter I suppose; only ours had three wheels.

I shall always remember the time when my brother and I made our first four-wheeled device; we called it a 'trolley'.   Using the axle and wheels from an old pram. One of us pushed while the other rode what we considered to be our unique machine, hauling it up the hills by a rope attached to the front, and riding back down.   One day we were both feeling quite venturesome and we had pushed and pulled the machine (I say machine in a loose sense) nearly halfway up Ewden Beck hill taking it in turns to ride back down again.

However on one occasion we went a bit further than we normally did, in fact nearly to the top. And it was my turn to ride back down, so I climbed aboard and off I went. I gathered speed down the first straight bit of road and I just managed to career around the first sharp left-handed corner. As the road became steeper I went faster, faster than I had ever gone before. Unfortunately we hadn't provided the trolley with any form of brakes; we usually relied on using our shoe to press on a front wheel to slow down.

On that occasion however one shoe wasn't good enough, I had to use both pressing as hard as I could on each of the speeding front wheels and I just about managed to slow down enough to swerve into a steep banking, where the trolley promptly overturned.

So there I lay in the gutter with my shoes smoking, then my feet started to burn.

I remember having to quickly snatch my shoes off to stop the burning sensation, and that was when I discovered that there was a hole burnt almost through the sole of each shoe, in the shape of a trolley wheel! As I stared at the smoking shoes I suddenly remembered they were my new school shoes bought especially for the new term starting the following week, and I had only been allowed to wear them that day to break them in before the term started.

Even though I went home slightly injured by my experience of being upside down in the road I received a sound clouting when mother discovered what had happened, not only that my brother Lewis also received his share of clouting for aiding and abetting.

As for me I had to wear my old shoes again until mother had saved for another pair, I remember my old shoes were so tight they were ready for bursting all day at school until my big toe poked through the front relieving the pressure. We were both very careful after that escapade when we were indulging in any unusual activities especially involving anything to do with school clothes. You could say it had taught us both a lesson!

On another occasion we, my brother and I, had pushed another version of our series of home made trolleys part of the way up the steep Ewden beck hill and turned it around so we could both climb aboard. This latest exercise was to test a two-seater version we had finished that very morning. Once we were away we gathered speed rapidly but for some reason the machine didn't respond to the steering ropes like all our previous trolleys had done, consequently we ran into a stone wall before reaching our farm gate, our intended destination.

The trolley overturned and a big nail we had so painstakingly looked for and found in a box to fix the wheel onto the axle, dug into my leg causing what we thought at the time was almost a terminal rush of blood. The trolley was promptly abandoned where it finished up and I limped into the house to seek attention.

The attention included a good shouting at by mother, then an application of iodine a medication both my brother and I dreaded. I was soon outside again, walking with a pronounced limp – partly for effect - to collect the abandoned trolley.

Luckily the trolley was none the worse for its experience. As we studied our twin man trolley we suddenly discovered the problem. We came to the unanimous decision that the back wheels were too near to the front –not far enough back- so we modified it, after that we had no bother at all it steered beautifully.

Now I remember the time when an old gypsy woman came to our house selling home made clothes pegs; she told mother if she would buy some of her pegs she would tell my mother her fortune for free.

Mother couldn't resist such an offer so she bought some of the home made pegs. In the fortune telling session my name was brought into the equation, the gypsy woman told mother that the boy (me) would be very good with his hands.

However that statement didn't mean anything to my mother for she already knew that I could take things to pieces and put them back together again, but she graciously thanked the old gypsy woman and sent her on her way. For during some of my escapades with anything mechanical items around the house, mother, or father would shake their heads hoping that I would grow out of the habit one day, but I never did.

My first encounter with powered mechanical machinery was I suppose when I was just two weeks old when my father took me with my mother to see our family doctor with his motorcycle and sidecar. Not that I can remember the event, but I do recall a few years later when I was old enough to be curious, lifting a dust sheet to have a look at what was underneath.

It was father's motorbike and sidecar the bike he had used for work during earlier years, it had a badge on the tank which declared it was a BSA. I have a copy of the log book here in my study stating that it was a 1928 500cc single cylinder registration number WE 2818.

After that first occasion I regularly lifted the edge of the cover up to creep

152

underneath to look at the BSA in the semidarkness, and wonder when father would start it up and take me for another ride. It was parked there for years, my brother, and me were both looking forward to when we were big enough to have a go.

Imagine our disappointment when one day we came home from school to find father had given it away. 'Yes, given it away.' He had traded the old motorcycle and sidecar for some extra manual labour, during a difficult time with the harvest. As you may imagine my brother and I were very upset at what he had done. In fact it was quite a while before I came out of a sulk only answering anything he said to me with the minimum of words.

Father had let me down big time, and I have never forgotten it.

But let's return to the main story.

As I became older I acquired a rather tatty two-wheeled cycle from somewhere and spent hours and hours restoring it so it was safe to ride. I can clearly recall demonstrating my riding prowess to a number of people who were watching at the time, including my Uncle Albert from Leeds.

I was able to ride freewheel down the little field behind the farm buildings known as the 'Croft'. The field wasn't steep, just sloping enough to ride the bike down without pedalling; in fact I couldn't pedal, for the bike was way too big for me so I couldn't reach the pedals properly and the freewheeling bit had to suffice on that occasion.

Anyway it impressed my audience sufficiently to keep my standing with them as being clever.

I wanted above all to be recognised as being clever, especially with mechanical equipment for all the people watching knew I had restored the bike I was demonstrating at the time.

However I was slightly miffed when my cousin Irene (Uncle Albert's daughter) climbed on the bike and rode it up as well as down the field without stopping. She was a little older than I was so her legs must have been longer, long enough to reach the pedals.

I was understandably rather jealous of her that day for she had stolen my thunder.

Uncle Albert and his wife Auntie May with their children Jack, Irene, and Colin came to see us at our farm a couple of times a year when the weather was nice. They lived in a street in Leeds almost opposite the main gate to Armley jail in fact they could see the big doors from their house where the prisoners were taken through.

153

Maybe some of those prisoners that they saw taken through the doors never saw the outside world again?

Talking about Uncle Albert brings to mind the occasion when father and me went on a visit to his house in Leeds. We must have travelled there by bus for it was much too far to travel by tractor. He took us to have a look at his allotment where both father and I were surprised to find he kept a couple of pigs. This was in the middle of Leeds City.

We went back to his house for a meal before coming home and Uncle Albert insisted on giving us a slab of his own grown bacon to take with us, when my mother later cooked the bacon it tasted of fish. Not like our own bacon at all and none of us particularly liked it.

So next time we saw uncle Albert father asked him why his bacon tasted of fish, and the answer he fed them of swill from the Leeds fish market.

Back to bicycles. As I grew older I discovered there were many discarded complete cycles and loads of spares associated with them laying around on local farms where the farmers sons or daughters had grown out of them and moved on to other means of transport. I began to beg them for free, or if I did pay for any I made sure there wasn't much actual cash changing hands during the change of ownership.

The lack of a cash part in any of the transactions was because I didn't possess any, not to any great extent anyway. Father wasn't a believer in paying me for doing anything on the farm which I suppose was understandable in a way for he didn't have much money either as there wasn't much money to be made on a farm just after the war years.

I produced some quite good serviceable cycles out of the bits I accumulated, I even managed to sell a few newly restored examples to friends or visitors to the farm, which raised some much needed funds for me.

I remember one of them was so light I was able to hold it up by the proverbial fingernail so I decided I would keep that one for myself. Especially to use on my regular trips to see Trevor Cotton a friend of mine who lived on a farm towards the Strines Inn.

Together we rode our cycles around the local roads during the long summer evenings, especially when there wasn't any work to do on our respective farms, and between us we enjoyed the freedom of the road and exploring the local area.

It was late 1945 just after my ninth birthday when I became actively involved with motorcycles. My cousin Bernard Dyson (Bud) from Wigtwizzle came to see us at Garlic House. He told us the news that he had just signed on to do an extended term in the military forces, and one of his duties was to serve as a guard outside Buckingham palace London. I remember it well; it was just a few days before he was due to go away when he appeared in our farmyard to declare he was giving me his old Ariel motorbike as a gift, If I wanted it!

I was as you can imagine (In modern parlance) Gob smacked. To say the least!

Cousin Bernard was my mothers brother Uncle Jim Dyson' son. A few years older than me, but as he explained when he had finished his military duties and had come home again, if he were still interested in motorbikes he would probably want a newer one.

He knew that I was mad keen on bikes and motorbikes so he thought there wasn't a better person than me to give his old bike to.

The bike was quite old, he considered it wasn't worth much so if I wanted it I could have it for nowt - so to speak!

I was obviously delighted to accept the generous offer, father said it was OK so long as I was careful, but mother wasn't at all pleased I remember she had a rather loud animated altercation with her brother Uncle Jim, Bernard's father, concerning the matter.

But she finally calmed down sufficiently to allow me to have it when father declared the bike would probably be helpful around the farm anyway.

The bike was a rather tatty ancient Ariel 350cc rigid with girder forks, it was all right, it ran and sounded good, but it was very heavy, it dwarfed me to certain extent.

After many aborted attempts at starting it I eventually discovered the best way was to park the bike with the left-hand side footrest propped on one the flagstones in the farm yard. Set everything up then jump with both feet onto the kick-starter as Cousin Bernard had instructed me. After a few attempts the roar from the exhaust rewarded me as the engine started.

Once I was underway in a field I was OK. I found the bike similar to riding my pushbike but much heavier of course. I soon removed and discarded much of the unwanted equipment and I quickly became a proficient rider, (in the fields) even though I say so myself.

When my school friends heard of my new acquisition I was inundated with requests to allow them to come to our farm so they could have a go. In the short term that was OK but in the long term I quickly found out that the Ariel used petrol. So the tank needed filling occasionally, and that cost money.

Money I didn't have. After many arguments with my father I had to admit we/he couldn't afford the petrol for my friends to go careering around the fields.

So father decided to tell them all that it was a farm bike, and he wouldn't allow anyone to ride it other than me, that effectively put a stop to that caper! I don't know whether my friends believed it or not but something had to be done, and it had.

Eventually however the novelty wore off and I just rode the bike when father wanted me to do a chore around the farm. In return father provided all the petrol I needed to run the bike!

My friendship with Trevor Cotton continued and we rode our bicycles whenever we had the opportunity. I went to his place or he came to mine, and we enjoyed each other's company with our mutual interest in bikes.

As we became older, and our respective parents had intimated there wasn't any pressing work to do, we went for longer rides into such areas as Derbyshire (I have a couple of photos) we relished the tourist atmosphere of such places as Castleton or Bamford.

One Sunday as I recall we even rode as far as Buxton and back. When I look back I think that may have been as far as Trevor's energy would allow him to ride, for when I suggested we next ride to Matlock, a few miles further he declined saying it was too far for him.

Eventually I did the trip on my own I remember it took me all day to ride there and back.

If my memory is correct it was pitch dark when I arrived home after that trip, and I didn't have any lights on my bike. Doing that trip I probably discovered the limit of my energy for I can only remember doing it once.

On a farm not too far away from Garlic House I discovered a good example of the sit up and beg gents bicycle manufactured by Wigfalls, a cycle shop in Sheffield. They had named it the 'Wigfalls Royal'. I liked the look of it so I actually bought it for two pounds. I had at that time recently started night school in Stocksbridge so I needed decent transport; the Wigfalls cleaned up nicely and I eventually got it to look like new. It was quite presentable to arrive and be parked with the other bikes outside the college. One of its biggest drawbacks was its weight as it was equipped with heavy wheels and frame. Quite all right for going downhill to college but unfortunately most of the going was uphill riding back home again. This dulled my enthusiasm for night school to a certain extent. However by then I was nearing sixteen years old and I had started thinking about motorised transport when I read somewhere about an innovation that would transform an ordinary bicycle into a motorised cycle just by attaching a little engine.

I knew my parents wouldn't offer to buy me one so I had to start moaning about how hard it was to travel with the Wigfalls (It was true really) but I exaggerated somewhat the difficulties until they gave in and agreed to buy me a Mini Moto.

The Mini Moto was a small petrol engine attachment that could be fitted to the rear carrier of a standard cycle to drive the rear tyre via a roller all controlled by levers attached to the handlebars.

By the time my 16th birthday came on the 16th July 1952 I had already passed my motorcycle road test in Sheffield on the Wigfalls royal with the mini Moto attachment, and the bike was taxed and insured ready for the road.

However when the newness wore off I found the bike was all right on the flat and down hill but I had to assist the engine on the steeper parts. So in effect it had two speeds, slow and very slow.

I suppose I had contributed slightly to the lack of power by attaching an extra dynamo in anticipation of gaining extra lighting, but the effort that was required of the engine to drive the dynamo outweighed any advantage gained.

Anyway as I have said it was better than nothing, so I persevered with it until I had saved enough funds to look for something better?

This came in the form of a 123cc BSA Bantam which I bought on the never, never through the advertising pages of a motor cycle magazine.

That little BSA started my entry into the realms of being a proper motorcyclist. I know it had only a 123cc engine but it was actually streets ahead of the Mini Moto. From then on I started to enjoy going to my night school activities.

My friend Trevor Cotton had also joined the ranks of being a motorcyclist. He had acquired a somewhat dubious rather ancient 250 BSA rigid. It was stronger and faster than my bantam but that didn't matter to us as we carried on with our evenings touring or should I say speeding around the local lanes.

It was during my first month of being a proper motorcyclist that I recall having a very unfortunate experience whilst riding with Trevor Cotton from Agden Lodge farm.

We were as usual both riding (speeding) along a lane near low Bradfield. Along a lane I didn't know very well. So I was following Trevor, he suddenly keeled over for a sharp left hand corner when sparks started to shower from his left footrest, obviously as I didn't know the corner I wasn't to know it tightened up considerably, so much in fact that I ran out of road.

I dived rapidly into an ochre filled ditch on the right hand side of the road; it was full to the top with horrible evil smelling yellow/orange-coloured sludge. Eventually Trevor came back looking for me, he found me trying to extricate my BSA from the gloop. When he saw me he just fell about laughing. After his laughter subsided I managed to persuade him to help me out, eventually between us we managed to get the bike back onto the road

I tried a few tentative jabs at the kick-starter not expecting it to start. To my amazement it started but as I was still covered in the orange stuff, even my cap was full, I decided there and then to abandon my evening ride and go home instead to get changed and cleaned up.

Trevor also went home but I could see he was still laughing to himself, as he no doubt continued to think about my misfortune. Soon after that episode I converted the BSA to a competitions machine which started me on a new career as a trials and scrambles rider, which has lasted to the present day. So I'll not go on about it for it is well documented in another of my books.

Seventeen

Tramps, Gypsies and Scrap men

During the summer months of the years when the weather was kind we always had an influx of tramps and gypsies calling at our farm. Turning up unannounced at the house door, in the farmyard or even in a building where we were working.

They were what one might call wandering men of the road, and they all had a certain aura of poverty about them. I suppose it could have been the way they were dressed for they were all ragged individuals.

But saying that so were all the farmers, for they were ragged individuals including me a farmer's son. For tattered clothes were our normal working attire especially during the time I lived at home anyway. When we were working outside on the land we wore clothes that were falling to bits, full of holes and probably someone else's cast off's anyway, for they had certainly seen better days. We wore the clothes that kept us warm because that was all that mattered it certainly wasn't a time for airs or graces.

Father always wore a blue jacket length 'smock' made from a heavy-duty material similar I suppose to the cloth they used in the manufacture of jeans, whereas a number of other farmers in our area wore the brown coloured variety they were the same really just a different colour.

Taking this a bit further, my Uncle Jim Dyson the farm bailiff of Broomhead farm always wore a long brown smock, none of the other workers employed on the Broomhead estate were allowed to wear long brown smocks, just uncle Jim. Otherwise they could wear whatever they wanted during the working day.

Except of course the estate gamekeepers, when they were working they had to wear the traditional plus four suits supplied by the estate.

Where were we?   Oh yes. All the tramps, gypsies or even the Scrap metal collectors for that matter referred to father as 'Boss' with their respective requests for food or scrap iron. A local saying declared that one was on the make and the other was on the take.

A sentiment that was probably true.

A genuine tramp could be well satisfied with a slice of bread and a cup of milk or water and then be on his way.   We always found that most of the tramps were quite gentle fellows grateful for anything we gave them.   But if one came late in the day to ask father if he could bed down for the night in the cart shed, he had to agree not to smoke or try to light a fire. If the tramp wouldn't promise to keep to that ruling they were just told to be on their way. At one period I remember we had an influx of tramps knocking on the house door asking for assistance, whether it was for food or for a place to bed down, it became so regular in fact that father confronted one of them demanding why we were being, as father put it, 'Targeted'?   He (the tramp) promised to tell father why, if he could see his way to provide some grub and a place to rest for the night.

In return he would let into the secret.

It was quite obvious when he showed father the sign scrawled on the wall inside the cart shed it said in tramp language that this farm (ours) didn't refuse anyone any request for food or drink or a place to bed down.   Father promptly erased the sign whilst the tramp was watching, after that visits from tramps lessened considerably, until once again it was rare to see one come wandering into our farmyard.

Father made sure the sign was never restored, by making regular visits to the cart shed to have a look to make sure.

On the other hand scrap men wanted anything they could see, insisting they could pay over the odds whether it was actually scrap or not. However dealing with scrap men was a different thing all together. Sometimes even turning into quite a traumatic experience for my father at least, as scrap men always worked in pairs and that in itself was intimidating.

For some reason father could always tell when they had come to buy or just

160

to eye things up with the real intention of returning when we weren't around. Then taking everything they wanted that wasn't bolted down. All this meant that there were two kinds of scrap men, the genuine ones and the sly ones, each had to be handled in a different manner. Father had of necessity to be always vigilant even when he wasn't actually around the farm so he began leaving a dog loose around the place preferably our most savage cow dog to try and deter such visits by what he called undesirables.

As father explained all his equipment had been bought with hard labour, very hard labour. So he didn't want such people as scrap men taking it as and when they thought fit.

When the price of scrap iron went up slightly the scrap men started to come around more often even every week in some cases, not necessarily the same ones either, for some of them were complete strangers to us.

But make no mistake some of the scrap collectors were undesirable and they could be quite persuasive if the farmer showed any weakness.

Father knew he would never receive anything like the value he thought any scrap metal was worth, but he was always open to offers especially by his favourite scrap man. When the haggling started father would have a figure in mind, so had the scrap man, but to get the two to match was an extreme and long winded business until one or the other gave in and the deal went ahead or rejected. Sometimes the haggling was so long winded father would suddenly agree to a price just to get them on their way, as he always had other pressing jobs to attend to.

As soon as the scrap man thought he had won their wreck of a lorry was quickly brought to the scene to break the old machine or whatever down into pieces for it to be carried away.

But father never left the scrap men on their own even his favourites, for there was always the danger that something else, something important could go missing.

The important part as far as father was concerned was the settling up, that was always nerve racking. When the stuff had been loaded onto the lorry the scrap man would say 'How much do I owe you Boss'? And the haggling would start all over again even though a price had been already agreed. By then of course after the scrap had been loaded, the scrap man was convinced he was paying too much. To stop that malarkey father began to demand payment in full before they even started the breaking process.

On other occasions another delaying tactic of the scrappy was to suggest that whilst they were actually breaking the machine they may uncover even more scrap to add to the haul thus raising the monetary value even further. But father soon became wise to that ruse as well.

Yet another annoying 'trick' the scrap men would try to pull, and this could happen before they had even come into the farmyard.

This was for one of the scrap crew to quietly slip away, disappearing rapidly behind the farm buildings with the sole intention of looking to see if there was anything around or behind the buildings suitable for scrapping?

And then the fellow would re-join the party when everything was about to be agreed, and then the leader might come out with 'What about those old bits behind the barn Boss'?

O Dear, that was guaranteed to make father mad. He knew right away he had been tricked and they would be immediately sent on their way assisted by our most savage dog.

Any regular scrap men who came to our farm soon realised they must not attempt that particular trick on my father. It soon became common knowledge amongst the scrap collectors that when father was mad he would more than likely tell them to remove all the scrap already loaded onto their wagon and to clear off forthwith.

Yes indeed, there's no doubt it was a traumatic experience when scrap men came to call at Garlic House Farm. As for me, I always kept well away, I didn't want to become 'involved' as it were, and it was the same with my brother Lewis he being the baby of the family was too small, so he stayed well away. Even so we could hear what was going on by the shouting and swearing but as I said we kept our distance.

I recall vividly one particular occasion when father decided that the two old horse drawn mowing machines lying around in the grass were no longer needed.

So father pointed them out to his favourite scrap man to make him an offer, to break them up and take them away.

Horse drawn mowing machines were notoriously heavy things, completely made from iron and steel, so the figure suggested by the scrappy sounded quite reasonable to father.

And the deal was done. It took them a while to break the machinery, load it all on to their transport and take it away. Father was pleased as he had a couple of pounds in his pocket, instead of the old scrap mowing machines lying around in the field.

However the good feeling only lasted a couple of days as something happened

162

which I can't recall exactly what, but we urgently needed a length of steel with holes in it all the way along to repair something of importance. Father's first thoughts were he could use the 'Bed' off one of the old horse drawn mowing machines lying in the long grass. That would fix the problem!

But no, the horse drawn mowing machines had been taken away by the scrap man that same week. Father was so mad and disappointed with himself he was upset for days.

However he still needed to have a length of steel with holes in it to fix his latest problem, and when he eventually found and bought what he wanted it cost twice the amount he had received from the scrap man.

I mentioned 'Bed' which to the uninitiated is a long length of strong heavy metal where the knife sits and runs backwards and forwards at a great speed cutting the grass. If all the fingers were taken off the bed what is left is a long length of steel with plenty of holes in it. Just the job for what father wanted. He would even have had two!

Shortly after that debacle father started to tell every scrap man who came to call

'No I haven't any scrap today!'

And then the scrap man might enquire

'What about that old bit over there Boss'? Pointing to some useless bit of old machinery.

Father's reply would always be 'No! It might come in handy one day'.

So over the following years our farm became littered with broken machinery left in the long grass which father insisted, might become useful some day!

Later when tractors and bigger heavier machines became destined for scrap the monetary value was of course much higher but the number of scrap collectors dwindled to a certain extent. It may have been I suppose because the bigger stuff needed bigger lorries with lifting kit attached to be able to collect bigger machines. Gone it seemed were the little scrappy with a sledgehammer and a chisel, and a wreck of a vehicle.

As at one time they were the only tools needed to set up in business being a small time scrap collector.

As for the tramps well there were still a few around. However even scruffier individuals started to appear on the scene, and they were always looking for a place to stay. Namely wandering travellers, with their mobile homes and caravans. Any farmers with gates opening onto the road were advised by the NFU to make sure they were closed, and chained, especially during the summer months when the countryside became 'invaded' by the so called 'wanderers'.

Not the traditional gypsy, for they could be controlled, and were all right as long as they left us alone or should I say we left them alone.

During this later period the occasional gypsy type horse drawn caravan could be seen passing our farm gate. But one could never tell whether the occupants were genuine gypsies or mere holidaymakers. Some companies in the leisure industry hired out the typical gypsy or Romany type caravan drawn by a horse and some town's people hired them to sample the simple way of living for a week or two. 'In the Countryside'.

Even so one had to watch where they went for they weren't above parking their vehicles in any field or gateway they fancied, or tethering their horse in a best mowing grass field overnight before moving on next morning, leaving such a mess you wouldn't believe.

I remember father having to move what he called 'Gypos' on from the gateway just up the road from our farm.

The gate was set back slightly from the road so it had a short track before the field gate. One morning we could see from our yard a rickety gypsy caravan parked there.

It wouldn't have mattered if they had moved on early.

As really they wouldn't be doing any harm as such. But father wanted to use that particular gate to get into the field so he had no alternative but to tell them to move on.

When father went up the road to demand their eviction from the gateway he found they had opened the gate and tied the horse to the gatepost, with a long rope.

The horse was then able to eat what it wanted and flatten a huge area of the mowing grass to the full length of its tether.

It's was a good job father had taken one of the cow dogs with him for back up as there were a couple of quite burly individuals amongst the family. They eventually went quietly on their way after father had soundly berated them about the damage their horse had done.

Father also had problems over the years with weekend picnickers. They came from the towns with their cars, drove up into any gateway they fancied spread their things around to have their picnic completely blocking the gateway until they had finished before clearing off.

That was OK if we didn't want to use the gateway, no harm done.

164

One of the fields affected in this way by picnickers was the one down the road, that particular field couldn't be seen from our farm without going across the road and standing on the top of the gatepost. On a couple of occasions the first we knew something was amiss was when the bunch of cattle that was supposed to be in the field suddenly turned up at the farmyard gate.

So we drove them down the road back to the field only to discover the open gate. With all the picnickers rubbish strewn around amongst the grass just waiting for the cows to pick something up and get it stuck in their mouths or in their feet. The loose animals could just as easily gone the other way and drifted for miles or caused an accident on the road.

Obviously someone had opened the gate and had their picnic but failed to close it again before leaving. I can recall the one-day when father did actually discover some people still having their picnic in that particular field, I remember him storming down the hill to demand what they thought they were doing?

During a stormy confrontation he demanded their home addresses.

When asked why, father told them because he was coming to their house to have a picnic on their front lawn, to see how they liked it!

Obviously the request didn't go down very well with the trespassers. For they packed up and cleared off pretty quick. But as far as I know no home addresses were recorded.

Eighteen

Aeroplanes

When father went outside our house early one morning to start his daily routine, in early August 1942. He suddenly shouted to mother 'cum here lass and have a look what's that thing ower yonder' he was pointing at something across the beck. Mother went to the door to see what he was shouting about, and from our farmhouse door it looked as if someone had built a new tower block on the skyline above Middle Moss moor.

In case I have lost you? Sometime during the night a large aeroplane had crash-landed on Broomhead moor in the area known as Middle Moss. What my parents were looking at from their vantagepoint across Ewden beck was one of its wings; the wing was sticking up in the air showing above the skyline, the other wing was buried quite deep in the soft peat on the ground.

When it was viewed through field glasses it looked like a new statue had been erected in the middle of the purple heather clad moors. But, as far as I can recall the aeroplane hadn't caught fire or anything. Through the glasses it looked to be more or less complete even at that unusual angel, although it must have been quite a mess.

The new arrival quickly became a talking point amongst the local populace. A few days passed by before any activity could be seen around the wreaked machine, then one day a heavy lifting machine lumbered from of the back of a low loader, we supposed they had come at last to take it away, but it didn't happen like that. Apparently the recovery crew had miscalculated how soft a peat moor can be, even in summertime! As the lifting kit they had brought to do the job proved to be more or less useless.

This caused another delay until something more suitable was brought to the scene to allow the recovery process to begin. After that it took a week or more of concentrated effort by many personnel before the huge machine finally disappeared completely, it left a scar on the open moorland for many months until the heather finally grew back.

All the time they were working on the crashed plane we could see armed military guards in attendance, as they paced around the site and I do believe they had guards on duty throughout the night as well.

Then late one afternoon during early autumn of the same year a huge Lancaster type Aeroplane suddenly appeared over our farmhouse. It flew so low we could have hit it with the proverbial stick. It was so low it only just missed one of our two chimney pots.

In fact the noise and vibration was so loud and intense we actually thought it had broken some of the house windows.

The aeroplane was flying so low; one of its wings hit the top of a young oak tree growing just below our farm buildings. Effectively snapping off a fairly thick branch, leaving quite a lot of debris on the road beneath the tree. We could all see the bit of branch sticking out of the aeroplane wing as it roared on its way down the valley.

Even today if you look carefully at the oak tree that is now old and mature, the damaged remnants can still be identified high up near the top!

The plane continued without pause towards Broomhead Reservoir. We didn't of course at the time know why the aeroplane was flying so low. The disturbance continued for a few days, making the cows gallop around the fields like loonies, they could have quite easily broken a leg.

It became so bad in fact father was all for finding out whom was responsible so he could report the inconsiderate pilots to their superiors for their unreasonable behaviour.

But it stopped just as suddenly as it had started. It was only then that we learned they were testing out Broomhead Reservoir as a suitable site for military manoeuvres, this included flying over stretches of open water testing a 'Bouncing bomb'!

The exercise was known as 'Operation Chastise'. Subsequently the operation became known as the 'Dam busters'! As I have said the exercises over our area lasted a few days until they moved on into the next valley doing the same thing over the Strines and Bradfield Reservoirs.

A week or so later we learned they had gone completely from our area, this allowed the normal peace and tranquillity to quickly return. Much to fathers relief.

They had actually moved on into the Derwent and Ladybower valleys in

168

Derbyshire where apparently they found what they were looking for and stayed there for quite some time.

We didn't envy them at all!

I remember clearly, the day a huge dark coloured aeroplane flew very low over Bolsterstone School. It was playtime and we were playing outside in the yard. We followed it with our eyes and mouths open wide with wonder, even more so when we realised it was leaving in its wake a shower of thin strips of shiny silver paper which fluttered slowly down to us.

A lot landed in our playground so there was a scramble to see whom could gather the most to show the teacher. The actual plane wasn't identified so we didn't know whether it was friendly or not.

Later the same year another even bigger American marked aeroplane came flying very slow and low over Bolsterstone village, this as I recall came from the Sheffield direction.

We could all see and hear it as we sat at our worktables; the complete class followed its slow progress with staring eyes and growing excitement.

Our classroom lessons had by that stage in the War included being shown pictures how to establish whether any passing aeroplanes were friendly or not, we were allowed to wave to the friendly ones, but we were told to hide from the other type. As the big aeroplane drew nearer we could clearly see the American star on the side so everyone established it to be friendly.

Suddenly a stream of what appeared to be small white objects started falling from the fuselage fluttering down to land on the ground as the plane slowly droned over our playground.

You can imagine our excitement when Miss Gill our teacher, allowed us outside to see what the small white things were; they were in fact little packets of soft toffee (candy).

We were instructed to gather as many of them as we could and place them in a pile, we were even allowed through the gate into the village square and then across the road into a field known as the rocks to pick up any stray packages. As you can imagine some were eaten before they were taken into the school, (well what would you expect)? We were starved of sweets, they were rationed and we didn't have the choice, so sweets falling from the sky was heaven sent as one could say. But as for those that did make it to the collecting point they made quite a pile anyway. Later our teacher declared it was all right for us to eat some if we wanted. We didn't need any further encouragement, as we obliged with tremendous gusto! 'What a treat'! Some ate so many they were sick.

Slightly later in the War something happened up the Broomhead moors behind Spencer Stewards farm. Then it was confirmed that a Wellington bomber had crashed near Margery Rock.

Soon huge military recovery vehicles started to congregate around our area, especially down Spencer Steward's lane three or four fields away from our house. My brother and I were so exited we trotted along our bottom fields to have a closer look at what was going on. We climbed on to the rungs of the wooden five-barred gate at the end of our last field, to see for ourselves first hand. From that elevated vantagepoint we were within touching distance of the soldier guards and recovery personnel, in their uniforms and helmets awaiting orders. We were absolutely wide eyed with the intrigue.
In fact we became so much into the operation that a sergeant came over to us to speak with us.
We both quickly jumped off the gate and stepped back a pace or two in the grass field to keep our distance, until we accepted him as not about to do us any harm!
When he spoke to us. He declared that he wished to give us a gift, a part from the aeroplane they were recovering from up above Margery Rock on Broomhead moor.
My brother and me were completely over the moon about having a part of an aeroplane given to us. A soldier had been directed by the recovery staff to deliver to our farm a cockpit radio.
A cockpit radio! 'Wow'. 'Wow indeed'. And a couple of days later we had in our possession a genuine Wellington bomber radio. It wasn't smashed up as it could have been I suppose, it was complete with as many dials and switches one could wish for, it was conveyed by the soldier into a cowshed, and placed carefully onto a window sill for us.
We quickly found out how we could contact anyone anywhere in the world, and other aircraft in the area (all pretend of course for it was broken and didn't work) by just flicking a switch here or there and talking into the front of the Box.
Thinking back later. By giving us the useless radio was an effective way of getting rid of us.
It worked for we didn't go to watch them again; we had our prized radio to play with instead.

170

A few years later when I had become a regular grouse beater during the shooting season on Broomhead moors and I had eventually become a member of what some may call elite 'Top drive'. Our first top drive was of course actually the second drive of the day for the shooting gentry. Then we had our lunch in the Cabin followed by a half-hour or so rest, as soon as our time was up we- the top drive gang, began our long walk via a well-worn footpath back up the moor towards Margery Rock to start all over again. Before we had reached our intended positions we always had a rest after the first two miles or so with a sit down for a breather.

If it was raining we took shelter underneath an aeroplane wing.

The huge aluminium wing was perched across a gap between two boulders with each end embedded in the surrounding peat banking. It was obviously quite mangled as the wing had at one time belonged to a crashed war time aeroplane.

Someone over the years had made a seat from a plank of wood making the underside nice and cosy where we could sit down and have a rest, and some could have a fag.

The area close by was littered with all kinds of lumps of tangled aluminium.

Of the many occasions I can remember sheltering under that wing we sometimes we had to wait out a mid August thunderstorm, and the rain rattled on the top making a tremendous noise!

I suppose that wing might even have come from the same Aeroplane as the radio my brother and I had been given earlier.

Some time after the war ended small pieces of aeroplane started to become noticeable as they had washed down Ewden Beck, collecting in obscure places where water swirled in slow moving circles, in corners or areas where debris collects. Things such as shiny nuts and bolts attached to pieces of mangled aluminium material, lengths of rubber pipes, strips of canvas or on occasion I saw what looked to be part of a seat frame wedged in a crevice.

We were led to believe that most of the crashed aircraft on the Broomhead moors had been buried deep in the peat. But obviously some pieces weren't buried deep enough as eventually they came back onto the surface and washed down the river. They had certainly underestimated the power of the lashing rains and wind on the open moors; some of the bits and pieces became fully exposed even before the war had ended.

But saying that forty years later new pieces were still coming down the river. Especially after a hard winter, or the river had been flooding after a thunderstorm.

In what was known as the 'Top drive' group of beaters we had Nelson Kaye, Leonard Kaye, Spencer Steward, and Willie Hague and sometimes Rodney Seddons with my father and me completing the line up. I was always the youngest member of the group.
My father was first to be left at his starting position, and then it was my turn to reach my position. Whereas some of the others such as the Kaye brothers had to walk more than a mile further to reach their starting place on the top boundary.

To get there they had to pass an area littered with war time aeroplane debris which was sometimes an avid talking point amongst the beaters as they rested in the lunch cabin. I was always interested in their discussions so I listened in to their banter whenever they were talking about the huge wheels and hydraulic axle parts they saw sticking out of peat bogs as they passed by. I should have liked to see them for myself but I was never directed to go that far up the moor.

Nineteen

War time

During most of the Second World War years my father worked shifts at Samuel Fox and company the steel makers of Stocksbridge, his usual mode of travel was with his trusty BSA motorcycle and sidecar. However to occasionally have a change he would sometimes walk to work instead via the fields, lanes and footpaths. The distance was several miles each way using all the known short cuts, but as he liked to have a change, so he didn't mind walking.

On one notable occasion when he had walked to work and was almost home again in the early hours, it was still quite dark so he had to be careful whilst climbing over the last stile into one of his own top fields, when he suddenly fancied a cigarette. He stopped to light one up, before he had had time to take the first puff a noise somewhat similar to a hornet buzzed past his ear to be followed by the sharp crack of a rifle.

He quickly ducked for he realised the noise had been a rifle bullet, quickly putting his newly lit fag out he marched the rest of the way home rather shaken. He realised he had made a mistake for he had been warned/advised not to smoke in the dark for the tell tale red glow could be dangerous! The following day he reported the matter to the commanding officer of the American army controlling the area, this resulted in extensive enquiries and the interrogation of a hapless GI private who was on foot patrol that night. The soldiers excuse was he had suddenly noticed the flare of a match about half a mile away, and without thinking he had taken aim and fired his rifle. The result of his 'not thinking' caused the unfortunate GI to endure a lengthy spell in the glass house to cool off.

Our farm and all of the surrounding area was in the control of the American military forces for a number of years. With road barriers and armed personnel controlling the road from Midhopestones to the Strines Inn area day and night.

But I couldn't say whether their powers extended to shooting first and asking questions afterwards, I should have thought it would have been the other way round!

When the Second World War was at its peak it made things more difficult even in our remote area of the open countryside. There were times when we could hear the explosions as the bombs were being dropped on the Stocksbridge steel works of Samuel Fox and co even during the daytime when the men were at work. A couple of minutes later we could see and hear the big airplanes flying across over Ewden valley towards West Nab farm, we presumed they were heading back home to reload and come back on another raid.

On other occasions we could hear and see the slates rattling on our stone barn roofs as the German bombers raided Sheffield. At other times we could hear them from our hiding place down the cellar under the big stone slab, the slab where we normally salted the pigs.
It was strange really because Sheffield was at least 10 miles away from our farm in the Yorkshire Pennines. When the latest raid had finished, and the Stocksbridge all clear siren (which we could hear quite plainly if the wind was in the right direction) had finally stopped, we came out of hiding. By then of course the dust around the stone slates on the barn roof had settled.
Then father would declare it safe enough for us to enter the buildings to begin picking up the bits of plaster and broken slate lath from the top of the haymows and on the piles of oats and barley in the corn chamber. But when I actually did hear aeroplanes roaring high up over our farm in the dark, I always wondered what it must be like to be living or working there in Sheffield.
But anyone saying they only dropped bombs on Sheffield or on the steel works would be telling a lie, actually, for they did drop a few in our area... in the open countryside.
From what local inhabitants suggested or surmised, the German planes were just getting rid of spare bombs to save weight so the aeroplanes would be lighter. It was said they must have thrown them out any old how so their fuel would last back to their base.
The craters in our area that may have been caused by German bombs were nearly all on farmland in the High Bradfield area. Especially in and around the large flat area behind Swan cottage, where the craters were reported to be quite deep as I recall.

174

I'm sure that if the crew in the aircraft had been aiming at a specific target they would have been far more accurate, so when the local wags suggested the aeroplanes were just getting rid of excess weight they were probably right.

But saying that, there was in fact a small bomb or shell that landed down the side of the boundary wall in our bottom field below our farm buildings, but it didn't explode. It was rediscovered 40 or so years later when the Natural Gas pipeline contractors dug it up with their machinery. It still didn't explode, so it must have been a dud.
But I can't remember whether they reburied it or took it away to be destroyed?

The first time I ever went to Sheffield I would have been ten years old, when my Uncle Steve Draycott took me there. He had earlier promised to take me for my first ride on a train from Deepcar railway station to Sheffield then on to have my first ride on a tram in the city centre.
We had to walk to Deepcar of course for we didn't have a car at our farm; Uncle Steve didn't have a car either. He had travelled from Sheffield by the morning workers Bus to Stocksbridge, then changed to a Huddersfield workman's Bus, to get off at Midhopestones.
From there he had walked the last few miles to arrive early in the morning at our farm.
As soon as I had finished my work in the yard with help from Uncle Steve we were able to walk to Deepcar to catch the promised train to Sheffield.
I think my experience of the Train and Tram rides were overshadowed by the experience of seeing the huge city of Sheffield, even though it was in such a damaged state. Our visit wasn't long after the war had ended and we could see all the dereliction of the demolished houses and business premises in the city centre. In some cases instead of houses and shops there were just piles of rubble.
Steve Draycott was in fact an acquired uncle; apparently my father and Steve had worked together as farm labourers around Chesterfield and the surrounding areas, when they were teenagers. As each married, the other was the best man; they were at that time inseparable. They had maintained close contact all through the wartime, my father was excused wartime service because he was a farmer, and Uncle Steve was excused because he worked in the munitions industry making parts for guns, all sizes of guns.
He related to me once about the time when he was involved with a huge gun

intended for a destroyer or battleship.

Apparently his job entailed machining out of the inside of the gun barrel, and the bore was so huge Steve declared if he could bore an inch out in an eight-hour shift he was very pleased.

I have mentioned somewhere about the no- go area that surrounded our farm during the Second World War and that the barriers were manned by the American army.

It all came under an act of parliament by the name 'Visiting Forces Act 1942'.

Over the time the American Army were controlling the roads in our area they came to our farm quite regularly to buy - what they termed 'hen fruit' an American expression for hens Eggs - from mother. My brother and I never missed an opportunity to be around when the Americans came to call in their Willys Jeep. For without fail they would bring us a small gift of either candy or chewing gum. But I must say as far as I was concerned I wasn't fussed on the latter as I'd much rather have had the soft toffee known as 'Candy'.

I was always disappointed when they only produced chewing gum when it was time to dish out the treats.

At the top of Ewden beck hill just over the skyline is the little 200acre or so heather clad moor of Barnside, part of the Broomhead estate. During the war the military built a service road up this moor and finished it with hardcore. The road hugs the skyline for more than a mile and is known locally as the 'Bomb road' it runs in a straight line to where the Americans had set up a facility to train the gun aimers who worked in the gun turrets of armoured tanks.

The facility comprised a couple of camouflaged brick built bunkers, spaced about two hundred yards apart with a narrow gauge railway line connecting the two. In each of the two bunkers were housed donkey engines working winches to drag a huge target backwards and forwards along the railway line.

Apparently the idea was for the military tanks to fire at the target from where they were positioned, which must have been almost a mile away. If the wind was favourable we could hear the sound of the guns from our farm as they fired at the target; sometimes we could even hear the sound of the shells exploding when they hit something. We were told that the target speed was quite variable catering for novice or expert gunners. Slow for the novice and faster for the expert. Until they all became experts I suppose?

However, some of the gunners'couldn't hit the target even at the slowest possible speed, missing completely. And because the tanks were firing up hill at the moving target, some of the shells just whizzed by the intended destination to carry on over the skyline coming down on the other side of the hill, where some landed in our fifty-acre field!

At various times of the year father had a number of animals in that fifty-acre field, animals he was fattening up for market. So occasionally when he was checking around he'd discover a dead beast with a hole straight through it where a wayward shell had made a direct hit. In such cases father had to report the matter to the military who would quickly send a detail out to bury it where it fell in the field. And from then on there were many varied claims forms to be completed claiming compensation for the loss.

I remember once when father enquired about the accuracy of the guns? He had addressed his enquiry to the commander himself. The commander somewhat bluntly replied that the guns on his tanks were serviced regularly and they were always accurate. So the problem had to be with the gunner or aimers, from then on we all imagined any wayward gunners or aimers would be thrown in the cooler (military jail) to remind him to learn to aim or shoot better.

On the adjoining Midhopestones Moor was the site of the American army workshop facility.

This facility had been set up to service all the military vehicles used in the training exercises in our area such as tanks and their transporters, personnel carriers, jeeps and I suppose the target training equipment up on the Broomhead Moor.

A few years after the hostilities had ceased; when I had become a regular member of the Midhopestones Moor grouse beaters. I remember we had to walk quite a way up the moors on grouse shooting days to reach the shooting cabin, along the way we passed by the roadside the remains of the concrete bases where the workshops had stood all those years earlier.

The complex had a wide concrete access road and the entrance still had the wartime barrier in place for many years long after the war had ended.

We all presumed Walter Salmon's the Midhopestones Moor head gamekeeper had the key for the gate for it was always opened for grouse-shooting days.

The gate and barrier were just outside the little village of Upper Midhope in an idyllic quiet country setting, surrounded on three sides by the expansive heather clad Midhopestones moors.

One morning either during or soon after the war, Grandad Dyson could be heard shouting outside our farmhouse door.

'Wheers ahh lass' he hollered 'come here a minit arve summat to show thee'. When mother finally made it to the door. Fred fished in his ferret pocket to produce a tiny red bundle 'Will tha put this little bugger int'oven lass afoor it dees'.

He wanted mother to place the little bundle in the black kitchen range oven where it would be warm, but not particularly hot.

Later mother called my brother and me to have a look what Grandad Dyson had brought in that morning. When she brought the little bundle out of the oven we could see it was a tiny pup, and we all wanted to hold it.

Mother gave it some milk to lap, and it grew up to be one of our most unforgettable and best cow dogs off all time. We named him Jim. Earlier that month, one of our farm cow dogs had gone missing, we knew she was in pup so we presumed she had run off to have her litter somewhere on her own, which sometimes farm dogs did. We didn't know what the father looked like so when Grandad Dyson brought that little pup for us we presumed it could have been a pup from our own dog.

Grandad Dyson explained he had been walking across the little Barnside Moor above our farm on his daily gamekeeper's rounds looking for predators, when he heard a whimpering sound. He traced the sound to water filled tank rut where he could hear the noise a little louder. He knelt down and carefully reached inside a hole, and to his surprise pulled out the little bundle.

At first he thought it could be a fox cub, but on examination he discounted that theory, if he had been certain it was indeed a fox cub, he would have killed it there and then.

He placed the tiny bundle in his ferret pocket and hurried down the hills to our farm to give it mother to warm up in the oven.

As I have said it grew up to be the most handsome dog you could imagine, it was fox coloured with a long brush for a tail and splashes of white on its face and four white feet.

Grandad Dyson always warned us not to let Jim roam around the farm on his own for if any of the other Broomhead gamekeepers saw it they would automatically regard it as a fox on the prowl and would shoot it without hesitation.

Everyone always said our cow dog must have mated with a fox that's the only explanation.

As for Jim, because he was small and very quick, it took a lot of time and patience to train him as a cow dog.   We had another cow dog of course but Jim didn't seem to want to learn how to do things by watching the other dogs work, he always wanted to be in there first.

Eventually he matured enough to become one of the finest cow dogs in the area.

Unfortunately Jim had a bad habit, and that was he could not resist having a quick nip at ankles anybody's ankles whether it was cows or people.

So when visitors came to our farm we had either to chain Jim up or make sure our visitors knew what the score was, so if they did get nipped it could be said it was their own fault, as they had been warned.   Father had tried to stop him by using many varied methods but to no avail, he still did it.

Twenty

Mortimer Road

Mortimer Road as we know it today was established around c1775, so the history books will have us believe. It entailed constructing new roads and bridges, from the little town of Penistone in Yorkshire across the many miles of open moorland to the village of Grindleford, which is of course in Derbyshire. Apparently there was a thriving wool trade between these two areas at the time, and the carriers needed a better road system to transport their goods along with their horses and wagons. To get their money back the road builders imposed tolls on anyone or anything travelling along the new road.

Here is an interesting fact; along the Mortimer Road at the top of Sheephouse hill between Midhopestones and Penistone there is a stone set in the wall at the roadside inscribed 'Take off'. So now lets go towards Derbyshire for quite a few miles along the same Mortimer Road, and just outside the Strines Inn can be seen an identical 'Take off' stone set in the roadside wall.

It is interesting to note that they are both at the top of very steep hills with a sea level benchmark shown on each of the stones.

The distance in miles between both these take off stones is probably 8 miles with quite a few very steep hills both up and down along the way.

Could it be that a traveller with a heavily loaded wagon have hired extra help in the form of a horse or horses to help him 'the operator' complete the distance between those take off stones in safety? Could these stones mark the point where the extra horses were usually unhitched?

It's an interesting point!

We can't ask the road builders for an answer for they have long since gone. I /we presume that if some were late night travellers who had finally arrived at the Strines Inn they could then hire a stall and buy feed for their horses. And maybe hire a room for the night?

However none of this appears to be so at the Penistone end where the other take off stone is located. For here at the top of Sheephouse hill there are none of these facilities visible. It may be that at some period in the distant past, a similar range of buildings providing facilities similar to the Strines Inn was available, but over time have disappeared without trace!

Mortimer Road is still there, for it goes past the farm where I was born and brought up.

However modern day travellers can rest assured that they can now ride their horse or drive their motorcar along the road without the fear of being stopped by a toll keeper.

Garlic House Farm where I was born is situated halfway up/down the 1 in 4 Ewden Beck hill, or so the signpost outside the farm gate declares. But it is much steeper further down the hill, more like 1 in 3 in places, as some travellers in motorised vehicles have found to their cost.

I remember when my brother and me were of school age and later, all manner of vehicles came to grief whilst they were trying to negotiate Ewden Beck hill whether they were going up or down was immaterial.

One of the first serious accidents I can recall happened whilst I was at school, during the War years. The crash happened down below our farm on what we have always known as the 'Big corner'. A military canvas covered troop carrier ran away going down the hill crashing through the wall and down the drop on the big corner continuing down the woodland banking and coming to rest against a big tree on the edge of a cliff. Inside the back were soldiers who were being transported somewhere. It was said that they were all knocked out by the accident and several lost their lives. Apparently their hair or helmets became caught in the top of the vehicle as it tumbled down the drop snapping their necks in the process.

Many cyclists have come to grief on the same corner after riding much too fast down past our farm and coming off their bikes lower down the hill. To prove it we had many damaged cycles left for safe keeping in our farm buildings whilst the owners recuperated from their injuries.

Sometimes it was many weeks before they came back to claim their damaged property.

I can recall one special occasion when a cycle ran away down the hill and the rider managed somehow to turn left (the actual road turned sharp right) and he collided with a stone gatepost just inside the woodland area. The resulting impact snapped the substantial stone gatepost clean off just above ground level (I believe the stump is still there), the rider and his bike were thrown clear over a barbed wire fence.

Understandably the rider was unable to ride his bike again that day because of his injuries but his bike surprisingly escaped heavy damage. His bike was stored in our empty pigsty for quite a while until he came to collect it sometime later.

A similar collision occurred where a cyclist came rushing down the hill much too fast to negotiate the right hand corner, and ran to the left - similar to the above rendition.

My brother and I were both sitting up on the bank in our bottom field and saw the whole thing happen. The cyclist hit the wire fence, and of course the bike stopped dead, but the rider continued he somersaulted over the fence landing in a untidy heap a least 20-foot further into the woodland. After a moment or two he stood up and looked around sheepishly, finally he clambered back over the fence to recover his bike. He looked around it for a minute or two adjusting things that had been pulled awry turned the bike the right way round climbed on board and continued down the rest of the hill. He was one of the lucky ones.

My brother Lewis reminded me about the time when we had a cycle stored in the pigsty for quite some time for many weeks in fact, and father finally decided we could play with it.

Obviously all the front end was damaged beyond easy repair but when the front wheel had been removed it didn't look bad. I went in search of a replacement wheel without success.

My brother and I had just completed a trolley made up from an old pram; the pram had been one of those affairs with the back wheels bigger than the front.

It only took a minute to affix one of the big pram wheels into the front of the wheel less cycle, and it worked. I know the cycle had a distinct forward lean but so what, it was ride-able and beggars can't be chooses (as someone once said).

My brother and I had quite a lot of fun riding our own produced version of a Penny-farthing type bicycle, - before the owner came into our yard one day to reclaim his bike!

Obviously we had to apologise for using it, but he didn't moan too much after father pointed out about the particularly long time it had taken him to come and collect it. We took our pram wheel out and gave him back his bike and a badly buckled wheel to go with it.

From then on we didn't presume anyone wouldn't come back for his or her property even if it were parked for months in the pigsty.

One of the more exiting vehicle crashes was when a beer lorry driver apparently became lost. The story goes: - This huge lorry had laboured up most of our hill with a full compliment of barrels on board, when suddenly one of the barrels came loose and fell off the back.

The barrel rolled with ever increasing speed back down the hill. The driver had noticed the errant barrel, but unperturbed he continued to the top of our hill where he was able to turn around to go back down the hill to recover it.

We at the farm were surprised to see a beer lorry going up our hill in the first instance but we were even more surprised to see the same lorry going down again a few minutes later travelling much too quickly for its own good.

Further down the hill the lorry apparently jumped out of gear, then the brakes failed. Consequently it ran away finishing up over the wall at the big corner careering down the woodland banking finally landing upside down in the beck with all the barrels smashed, and the lorry a write off. There's a moral here somewhere!

As for the driver! Luckily he survived to tell the tale.

Another highlight I remember was when my brother and I were playing near the road and a big box type lorry rushed past our farm gate, we could tell there was something wrong for it was gathering momentum all the time. We watched as it disappeared rapidly down the hill out of our sight. It continued to career down the hill as far as the big corner where the driver managed to steer the vehicle left instead of right then it overturned. It finished up perched precariously on the edge of a very steep drop.

The impact loosened the sides of the lorry allowing its load of loose 'Soap flakes' to escape and to pour down the hillside towards the river below.

184

Obviously we at the farm didn't know what had happened, until some time later, when the somewhat dazed and bedraggled lorry driver came staggering into our farmyard requesting the use of our phone.
He was disappointed when we had to tell him we didn't have one, but he stayed long enough to have a hot cup of tea before he went off to see if he could make the call from Broomhead Hall instead. Needless to say father, my brother Lewis and I went down the hill with him to have a look. What a sight, there were soap flakes everywhere.

Later when the wreckage had been cleared away, and not missing the opportunity, we all went down to the accident site with sacks to collect as many of the slippy soap flakes as we could.
Mother didn't have to buy any sunlight soapflakes to do the weekly washing for many weeks afterwards!
I remember the river frothed up like a bubble bath, as did the Broomhead reservoir piling up on the shore in big dirty coloured cloud like heaps. And there was a decided smell of soap in the area for months after that spectacular crash.

As my brother and I became older we started to go down the hill quite regularly on nice fine Sundays to sit up on the bank in our bottom field overlooking the big corner where we witnessed many of the crashes, some were more notable than others.
We didn't know it wasn't nice to watch other people's misery we thought it was just exiting. Which it was at the time?
There was another quite notable accident. That neither my brother nor I saw personally, it was the time when a 'Barber Green' tarmac-paving machine ran away.
The first we knew anything about it was when we were on our way home from school in the Taxi driven by Lewis Scholey himself. He had just driven over the bridge at the bottom of Ewden Beck Hill where he stopped to engage low gear.
After restarting we slowly rounded the first right-handed corner, and suddenly we were confronted by debris scattered on the road, at that point the road is too steep to stop with safety, so Lewis carried on successfully negotiating the rubble.
We continued up the hill. After we had rounded the big left handed corner we were all surprised to see a huge gap in the left-hand roadside wall, just

below Ewden Wood gate. This new development was intriguing to say the least.
So as soon as the taxi stopped to let us get out at our farm gate I was out of the door hotfooting back down the hill to have a closer look. As I looked over the gap in the wall below the wood gate I saw all the vegetation had been flattened as if a giant roller had been there, but I was none the wiser as to what had happened, so I went home rather puzzled.
Later we learned a tarmac paving machine had run away as it travelled down Ewden beck hill.

It had crashed through the stone wall below the wood gate continuing down the steep woodland (about 150 yards) finally knocking down the lower boundary wall of the wood to land in the road below. Luckily the heavy tarmac machine had landed the right way up and was relatively undamaged. We also learned from a council worker, that the machine driver was so shaken by the experience someone else had to drive it the rest of the journey to where they were going, leaving all the mess still in the road.

All the above renditions suggests that all the vehicles were travelling down hill before they crashed; but you may be surprised to learn that there were almost as many crashes whilst the vehicles were going up Ewden Hill.
My brother Lewis and I have over the years, witnessed innumerable vehicles coming slowly up the hill struggling around the very steep left handed corner. Only to come to a stop with a final gasp further up the hill where they had either stalled the engine or the vehicle had jumped out of gear. Then everything would happen suddenly, the vehicle would come rushing back down the hill backwards swerving around violently to finally come to rest either upside down in the road or imbedded in the roadside wall below our feet.
Some of the antics we thought were hilarious. We have on many occasions witnessed motorbikes with sidecars attached coming round the big corner, with numerous people pushing, the engines revving hard, all accompanied by billows of smoke.
Or on other occasions when cars have come rushing down the hill amid clouds of smoke coming from all four wheels.
You must remember there were no seat belts in those days, they hadn't even been thought about never mind invented. So the drivers and passengers of crashed or damaged vehicles either tumbled out uninjured through the doors or the broken windscreens.

186

If they were injured the ambulance had to be sent for. The nearest public telephone at that time was the phone box at Midhopestones cross roads on the A616 Manchester road about six miles away. Sometimes it could be quite a while before we heard the ambulance bell clanking coming to collect the injured people being attended to by other road users. My brother and I were too scared to get down from our vantagepoint on the banking, so we either continued to watch or we went home.

I recall the occasion when there was quite a pile up on the road just below where we were sitting. The first indication something was going to happen was when we saw a little Austin seven saloon suddenly come into view rushing down the hill. My brother Lewis and I voiced the same idea it was going to crash, and it did. As we watched, it unbelievingly succeeded in negotiating the very tight right hand corner but failed to straighten up, instead it finished up on its roof. No sooner had we both taken in that dramatic spectacle than another identical Austin seven came down the hill and did almost the same thing.

During the next ten minutes or so there were even more Austin sevens littered around the area causing quite a melee in the road. All the drivers appeared to be unhurt, but some of their cars were quite badly damaged.

My Brother and I were of course mesmerised we knew we were too young to do anything so we stayed where we were sitting side by side watching and taking it all in, it made our Sunday exciting. I wouldn't say we were ever scared but let's say we were sometimes rather anxious.

That particular bit of the road known to us as the big corner was I suppose more of an acute angle somewhat similar to a horseshoe, and I can't imagine how the road builders managed to construct it in the first place. I remember they used steamrollers to roll the road when they had completed any repairs such as tar spraying or regritting. The steamroller the council used was a massive green and black Fowler machine, it belched steam and smoke as it clanked and banged its way past our farm. There's no doubt Ewden Beck hill was by far the steepest hill with the sharpest corner along the entire length of Mortimer Road.

Fred Chantry the agricultural contractor always had difficulty when he wanted to move his threshing kit up Ewden Hill from Broomhead Hall farm to our place when he was threshing corn in the autumn and winter months.

During his early days Fred used a Field Marshall tractor to work his kit. So when the time came for him to move his machines across the valley to our farm he arranged to borrow a tractor and driver from Broomhead to help him up the steep hill to our farm.

Fred had learned from mistakes in the past that it was better to attach the second tractor at the very bottom before attempting the 1 in 4 hill.

So he would stop completely on Ewden Bridge to hang on the extra tractor borrowed from Broomhead. A lot of shouting and swearing later the two tractors would attempt the hill as a team. I remember it all, as I would be standing well back out of the way watching it happen.

Broomhead had at that time one of the popular tall Fordson major tractors.

By using two tractors to tow the kit up the steep Ewden Beck hill made the job look easy so it was always successful. However a couple of years later Fred bought a relatively new more modern four-cylinder Nuffield tractor; and by doing so he probably thought his problems would be over when the time came to tow the threshing box up Ewden hill.

He was of course deluding himself. As I can recall, it were all hands on deck one day when Fred attempted to tow the kit up our hill with his Nuffield tractor without asking for the extra assistance. Fred's Nuffield was no doubt stronger but it had one drawback it hadn't got the grip, consequently the tractor ground to a halt on the steepest part of the hill with the rear wheels scrabbling for grip. Soon the whole outfit slowly started going backwards. Franticly with much shouting and swearing Fred's helper un-shipped all the wedges they carried with a few wall toppers from the roadside wall for good measure to wedge under the wheels of the threshing box and tractor to try and stop the plot gathering momentum.

The sliding backward motion was successfully stopped, but the threshing box and the Nuffield were stuck there in the road unable to start again. I remember rushing home to tell my father about the situation. He quickly went to have a look and decided to take our pair of workhorses down the hill to hang them on to the front with heavy chains. This helped to hold the kit steady until the Broomhead Fordson tractor came to save the situation.

Needless to say Fred never tried to do it all on his own again as far as I know anyway.

In the late 1950' a strange but surprising thing or even phenomenon suddenly

188

started to happen. At certain times every day a biggish car would roar past our farm gate, always going uphill!

We could set our clock by its regularity. Soon we began to take more notice of its regularity and we could hear tyres screaming on every corner coming from beyond Broomhead a mile away.

It must have been summer time because one of the times of day it was due was the time we fetched the cows in for milking. We had to change milking times slightly so that we weren't walking cows on the road when the car was due to appear.

My brother and I went down Ewden Hill to sit up on the bank in our field to watch as it came careering around the big corner, there was tyre rubber all over the road. The car was covered in something like black canvass stuff, matt black certainly no shine at all to the body colour, it had tinted windows so we couldn't actually see who was driving.

This went on for a couple of weeks or more, I recall one day when I was standing out side our farm gate to watch it go by, I could hear it coming up the hill, when it suddenly stopped. It had stopped just below the big oak tree below the farm buildings, as I watched, the driver got out and raised the front bonnet to have a look inside, I was so exited I quickly trotted down the road to try and get there before he drove away again.

As I skidded to a stop on the steep road surface the driver slammed the bonnet shut yanked opens the drivers' door and roared off amid a cloud of rubber smoke. I was devastated. I was so close I could have seen the driver's face if he hadn't been wearing a crash helmet at the time.

As I have said the whole exercise only lasted slightly more than two weeks, I waited many times outside the farm gate for another opportunity to have a look but the car never stopped again.

We heard later that the car went through upper Midhopestones village, up Woodhead pass, through the small town of Hayfield, down the Snake pass, past the Strines Inn before coming by our place. This went on regular as clockwork for five days a week for a couple of weeks.

We heard later one of the drivers had long blond hair sticking out of his crash helmet (Just like the one I had seen) and his name was Mike Hawthorne. Who I discovered later was a racing driver. We also heard the car was a prototype Rover 2000 and there was a service facility set out at the end of the Strines road.

At the time that information didn't mean anything to me. But it's all-true.

My only regret about the whole incident was not having time to say hello to the driver that day, before he took off all of a sudden.

Twenty-one

Local villages

I lived all my early years on a farm in an area known as Ewden Beck, where the full title address was Garlic House Farm, Ewden, Bolsterstone, nr Sheffield. However government departments and such people insisted on spelling the word Ewden as Yewden, maybe it was the correct or even an old way of spelling it but father liked to spell it his way. Without the 'Y'. Midhopestones was our nearest village, but all the local population liked to call it by the shortened version of Midhope. Without the 'stones'. Or just 'Middup'!

Midhope village was graced with a Post office with a shop, a primary school, a chapel, and a public house 'The Club Inn'. Midhope also boasted a disused blacksmith's shop, so it had a right to be called a village. A mile or so along a narrow lane was Upper-Midhopestones or Nether- Midhopestones, or as the locals called it Upper- middup. All three of them were commonly used names for the same village. I always wondered why such a little place had such a long-winded name!

For Upper Middup didn't have a shop, a school, a pub or even a chapel, or for that matters any of the attributes of its nearby counterpart Midhopestones so it didn't qualify as a village at all, it was in fact a hamlet, or a cluster of houses.

If we now follow the little narrow winding road a little further over a reservoir embankment, we enter the village of Langsett. The village of Langsett is somewhat split in two by the A616 Sheffield to Manchester trunk road. Langsett boasts an excellent public house the 'Wagon and Horses' otherwise known locally as 'Billy Greens', and a village shop, with a working farm all built in Yorkshire grit stone huddling together as if cringing away from the roaring traffic.

When I was a teenager I regularly rode my bicycle to the A616 Manchester to Sheffield main road at Midhopestones and then up to Langsett where I stopped to have a rest before continuing through Upper Midhope back home, all done just for fun.

I remember one day as I leant against the stone wall on the corner across the road from the village shop to have a breather when I suddenly noticed how busy the little shop cum café was on that particular Sunday in the summertime. Then I noticed the many cycles that there were around the place some leaning against the shop wall, with many more propped against the wall alongside the main road. There was a blue plaque attached to the wall by the doorway. So I went to have a look, and it depicted the legend 'Cycle Touring Club', and the shop was on the cycle clubs accredited list for supplying snacks and refreshments to bike riders passing through, especially, during the summer months, when the whole area became a popular tourist destination.

Just around the corner on the side of the lane from Llangsett to Upper Midhope is a mock lodge/castle structure, which at first impressions appears to be keeping guard over Langsett water works reservoir. It is in fact where all the pumps and gauges are housed which control the water levels in the reservoir. Langsett reservoir was the largest single expanse of water owned by the Sheffield water works covering 125acres, it is 97ft deep, and holds 1,408 million gallons of water. Another feature of the Langsett reservoir is the road, which runs across the embankment, it is said to be the longest single carriageway across the embankment of any reservoir in Great Britain!
I have gleaned these facts from Jack Branston, s book 'History of Langsett'. There is another much smaller reservoir a mile or so away known by the name of 'Midhope reservoir' this was built on what was Barnside Common. But passers by do not easily notice it for it is hidden behind a stand of fir trees.

Completely in the other direction from our farm is the village of Bolsterstone.
Bolsterstone is a much larger village, both in the number of houses and people

who populate it.

The primary School in Bolsterstone village is the school I first attended as a five-year-old. At that time the village boasted a Post office, a grocery shop, a working blacksmith's shop and of course the School. Sadly most if not all of them have become lost in the mists of a past era. Nowadays only the Church of St Mary's and the Public house 'Castle Inn' remain. The School is now a recreational centre.

Bolsterstone village is 984 feet above sea level and was in earlier times an ancient Saxon settlement. Much older than the nearby bigger towns of Stocksbridge or Deepcar!

It was always a debatable topic as to how the village of Bolsterstone acquired its name.

One theory suggests, that there were two large boulders lurking in a area what is now within the confines of the churchyard, and these boulders, it is again suggested, is where the ancient name of Bolderstone started before it was later refined to Bolsterstone!

In the centre of the built up part of the village is the building known as the Porters lodge, where historical records suggests once stood the ancient Bolsterstone Castle.

It still has the ancient village Stocks housed inside railings to keep them safe I suppose - from vandals!

I remember in my school days when I attended Bolsterstone infant's school just across the village square the many times I would find myself standing up on the stone base of the village stocks, craning my neck to peer over the Churchyard wall at a large stone structure. What I could see from my vantagepoint was what can only be described as hollow stones. The hollow stones are about four-foot high, and legend or local folk law has it that the hollow (shaped) stones were where people placed their heads to be beheaded for certain misdemeanours. It always intrigued me, and I day dreamed that I could see people waiting in a line to have their necks chopped off by someone with a large axe.

For many years there has been a world renowned male voice choir based in Bolsterstone, and over the years the choir have won many competitions and awards both nationally and abroad gaining many accolades world-wide for their excellence.

Here's a little story, its funny now but it wasn't at the time.

In the centre of the village immediately in front of the Bolsterstone School front gate is another area surrounded by iron railings, these railings are supposedly protecting the redundant communal village water pump. Even though the large stone horse trough next to it was still being used to water passing horses. The bars of the railing around the pump were set close together with spikes on the top to stop anyone venturing inside the 'forbidden' area!

If one looks closely at the railings on the side facing Sundial Cottage, across the road, one can still see an area that has been damaged at some time.

What local people may have forgotten is how the damaged area came about! It was like this. It happened during the year of 1935 the year when driving tests were first introduced for drivers of motor vehicles to have a licence to drive.

At the time of course my father was already an experienced motorcyclist and someone who lived in the village approached him asking if he could spare the time to give a few practical lessons of how to ride a motorcycle correctly so he could take the newly introduced driving test.

In the process of these 'lessons' father had taken the potential new rider up Heads lane carefully following his pupil on his own machine. When they came back the prospective new licence applicant turned the corner from Heads lane outside the school gate far too sharp and crashed into the newly erected iron railings surrounding the redundant water pump.

The resulting melee and chaos brought some of the local people out of their houses to watch as my father and the somewhat humiliated unfortunate motorcyclist extricated the errant bikes front wheel from the badly distorted railings, eventually both of them rode away from the scene.

Later when the authorities tried to find the culprit, no one knew anything about it! Father always presumed it was because they were both well-known characters who lived in the locality and they, the village residents, didn't want to add any additional pain to the unfortunates.

The damaged railings were still there just as they had left them all through the period I attended Bolsterstone School as a pupil. They may still be like that now?

Whilst I attended Bolsterstone School Minnie Webster kept the Bolsterstone village shop, and I remember quite well the occasions when I had been instructed to collect either a loaf of bread or a number of her luxurious soft ½ penny tea cakes Mrs Webster sold in the shop. Mother had instructed me to collect them just before boarding the school taxi that carried me home after school. I remember on some occasions I would be so hungry the solid loaf sometimes arrived home resembling as if mice had been at it, as I had nibbled at it to presumably quench my hunger whilst riding home in the taxi.

Just over the playground wall of Bolsterstone C of E primary school is a road named Yew Trees lane, about a mile or so down Yew trees lane was the little hamlet known as Ewden. I say 'was' in the past tense, for at one time there were very few dwellings in the Ewden area until 1916 when more than thirty wooden 'Houses' were erected for workers to live in whilst they were constructing the two new reservoirs in the valley.

The inhabitants of the wooden houses raised Ewden hamlet to village status so it quickly became known as Ewden Village.

It had by then acquired a shop run by the Stocksbridge Co-operative Society, a mission hall, a canteen and a recreation hall for village meetings. You may be excused if you are starting to wonder how I can recall the wooden 'Huts' in Ewden village in 1916? When I wasn't born until 1936. Well, I have to admit looking up that little snippet of information in Jack Branston' historical book entitled 'Pennine people and places' otherwise I wouldn't have been able to continue with what I was writing about! The huts were still there when I was old enough to remember the children of my age who lived in them, and most of them attended the same schools as I did. For the best part of my early teenage years I often rode my bicycle especially in the long summer evenings down and along the footpath through Ewden wood to the iron-bridge below Wigtwizzle. Where I had to lift my bike over the railings to continue along the metalled road around Broomhead reservoir and down the private road known as 'the private' to Ewden village to see my many friends, who lived there, in the 'Huts' as they were called.

If the gate was locked at the top of 'the private' as it sometimes was, I had to either lift my bike over the top or push my way through the undergrowth to get around the barrier and back onto the road to continue. All the huts I went into were very nice just like conventional bungalows. I believe it was as late as the 1960's before the last of the wooden bungalows were finally demolished.

It was during one of my summer evening visits to the village that I had inflicted on me one of my biggest most painful accidents. I was I suppose fourteen years old. I was on an escapade that had all been arranged at school for a small gang of us mostly from around the village. There were I suppose ten or so of us. We were going to have a look inside one of the control towers controlling the water levels in the Broomhead reservoir.

One of our 'gang' was the son of the keeper or manager of the tower in question and he had proclaimed he could acquire a loan of the key to the building? However by the time everyone had joined our party it was already becoming dusk, the operation entailed jumping over a low coping stone wall down into a dry cobbled floored overflow duct. Quickly the other members of our gang disappeared rapidly over the wall leaving me the last to jump.

That wall was a much, much higher than I had anticipated so the resulting landing on the cobble stone floor below jarred my heals and legs so much I collapsed.

Recovering slightly I was able to stand up, but it was certainly painful and difficult to walk.

It resulted in my arriving at the rendezvous well after the others who were impatiently waiting for me at the door of the building. After we were all accounted for our guide produced the necessary key, and we went in. We all stood there awe-struck as we looked at the myriad of levers and dials all around the walls; we only stayed a few short minutes before we went back outside again. Our keeper of the key quickly locked the door and we made ourselves scarce, for we shouldn't have been there in the first place! Luckily we went another way back to the village but my legs were terrible I'm almost sure I had to push my bike all the way homes that night because I wasn't able to operate the pedals. I always blamed myself into agreeing to go somewhere where we weren't supposed to go. So what happened that evening served me right.

But I shall always remember the pain I had in my feet and ankles for days afterwards. I became convinced I had broken something somewhere, but I didn't say much about how I had acquired a sudden limp. I remember having to invent various excuses when anyone questioned me about it, eventually the pain diminished and finally the problem went away.

There are far too many names to mention amongst those of my friends who lived in Ewden village. However I must mention one, his name Peter South. Peter South and I became more or less unseparable friends at school and at play, making it a priority to call at his house everytime I cycled to Ewden village.

As he became older he began to come to our farm to see if he could help with anything what was going on. One of the advantages of this was we were able to get away earlier so we could have a ride around on our bikes. He came to visit our place from Ewden village the same way as I did, by climbing over the railings by the Iron Bridge then riding along the path by the river up to Ewden Beck Bridge and up the hill to our farm.

I clearly remember him arriving in our farmyard one summer's evening absolutely soaked to the skin for he had apparently fallen in a deep pool by the old bridge. Apparently he had wanted to have a go at crossing the old dilapidated wooden bridge over the river for a long time but daren't. But for some reason he had finally succumbed to the temptation and decided to have a go on the day he was on his way to our farm.

The wooden bridge at that time was in a particularly bad state of decay, Peter had apparently only managed to get half way across when he slipped and fell off the narrow slippy plank into the deep water swirling around underneath.

I told him he was lucky the water was so high. For he could have been injured if the water had been low, as the riverbed was littered with big rocks directly under the bridge.

It became a talking point for a long time amongst our group of teenagers, sometimes becoming a source of merriment when the story expanded to the time when Peter South fell in the river in Ewden wood and was attacked by a bunch of water rats!

Bradfield…Even in mentioning the name Bradfield! Can be confusing for there are two villages by the name of Bradfield one is Low Bradfield and the other High Bradfield connected by a quite steep narrow lane bordered some of the way by the high wall of the Church yard. I rode my bikes both cycles and motorcycles through both the Bradfield villages many times over the years. But really they were just that little bit too far away from home for me to know anything much about them. Except that Low Bradfield boasted a cricket team, and it had its own pitch.

Nearby was the pub known by the rather quaint name of 'The Hay Chatter', which I am told has now been closed or even demolished. In the village centre is 'The Plough Inn'. This is regaled by its many patrons as excellent.

High Bradfield on the other hand is a village we would often pass through on our way to Sheffield; if one could call the short experience 'passing through'. For if one were driving through the village of High Bradfield the village would suddenly appear in ones sight then next minute you were through it! Yes it's that big!

As I recall High Bradfield doesn't have any distinctive features other than the popular 'Old Horns Inn' public house and the remains of a Norman castle hidden somewhere behind the only farm in the village but we mustn't forget of course the village ghost.

Legend has it a figure in white appears on the road outside the church during late evenings on the narrow lane leading down to low Bradfield only to disappear suddenly when anyone walks down the lane towards it. I know of several people who claim to have seen the figure but I am still sceptical about the 'legend'.

For all those who say they have seen the 'apparition' were all passing the churchyard after visiting the local public house. The 'Old Horns Inn' whether their sighting' were influenced by imbibing an excess of amber fluid I couldn't possibly say.

For I have yet to see it for myself.

The local name confusion continues when I look at my birth Certificate. It states that I was actually registered as being born at Garlic House Farm Bolsterstone in the registration district of Wortley, a sub district of Bradfield. Bolsterstone and Wortley are of course villages in South Yorkshire, whereas Bradfield is in the Derbyshire Peak National Park. Records can't get anymore confusing, can they?

Twenty-two

Tractors

The first tractor I remember encountering was when I was 6 years old during 1942.

I was sitting on the drivers' seat steering it on my own. The tractor was a small Caterpillar type machine, and I was holding on grimly to two handles used as steering controls. The left one to turn left, and the right one to turn right. I vaguely remember the tractor was pulling a wheeled trailer full of manure across a newly ploughed field, and my father and another chap were spreading the stuff off each side as we slowly travelled along.

I was told later, that each time we reached the headland the fellow on the trailer jumped down and turned the caterpillar around for me so they could continue spreading the muck whilst we travelled across the field going the other way. I couldn't do the turning manoeuvre myself, as my legs weren't long enough to reach the controls on the floor. Apparently when the job had been completed I was so exited to have been helping I wanted to stay on the tractor.

I had determinedly clung to the machine and wouldn't let go the only way they could get me off was to promise me that I could drive the machine again later.

That particular caterpillar tractor was a Ministry of Agriculture machine on loan to our farm engaged in a Government sponsored scheme, a scheme designed to encourage farmers to bring more farmland into food production to help the War effort.

Another government owned machine; working on our farm a year or so later

199

was a wheeled tractor known as a 'Case' (American). The case had been busy working in a field about three fields away towards Nether House Farm, ploughing and working the ground ready to sow grass seed. At the end of each day it was brought into our stack yard to be parked up for the night. But unbeknown to the driver my father had been covertly eyeing up the tractor with designs on using it one evening after the driver had gone home.

Father wanted a strong tractor to drag something somewhere that our own workhorses couldn't move; he didn't want to ask the driver beforehand, he preferred to do it his way. So one evening as soon as the driver had gone home, father took over. He had obviously watched closely how to start the engine, this he successfully managed without any problem. He even managed to move whatever it was successfully, without any problem.
After he had completed the task father returned the tractor to exactly the same position where the driver had parked it earlier, intending I suppose, for the driver to be none the wiser the next time he came to use it. Unfortunately he had failed to watch how the driver stopped it, father tried pulling this, pushing that until eventually he got into a right old flustered lather.
All to no avail as the engine wouldn't stop.
I can hear the engine now droning on and on in the background all through the night, until the operator came the next morning.
Father immediately somewhat shamefacedly owned up to having used the tractor to move something difficult. And he went as far as assuring the driver it wouldn't happen again!

Now I'll relate a situation involving a tractor, which became quite scary.
When it was time to take away or bring any Government owned machines to outlying farms the usual way was for them to be delivered or taken away on long flat-bedded lorries. Some of the drivers didn't even have a ramp to unload whatever it was they were transporting.
However the lack of an unloading ramp wasn't normally a problem, for all the driver had to do was find a suitable banking somewhere at the side of the road, back his lorry up tight against it to unload the tractor or machine. But on one memorial occasion it did become a problem.
The date I suppose must have been towards the end of the war, and I'm almost sure it was a D7 Caterpillar that was being delivered to our farm. The driver of the lorry had driven further up our hill from Garlic House searching for a suitable banking to unload. I vividly recall my brother Lewis and me trotting

behind the lorry as it was slowly driven up our hill to the chosen unloading area. The driver ever so carefully backed his lorry up against the banking as tight as possible, climbed out of his cab and climbed up onto the Caterpillar to start the engine.

It started with a cloud of black smoke and a loud roar. The driver climbed down onto the ground leaving the tractor engine running whilst he removed all the restraining ropes, chains and wedges. He clambered back in the driver's seat of the caterpillar gradually manoeuvring the machine around so he could reverse it backward off the lorry, onto the roadside grass banking.

That's when the fun began. For some reason as the machine was being edged off the back of the lorry the front end started to rise up off the ground?

As my brother Lewis and I watched we became so alarmed at this unexpected turn of events, we quickly climbed over a nearby field gate to be separated from the action unfolding.

Wide eyed we both watched as the lorry front end went up and up until it was almost vertical, we both cowered still further back not knowing what was going on, or what to do.

Then it happened. All of sudden the front end of the lorry returned to its normal position on the ground with such a crash it must have been heard in the next valley. Rattling everything you could imagine including our teeth, my brother and me were so scared we both clambered over a nearby stone wall and ran home as fast as we could.

Imagine our surprise when soon afterwards the lorry came down the hill driven as normal to our farm as if nothing had happened.

After explaining to our parents what had actually happened they too were surprised the lorry was operating as normal. They must have built lorries in those days better than they do in modern times, for if that same treatment had been handed out to a lorry manufactured in recent times I'm sure it would have immediately fallen apart all over the road!

Whilst we are relating tales about tractors – You may recall Fred Chantry the threshing machine operator I mentioned in my earlier book? Well, the Field Marshall used to drive the threshing drum with was a remarkable machine it was a British made Marshall with a single cylinder two stroke diesel engine (No valves) fitted with a piston reputed to be as big as a bucket. The cylinder lay horizontal with the cylinder head facing to the front of the machine with two large flywheels one either side of the engine.

I can hear it now Whump, Whump, Whump, whump. As Fred manoeuvred the threshing drum into it's carefully selected position in our stack yard. After making sure it was level all round, he placed the flat drive belt onto one of the tractor flywheels and gently tightened the belt to its correct tension. Before finally setting the handbrake on the tractor and stopping the engine.

With a lot of huffing and puffing Fred managed to remove the flat belt and rolled it up to store it somewhere in the dry ready for threshing day. Next morning I was there again this time watching Fred prepare to start the Field Marshall tractor.

First thing Fred did was to unscrew a winged socket in the side of the cylinder head, and carefully force into the socket end a wedge of blue paper.

After making sure the tractor was out of gear, Fred inserted the huge starting handle into one of the outside flywheels, and activated the decompression lever. Carefully Fred lit the blue 'touch' paper, when he was satisfied the paper was fully alight he blew it into a bright glow and quickly screwed it back into its locating hole. Then grabbing the starting handle with both hands Fred rapidly wound it round and round until he was satisfied the engine was spinning fast enough to flick off the decompression lever, and the engine started with a Whump…Whump…amid clouds of black smoke.

At that point a bystander informed me that occasionally even with the meticulous care Fred administered to the starting procedure the engine would fail to start, and then it was look out everybody! For Fred' already red face caused by the exertions of swinging the starting handle would turn purple as he snarled, snapped, cursed and raged.

Anyway every time I was watching it did in fact start at the first attempt.

It was almost time to get on with the work. But first the painstakingly prepared flat drive belt Fred had removed the night before was brought out ready to be refitted. Fred obviously had a knack somehow of putting the flat belt on the flywheel whilst the tractor engine was running. Firstly he placed the belt in position on the threshing drum pulley. And checking to make sure it wasn't twisted, he finally flicked the belt onto the tractor flywheel which was of course spinning around, There's definitely a knack to that manoeuvre for if Fred had got it wrong it could easily have sliced his arm off.

One day during 1947 father noticed a lorry travelling down Spencer Steward's lane, and securely strapped on the back was a David Brown crop master tractor, resplendent in its bright red livery paintwork. Father had previously heard that Spencer had ordered a new tractor but didn't believe the rumour until he saw the new red tractor that day, father was very jealous.

It was a very important occasion for Mr Steward in particular and for us as his nieghbour, for up to that day only Broomhead Hall farm owned a tractor of there own.

A couple of days later the red tractor could be seen travelling across grass fields and it looked as if it was pulling a set of chain harrows. Father became even more jealous by the day until he suddenly announced to mother that we must have a tractor for our farm, mother agreed, so father went to Penistone to see Mr Thorpe the bank manager.

Father came home later that day to tell us Mr Thorpe was coming out to the farm to have a look around to see if we could afford to borrow the amount of money required to buy a new tractor.

All that went to plan, but when father approached the tractor agent about ordering a new David Brown tractor he was told he would have to join the queue!

Apparently all David Brown tractors were in short supply. Father didn't like that idea, so he asked the Ferguson tractor agent the same question, and he was told he could have a new Ferguson tractor delivered the next day. And the cost would be cheaper into the bargain.

As an added bonus it would be supplied complete with a new two-furrow plough free of charge.

So our very first tractor was a Ferguson TE20. It was delivered to Garlic House Farm in 1947.

I remember watching through our farmhouse window as the lorry carrying our new tractor drove into the farmyard.

The delivery lorry had the name of Samuel Wilson and Son Bradfield road Sheffield emblazoned on the door. And securely tied on the back was a Ferguson TE tractor painted in a striking grey livery complete with the registration number KWA 137.

Attached to the hydraulics on the back was a two-furrow plough. We all watched with growing excitement as the lorry driver started the tractor and drove it down the two ramps to our level in the farmyard. Now we stood and drooled over it whispering amongst ourselves that we all thought it was wonderful. The lorry driver tidied all the securing straps away placed the ramps on the lorry bed before announcing that it was now the time for a demonstration.

He asked father which field he could try the plough in? Father declared the field below the buildings was due for ploughing anyway so why not show us how its done in there, so he did.

Most of the instruction was for father's benefit. But as I was 11 years old I was very interested and I took in all what was being said with growing excitement, for I imagined when the lorry driver had gone father would continue to plough the field, and maybe let me have a try. Unfortunately father's next question was to ask the demonstrator to show him how to remove the plough. Explaining to one and all that the tractor would not fit into the shed with the plough still attached. So all that happened later when the empty lorry had left was for father to drive the new tractor into the shed he had prepared previously and leave it there until it was needed.

But there was one big drawback with the new Ferguson tractor and that was its ability to guzzle such a lot of fuel, petrol. I know petrol was relatively cheap in 1947 but money to buy the petrol with was also scarce making the cost of fuel quite expensive.

Soon after the delivery of our new tractor Samuel Wilson and sons organised a trip to the Ferguson tractor factory in Banner lane Coventry. All the local farmers who had bought Ferguson tractors were invited. I remember a car came to our farm to collect father taking him to join a coach party starting from Sheffield; it was the first time my father had been to a engineering company's factory and it proved to be a very exiting experience. They were shown around all the aspects of making a tractor from a slab of steel to the finished product, in fact the statistics they were told suggested a new complete T20 Ferguson tractor left the production line at the rate of one every two and a quarter minutes. That in itself takes some believing considering all the different operations the machine has to go through before it gets to that stage. As I have said it was a quite exiting day for them all. The trip took a complete day finishing up with an organised meal in the factory canteen where they had a guest speaker and an entertainer that made for a 'reight good' day out.

When at a later date it was time to buy an additional tractor, a diesel powered version had to be considered to allay the running costs. Diesel was quite a lot cheaper and it went further as someone had told father earlier! So our second new tractor was the same type a grey Ferguson but designated the TEF signifying it was fuelled by diesel. The new tractor was good whilst working, but it had one very annoying drawback.

And that was as soon after the newness had worn off the engine began to get difficult to start with the self-starter, father contacted the agents and they sent out a fitter to have a look. After a cursory look around the machine the fitter intimated to us that most of the TEF Ferguson tractors had the same fault as ours had, and even the factory had been unable to find a satisfactory answer to the problem.

Being a diesel engine of course meant it was extremely if not impossible to be start it with the starting handle, even though one was supplied with the tractor. We soon found out that if the self-starter was used excessively it soon flattened the batteries. The only answer to the problem was to push the tractor out of the shed – every time we wanted to use it – into the road to run it down Ewden Beck Hill.

From there it was the case of going through a strict starting procedure. First we had to press the Kygas fuel-vaporising pump a few times, activate the decompression lever under the dash.

Select top gear 4th with the clutch pedal pressed down to the stop make sure the brake was off, we let the tractor roll down the steep 1in4 Ewden beck hill until it had gathered enough speed before quickly lifting the clutch pedal. That action would drive the engine, when the engine was running fast enough and white smoke could be seen coming from the exhaust chimney we released the decompression lever.

Usually the engine would then burst into life amidst a cloud of black smoke. If it was a particular cold day and the engine failed to start first time all the above mentioned drill had to be gone through again before the engine burst into life. It really was all a pain. And that's putting it mildly.

However once the engine had been running it didn't usually give any trouble for the rest of the day starting with the self-starter as normal. Unless the engine had again gone completely cold, then we had to go through the running down a hill procedure again to make it go.

Dinnertime was a worry and we took to leaving the engine running whilst the driver had his dinner especially if he was working in a relatively flat field, where there was no run off.

However if it was a nice warm day most of our worries were unfounded, as it would start on the starter. But if it didn't we would have the difficult task of having to release the implement off the back, before organising a tow to make it start again to continue with the work.

A couple of years' later Ferguson tractors brought out a new tractor designated the 35 series.

Still using a similar 4-cylinder engine as used in the previous model. It was slightly better at starting than the TEF but not by much. It looked slightly different by having a different shaped bonnet with a change of paint colour, now bright red instead of the traditional grey.

By then many Ferguson owning farmer' were loosing confidence in the brand and sales of new Ferguson tractors were at an all time low.

Suddenly we heard that Harry Ferguson had gone into partnership with the American machinery manufacturer Massey, and a new company had been formed to manufacture Massey- Ferguson Tractors. The new company in collaboration with Perkins engineering designed a new three-cylinder engine designated the AD3 this was introduced to the public as the Massey Ferguson 135.

With the new Massey Ferguson 135 fitted with the three-cylinder AD3 engine all the previous problems disappeared completely for it would start at any time whether hot or cold. It soon restored much of the confidence farmers had lost with the previous model.

Maybe it wasn't quite as powerful as the earlier four-cylinder Ferguson 35 machine but it had more features to aid the operator doing his work, and it soon became a best seller.

Topping the sales charts for quite a few years fully restoring the popularity of the Ferguson brand, it soon became known as the tractor to have. Especially if one wanted to be a successful farmer!

And to prove its longevity there are many thousands still in use today used as a small tractor around the farms where big tractors are now the norm.

Incidentally it was more or less the same Perkins AD3 engine with only slight variations that the Ford Tractor Company used to power their highly successful Ford Dexter small tractor range. And that also proved to be a best seller.

But all was not rosy at the tractor manufacturing plants. Massey-Ferguson accused the Fordson Tractor manufacturer of stealing ideas such as the hydralics, they declared the system fitted to the Ford Dexter range was virtually identical to the Ferguson System invented by Harry Ferguson all those years previously. There's no doubt they were similar if not identical, but we the farmers and operators couldn't have cared less all we wanted were tractors that would do its work without complaint.

Now we had a choice of two tractors both could work all day without complaint one the Massey Ferguson 135 and the other the Ford Dexter standard or a slightly better equipped version the Ford Super Dexter all of them very good small tractors.

Twenty-three

Market Days

Our nearest cattle market was right in the middle of the small town of Penistone Yorkshire. And early every Wednesday morning it was chaos along its high street with all the hustle and bustle of local farmers, their wives, children, and assorted dogs driving their livestock to the once a week market.

As our farm was situated several miles away, father had to employ a cattle truck operator to take our full-grown stock to Penistone market; these included such animals as fat bullocks, dry or barren cows or newly calved cows with calves. We transported our week old bull calves to market ourselves by trussing them up in cow cake bags to carry them in the tractor link box.

Market days were always regarded as special by everyone who lived in the surrounding area for sometimes it was the only day of the week when the farmer had a proper shave, and dressed up in better clothes. And for some of them it was a weekly ritual especially if they were intending to spend most of the day away from home attending to business or pleasure.

For occasionally the farmers' wife went with him to do some shopping in the high street or the outdoor market?

Some of the farmers kept what could be called a decent suite of clothes in the wardrobe, which only saw the light of day on market days. The outfit was finished off with a pair of brown market boots and leggings with a trilby for his head instead of a flat cap.

The resulting appearance of the farmer was quite striking to what he looked like for the rest of the week with his tatty work clothes, becoming quite respectable for a change!

When the business in the cattle market was completed, some of the farmers and dealers went into the 'Spread Eagle' public house amongst others houses of such ilk, to continue with their bargaining. Some said there was even more business conducted in those establishments after the cattle market had closed, than was actually done in the sales ring. These I can believe and could well be true!

My father only went to Penistone market when he had something to sell or he wanted to buy something either from the market or from the machinery dealers who had representatives attending market days.
Father didn't drink much as he couldn't afford to. He didn't go to the market all that often either as some did, but if he wanted to smoke during these trips he had to be careful during the previous week and save some some of his allocation for mother restricted him to 40 Players a fortnight cigarette ration.

There were many characters synonymous with Penistone cattle market. One of them was Tom Harris. Everyone knew Tom Harris as a local cattle dealer, and a very industrious wily person; he was short in stature, heavy build, with a round stubbly face topped with a mop of unruly hair. Tom Harris would spend almost every day of the week between market days wheeling and dealing around the farms, when he'd bought enough to fill a cattle truck he'd be ready for Wednesday, Penistone market day.
Tom would be there in the sales ring with the stock he had acquired/bought during the week, driving the beasts around with his cow stick showing them off to potential buyers, hoping to make a couple of bob. (His words) If they didn't reach the figure he thought they were worth he would withdraw the beast or beasts then try again at another market.

I shall always remember the occasions when Tom Harris came to our farm buying stock as I remember none of his visits were prearranged, he would just turn up at the yard gate to enquire if father had any stock for sale? If we had father would take him to have a look at the beasts; these could be either in a field or in a shed. If the beast' were in the field he always wanted them bringing in closer to be trapped in a corner where he could run his hands expertly around the animal or animals before considering what to offer. When a deal had finally been struck Tom's hand would go into one of his many inside pockets to emerge clutching a huge roll of notes. And I mean

208

huge! Tom would turn his back on father to peel off the agreed amount, turning back to hand the cash over.

All farmers doing a deal with Tom Harris always counted out the money themselves note by note, after Tom had handed the notes over.
Obviously a quicker method of counting the notes was to count each end of the wad to make sure the numbers were the same at both ends?
If the deal involved a larger sum which required a cheque. Tom would drag out of another pocket a handful of well-worn cheques. He'd leaf through these to find one suitable or near enough to the amount he wanted, sometimes the cheque or cheques were accompanied by a small cash adjustment to get to the figure required. On the back of each cheque were a list of signatures, as far as I know those cheques never ever bounced! This common practice of passing tatty cheques around when buying stock appeared to be normal amongst cattle dealers, some of the cheques had been around so long and were so grubby one could hardly decipher what the amount listed on the front was exactly. I don't know how the practice worked, but my father never questioned it.
As soon as the deal had been agreed and the cash or cheque handed over, Tom would ask father for a bit of luck (discount) only a small amount but it represented good will or intentions. That was also a normal everyday thing, in our part of the country, every deal involving cash had luck attached to the deal. But you had to ask for it.

My father's cousin Harold Hammond (known to us all as Uncle Harold) farmed Hollow meadows farm in Derbyshire. He would occasionally call at our farm when he had been to Penistone market, just to say hello. Besides being a farmer uncle Harold was also a cattle dealer, somewhat similar I suppose to Tom Harris, but dealing mostly in the Derbyshire markets of Bakewell, Buxton, or Bamford. Occasionally he would make the much longer treck over into Yorkshire, to attended Penistone cattle market, especially if there was something going on that was interesting or unusual.
When he considered it was time to go home to his own farm in Derbyshire he sometimes travelled past our farm along the way. So he would stop for a chat, a cuppa and a slice of mother's cake. My brother and me loved uncle Harold so we were always pleased to see him, for as soon as he saw us he would fish in his many pockets and produce a bag of spice (sweets) or a similar treat he had brought especially for us.

Uncle Harold always travelled in a big nice smart car, he was always dressed in a good suite, wore the obligatory brown market boots and leggings. And he always sported a pork pie style hat perched rakishly on his head, and he smoked cigars.

So rightly or wrongly we at Garlic House always thought Uncle Harold Hammond had plenty of money whether he had or not of course, we never discovered.

If we had a dry cow or a newly calved cow with its calf that father wanted to be taken to market he would ask or arrange for Tom Oxley to come from Silkstone common with his cattle truck. For Tom this would be a simple matter, but having to come to collect a bunch of highly-strung strong rearers from Garlic House was another matters altogether.

For it could be quite a traumatic experience for everyone involved when it was time to load the animals. We would have done all the preparation beforehand such as isolating the animals to be taken away by trapping them behind a gate in the corner of the yard or in a shed, but that wasn't enough sometimes, especially if the beast' didn't want to go.

Some of them could be so stubborn they just would not go up the ramp into the cattle truck even with the help of a couple of cow dogs and a few cow sticks. The worst scenario that could happen was for one or more of the beast' to escape. To rapidly gallop off into the distance!

So if the task of getting the beast back to where the loading could start all over again was too difficult, or the truck driver hadn't the time to wait, father would shout

'Just leave the bugger it'll come back when it's hungry'. And they always did!

A big fat bullock could be the worst and especially difficult to handle, we would have done all the preliminary work such as isolating the animal in a suitable shed or yard sometimes with a halter at the ready.

Everyone knew if the animal was allowed to break loose it could easily jump over any five barred wooden gate or barrier and wreak them or even break its leg in doing so.

So as you may imagine we were always pleased when Tom Oxley was able to raise the big door/ramp at the rear of his truck, and drive away with our consignment of livestock inside and complete. We knew Tom would look after the animals from then on, we also knew they would safely arrive at the market without further trouble.

210

On the rare occasions when father expressed his desire to accompany his livestock to the market Tom had to make room for him in his lorry cab amongst his dogs and cow sticks and various aids before father could climb into the cluttered passenger area. Travelling to market with Tom didn't pose a problem in itself the problem was how was father going to get home again later in the day.

So when he did finally reappear later in the day he could have come home by various methods such as walking from the bus stop at Midhopestones, begging a lift in a motorcar or even on the back of someone's motorcycle.

However there was an alternative market available other than Penistone. This was in the small town of Holmfirth, a few miles further away than Penistone, held on the Thursday of each week. Holmfirth market always had a good reputation for the disposal of the younger animals so father sometimes took our week old bull calves there especially if the 'grapevine' suggested calves were making more money at Holmfirth rather than Penistone. However market days weren't solely for the buying or selling of livestock, one could buy such things as hand tools or dairy essentials and representatives from the tractor dealers were always in attendance looking to sell a new tractor or machinery.

The machinery dealers were always on the look out for the farmer who had just sold a couple of cows at a good price during the day. They targeted such farmers and took them on one side or even bought them a drink in the 'Spread Eagle', where they could discuss, with them how to spend his or her new found wealth by renewing some of their ageing machinery.

The same applied to the bank managers. They would also be on the look out for farmers who had sold a couple of beasts, making careful note to stalk the farmer, and eventually corner him to suggest now was the time to pay off some of his overdue overdraft?

The cattle dealers always made a good living as could be seen from the vehicles they drove around in. They may have been scruffy, but they were modern and up to date. Whereas the farmers' vehicles were old as well as scruffy for they were in some cases used every day of the week either to tow a cow trailer or carry stock in the back.

Lots of them had such things as lights hanging off or wrong number- plates on the trailer.

It was the responsibility of the market inspector on duty on the day to make

211

sure the vehicles used to convey animals were fit to do so.

If he considered a vehicle not safe or fit to be on the road he would bring it to the attention of the police officer on duty attending the market that day. So sometimes one could see the police officer waiting patiently by a vehicle for the owner to make an appearance so he could have a word with him about his conveyance.

As usually in the first instance the policeman would give the owner verbal advice or warning about the his legal obligations whilst owning and driving a vehicle on the road. This usually did the trick, however some of the owners didn't take the warning seriously and by the time they had completed the day's business they would have forgotten all about it.

When a vehicle caught the constable's attention the first thing he looked at was of course the tax disc, he would peer closely at it taking in all the details listed, eventually he would either fish out his notebook or move on. If the owner of the vehicle was watching that was the time to approach the lawman to explain things. In most cases it was simple things like worn or bald tyres.

Maybe the numberplate on the trailer referred to a completely different towing vehicle; it could even be one the farmer had disposed of at some previous time, or the lights didn't work, or there was a missing light lens, or in some cases mudguards were missing completely from the trailer.

Boisterous animals in enclosed yards caused most of the minor damage done to farm vehicles, especially if the farmer had been foolish enough to leave the vehicle parked where bulls or bullocks could tamper with it. Any farm animal when suitably bored can take a delight in charging shiny things like wing mirrors, lamp lens's, radiator grills and hub caps so they could soon play havoc with any vehicle left unsuitably parked.

Some farmers were so poor financially that any vehicle they owned was always on its last legs, so any faults that were developing were either ignored or patched up this obviously made some of the vehicles unsafe or even un-roadworthy.

Of course all this happened before the introduction of the MOT during 1960's where all road vehicles over ten years old had to be checked annually before being issued with a Test certificate. In the long run the introduction of the Ministry of Transport examination made for safer vehicles. But a year is a long time especially in the farming environment so the farm vehicles were just as bad if not worse well before the next test was due.

If there were any decent vehicles to be found in the cattle market car park. You could bet almost anything they belonged to a cattle dealer, the local bank manager or an agent for agricultural supplies. As only those people had the money to buy new vehicles and the money to keep one in good condition. The average farmer bought a vehicle as of necessity to get from one place to another without having to walk. If any vehicle was bought in a reasonable condition it didn't last long under the arduous conditions of being used in the countryside. Its daily use involved traversing rough lanes, knee deep in cow muck. In effect, farm vehicles had to be strong and robust machines, capable of towing animal trailers with ease, whether loaded or empty.

It was late in 1947 when the Land Rover revolution started. For that was the year the Land Rover was first designed, and introduced to the home market. So by 1948 land rover had already become a by word for reliability albeit rather expensive. When the farmers started to buy the Land Rover it was a dream come true for they found it strong and well able to withstand the rigors of being used on or off the land, in short it was just what they needed.
It didn't take long for the green shiny new Land Rovers to be seen parked in Penistone on market days. First of all the better off farmers bought them as new vehicles then later ordinary farmers bought them when second hand examples became available.
They were always expensive but farmers soon realised a Land Rover would outlast quite a number of ordinary cars. Soon it became normal for most farmers to have a Land Rover to tow the cattle or sheep trailer around whether it was on or off the road.
This in effect caused the demise of many one man cattle truck operators as farmers bought or made their own cow trailers to transport cattle, horses or sheep with. Initially only the petrol versions were in production but by 1961 a diesel version was introduced as an alternative and this became a best seller. It didn't take long for the Land Rover to take over the role of the number one vehicle on the farm. When the ordinary family saloon car finally expired, it either joined all the other unwanted equipment behind the farm buildings, awaiting the attention of the scrap man or it was offered in part exchange for a Land Rover, which took over the role as the family car.

Twenty-four

Farmers year

A farmer's year doesn't vary much it's more or less predictable from one year to the next, the seasons follow each other as they always have done the only unpredictable part of the equation is of course, the weather.

When father took Garlic House as a rented farm the weather played even a bigger role in everyday farming as everything was done the hard way no machines just the farmer and his horses. He had to sow the corn seed or grass seed from a hopper strapped to the front of him so he could use both hands, filling the hopper every other pass across until the field was completed. The newly sown seed had to be harrowed or chain harrowed and then finally rolled with the flat roller all done with horse and manpower. If the field was to be grass the following year the grass seed had to be sown more or less at the same time as the corn, (Undersowing) then the field had to be rolled to try to save the seed from being picked up by the birds.

It was in the late nineteen forties I suppose before my father was able to persuade his brother in law my Uncle Jim Dyson, to lend him the Broomhead estates mechanical corn drill.

A pair of shire horses normally towed this masterpiece (it was in those days), around the fields drilling corn. And because our own horses weren't experienced with the equipment, the Broomhead horses came with the drill as well.

It not only saved a lot of time and effort on father's part but did a better job. For the disc drill planted the seed deeper in the ground this alone guaranteed to produce a better yield.

Then Broomhead bought one of the newly introduced fiddles to sow grass seed. I know it sounds a silly name for an agricultural aid, but the 'Fiddle' became an important part of a farmer's equipment. If operated correctly the fiddle transformed sowing grass seed into a successful operation. Previously sowing grass seed by hand from a hopper had in some cases resulted in some areas of a field being rather patchy mostly caused by miscalculations, or even a small puff of wind at the wrong time could cause havoc with calculations.

Father went to a farm sale somewhere and bought his own fiddle and from then on our grass fields became 'tidy', as patchy areas became a thing of the past.

However the era of the fiddle didn't really last all that long, for a few years later another machine replaced it, this machine was named the vicon.

The 'Vicon' was in effect a dual-purpose implement; it could successfully sow granulated fertiliser, grass, oats, wheat, barley, turnip or any other small sized seed.   On its own the Vicon caused a revolution in the machinery market doing away with numerous other traditional implements at one go, it fitted onto the hydraulics on the rear of a tractor driven by the power take off shaft 'PTO'.

The next crop to plant was the potato. First of all the selected field had to be given a liberal dose of farmyard manure then ploughed as deep as we dare without bringing up stones or breaking too many shares then worked it down to give a nice fine tilth. This was achieved by using spring drags and other cultivating implements until we were satisfied. Finishing the area with spike harrows or chain harrows to level it before rowing up the complete area with the horse drawn bouter. We planted the potatoes by hand in the bottom of the rows before closing the rows shut again with the same bouter, this effectively covered the potatoes with ridged rows of soil. All of it done by horse and manpower.

Later on, I suppose it could have been early in the nineteen fifties when father bought a two row bouter to fit on our Ferguson tractor and with it came the extra equipment to make it into a potato planting machine.

Not automatic, as they didn't come along until much later. On our machine the potatoes were still planted manually, but even so it was a revolution. It not only allowed two rows of potatoes to be planted at the same time but it did away with at least two jobs as well.

There was however one drawback and that was it required three people to operate it, two sat on the machine to plant the potato seed, the other was needed to drive the tractor.

At that time my brother Lewis was at school during the day so that left only two of us, father and me, the third person had to be hired bribed or even cajoled into helping us. Mother reluctantly did it some times but she didn't like the job as far as I can remember. With the ground already prepared and the sacks of new potatoes in the field, we could plant all the acreage we needed in more or less a single day with the new revolutionary planting machine. As the implement was pulled slowly along behind by the tractor a bell attached to a small land driven wheel rang at given intervals, this was the signal for each operator to drop one potato down the chute mounted directly in front of him. However if there was a slight problem, for example if something became trapped under the bell, causing it not to ring as it should confusion reigned, especially if the planters weren't paying sufficient attention.

So by the time the problem had become noticed quite a few potatoes could have been missed. A quick shout to the tractor driver was needed for him to stop so someone could get off the machine to clear the obstruction.

If we thought a few potatoes had been missed, we rectified the problem by going back a few spaces, pushing in seed potatoes by hand until we were satisfied there would be no gaps in the planting pattern.

In a way it was more stressful planting potatoes with the machine but it was easier and quicker.

As soon as the month of May appeared on the calendar it was time to drill turnip/swede seed and here another old saying comes to mind

'Make sure the swedes are drilled before sheep sheering starts'. Father must have acquired our single row swede drill, quite early in his farming career for I can remember trying unsuccessfully to help with the drilling when I was five or six years old.

After the field had been chosen, manure spread, ploughed and the soil worked down into a fine tilth, the next job was to row up the soil with the single row horse bouter into straight ridges ready for the drill.

Father always serviced the little drill well in advance, and drilling day had to be more or less perfect as far as weather conditions were concerned. It had to be dry with no rain anticipated in the near future.

To sow a complete acre or so field it only needed a little bag of seed so father had to be careful not to spill or loose any, whilst he was filling the seed box on the drill, then he was ready to go.

All ready to start drilling, one man with a horse and turnip drill could easily plant an acre in a full day.

However it wasn't a job to be rushed. For when the little plants came up everyone would be able to see and comment on the operators skill and handiwork, if the operator had any pride at all he did his best to keep the drill as straight as possible on top of the ridges at all times.

The turnip drill consisted of a front roller curved or hollow/dished so it shaped the row top into a nice smooth rounded profile. Just behind the dished roller came the seed box, connected to the adjustable coulter. The coulter scraped a little shallow groove in the newly profiled topsoil for the turnip seed to trickle into, finally a flat roller at the back of the machine flattered the row top effectively covering the newly planted seed with a layer of fine soil.

All very clever one must agree, and it worked.

Quickly we move on to hay time.

Here's another age-old saying in farming circles, declaring 'A load of hay in June is worth two in July'. And it's true! As the best quality hay was always made and harvested in June when the grass was young and tender. However sometimes the weather in June wasn't always conductive to gathering hay as I recall.

One particular year in the late nineteen forties was extremely wet, so wet in fact the traditional method of gathering loose hay became almost impossible. The traditional method was to cock up the hay in fork sized piles to finish drying ready for hauling, but one particular year all attempts to finish drying the crop was useless, because of the constant rain or showers.

Then one day father noticed Wilby Seddon had made a drying rig somewhat similar to a wigwam in shape, constructed from eight foot long willow or hazel nut sticks tied at the top and splayed out wide at the bottom. Wilby had then built the damp hay around the structure for the wind to blow through. It was all a desperate hastily made effort, but it worked.

Wilby Seddon!

Mr Seddon farmed Barnside Cote for many years, and was always inventing something or other so it came as no surprise when he was the first in our area to use the wigwam hay drying aid.

In fact the idea worked so well, soon similar structures could be seen in almost all the hay fields in our area. I even recall the agricultural merchants in Penistone market starting to stock a commercially made version. Buying them ready made saved one having to spend time looking for suitable long sticks I suppose, but father preferred to save the expense, so we made our own.

218

On another of his fairly regular visits to Penistone market father had noticed a new farming aid it was known as a Hay sweep! After he had taken a long look at it father decided it might be another way to help his fight with that years-wet weather haymaking season, so he bought one. The one father bought was a single horse version with the main cross member nine or ten foot long made from strong timber with long wooden fingers (somewhat similar to a rake) fixed securely to it.

The sweep was highly successful, and on a hill farm, such as ours, the sweep proved to be indispensable.

Its main function was to drag large quantities of hay across a field from one place to another without having to load it onto the cart or dray first, it was invaluable in those wet years of the late 1940'.

The four or five acres of root crops we grew at Garlic House always needed cleaning/weeding around the middle of August each year. But for some reason every field father decided to grow root crops in the dreaded weed known as Kecklets grew in profusion. Kecklet seed must lay dormant in the soil for years, for once a field had been ploughed the weed grew thick and fast, and the resulting outbreak could soon overpower any young root crops such as swedes, potatoes or kale growing in the same ground.

There are two varieties of that particular weed, the yellow flowered version, and the much stronger version with white flowers. We could pull the yellow flowered ones up with bare hands but if one tried that with the white variety you would have sore hands in no time at all as they had rough sharp prickles on the stalks, so we had to wear gloves to pull those.

The 'kecks' as we called them could virtually take over a complete crop of swedes or potatoes. We normally pulled them up by hand just before the flowers blew off, hoping I suppose it may have helped to reduce the following years infestation. But I don't think it made any difference.

However in later years some farmers controlled the nuisance by spraying, whilst I worked at home we didn't have a sprayer, even if we had, I doubt whether father would have been able to afforded the costs of the chemicals.

When the corn was ready for harvesting, a couple of days before the binder was due we had to open up the field around the headlands. It was much better if two of us worked together when we were opening fields out, father used the scythe, and I 'took up'.

Opening the fields out? This had to be done in each of the cornfields. The operation entailed clearing a swath of corn, wheat or oats- about 4-5ft or so wide around the edge of the field to allow the binder a clear passage around the field for the first time without flattening any standing corn. This eliminated waste.

Taking up? This was the process of gathering the newly cut corn into sheaf size bundles, and tying them tightly round the middle before standing them up against the field wall out of the way.

After the binder had finished the next job was setting up the sheaves into 'Kivvers' or 'Stooks', as some people liked to call them. It depended how heavy the crop was as to how many sheaves we built into a Kivver. Sometimes there were just six, sometimes eight or even as many as ten sheaves to a Kivver, we set them up in rows so that any prevailing wind could blow through the middle to help to finally dry off the newly cut corn. A few days later when the crop was nice and dry and ready to haul it was the case of everyone available working flat out to get the crop home?

I mentioned wet years earlier in this chapter. In contrast, some dry years caused problems with crops such as potatoes these were very vulnerable to such diseases as blight, which could in extreme cases ruin the entire crop. Swedes or kale were other crops to suffer if the year was too dry, producing poor quality or a smaller crop.

Another problem father encountered in certain years, all the crops seemed to be ready to do some work on at the same time. For instance, if it was a particularly dry spring. The grass could be late so it had to be left to grow for longer before it was ready to be cut. Sometimes during a dry year the corn crop would ripen early so it had to be harvested earlier than normal. At the same time the potatoes or swedes needed striking/singling or weeding. It was a nightmare for father, as he had to decide what was the best thing to do at any particular time.

I mention striking/singling. Because we grew swedes/turnips for the cows to eat during the winter months the plants had to have the space to expand and fully mature.

This is another case where a two-man team is an advantage once again. The two- man team worked up rows one behind the other. The first man up the row 'striking' with a hoe, in other words knocking out all the little plants in the row but leaving little bunches of undisturbed plants every ten/twelve inches or so.

The following worker had to pull out all but one of the plants left in these bunches making sure there was only one plant left growing in each position, this was known as 'Singling'.

As I have said it was a very important job, and it had to be done at the right time, such as when the plants were small but still big enough to survive this somewhat ruthless operation.

Potatoes were the next crops to be ready for harvesting. It was always better to time potato harvesting to be done during the School half term holiday, in October known locally as

'Potato picking week', when the youngsters from Stocksbridge or even as far away as Deepcar came looking for a few days work to earn a few (Bob) shillings picking spuds.

My father along with all the potato-growing farmers had to be quite selective when taking on casual labour. He had to ruthlessly reject the six, seven or eight-year-olds. Who all wanted a piece of the action (money) the older kids were expecting, so they were sent away I can see them now dejectedly trooping back home or on their way to try their luck on another farm.

We were always at a slight disadvantage at Garlic House when it came to employing extra help with potato harvesting, as we didn't have any means of transport to collect the kids from Stocksbridge so they had to walk. However, most of the kids were enthusiastic enough to walk so they didn't mind.

On the first morning we were expecting the pickers to arrive the first we saw of them was when they came over the big stile up on the skyline before they headed down the fields towards our farm via the footpath. Each with a bucket slung over one shoulder and a lunch bag over the other.

Sometimes they stretched to quite a long line walking along the footpath, and we could hear them laughing and giggling, as they were no doubt looking forward to a financially rewarding day. As they drew nearer some came directly to our farm, others branched off to go further on to Spencer Stewards at Ewden Lodge farm. All the kids worked hard during the first day or two, until the younger ones would understandably become tired or bored leading to some of them messing about. It made no difference how much father threatened them with none payment.

Sometimes a disturbance would suddenly flare up with the older kids too, and this had to be quelled early or spud throwing would quickly develop, when that started to happen father had to sharply nip the disturbance in the bud by shouting

'If I see any more of that no one gets paid today, do you hear'! But the farmers including my father had to be careful in so much as word would quickly spread if a farmer had mistreated the kids in any way, for this could cause a boycott making it difficult to finish the job.

So as I said before, when selecting workers father preferred the kids to be around twelve to fourteen years old. At that age they were usually strong enough to work all day without becoming tired or bored. And as an added bonus if the bigger ones sometimes stayed a bit longer to help with stacking the bags onto the cart or trailer they were usually rewarded with a little extra money.

When all the days potato pickers had gone home our day was only halfway through, we had to finish hauling in the remainder of the days harvest and empty the heavy bags onto the heap inside the specially prepared building.

When that job was concluded it was straight on to our daily ritual/routine of feeding the stock and milking the cows, all culminating into very hard tiring days so we were always very glad when the potato fields were cleared, and the resulting crop stored in doors.

In the really early days the potato rows were ploughed out with the bouter, unfortunately that way of rising them always managed to damage a high proportion of the crop, it didn't matter how careful one had been at the time. In the late 1940' father managed to borrow from somewhere a potato harvesting aid a machine called a spinner.

The 'spinner' was a heavy machine with large iron wheels to straddle the potato row to be harvested, and a tractor normally towed it. The heavy blade underneath scooped up the entire row of soil and potatoes straight into the path of a fan type spinning wheel. This spinning wheel in effect threw everything to one side, this action also separated the spuds from the debris making picking the potatoes so much easier to pick, and there were far less damaged potatoes to deal with afterwards.

However if the driver of the tractor went too fast the spinner threw the entire crop far and wide causing much wasted time searching, it was a case of a happy medium not too slow and not too fast.

After becoming a registered milk producer father started to grow Kale to feed to the milk cows during the winter months, it was at its best-chopped and fed daily. If it was a rainy day chopping and gathering kale was a particularly wet job so we had to wear fully waterproof clothing and a sou'wester or we would become absolutely soaked before we had finished filling up the cart or trailer.

Chopping kale could in a way be likened to felling trees in a rain forest, especially during a good kale-growing year. It could grow up to a height of five or six foot with stems up to one and half inches thick even though the stems were relatively soft it took considerable effort to chop through each stalk with one slash.

Gathering Kale each day had to be done in all weathers Sun, Rain, or Frost as it was a good source of vitamins for the cows. All the milking cows loved Kale!

Pulling swedes was another hard job that had to be done whether it was wet or dry. Swede pulling was better done if there were two people working together as a team, it was a job where you could work and have a conversation at the same time, so to speak! Excuse the pun!

Anyway father and I would work four rows between us he would take two and I would take two pulling topping and tailing and dropping the finished swede into a communal row in the middle.

It was heavy back breaking work but I always enjoyed pulling swedes. One could view the finished row anytime by just straightening up and looking back. It was such a satisfying sight to see the neat wide rows of newly pulled trimmed swedes.

At that time there were two curved turnip knives manufactured especially to harvest turnips or swedes. I liked the one that had the spike standing up, but some workers liked the other type which had the spike turned down. It didn't really matter which one we used for both did the same job; it was just a personal preference.

The worst example that I used was just after the war years, and father couldn't or wouldn't buy me a proper knife, I had to use the broken end off an old scythe blade which father had made to look like a swede chopper. If one missed with that thing it was lethal! The worst times I had were when we were pulling swedes on a wet day when the swedes became very slippery and difficult to deal with, and sometimes I would finish up chopping my hands so badly I had to wear gloves to do my other work. After one particular disastrous occasion father relented and bought me a proper knife.

I remember we always tried to complete the carting and tipping of the swedes into the clamp before Christmas each year. It was a work of art stacking the swedes into a steep sided long pile of swedes. We grew two varieties red ones for early feeding and the green ones for feeding later in the winter months.

When father declared the swede clamp to be complete, and it was all neat and tidy it was covered with a thick layer of straw then we dug a ditch all the way round throwing the soil up onto the straw covering the swedes. That did three jobs. One was to keep the straw from blowing away; two to keep most of the frost at bay and three the ditch drained excess water away.

The last season of the year was in some respects the busiest; this was, of course, the corn-threshing season.

On our farm threshing day was a big event entailing a lot of workers visiting from other farms in the area for most farms grew a crop of cereals especially if they were milk producers or livestock rearers.

Our farm was one of the ten or so farms where Fred Chantry the contractor threshed the corn with his Ransoms Sims and Jeffries threshing box once or twice a year (It all depended on how much acreage the farm grew).

It could be as early as October or as late as January before Fred turned up at our farm, usually moving his kit from Broomhead farm across the valley to our place Garlic House.

All farms have to have a routine and to have it disrupted all day from when Fred arrived with a crash bang wallop preparing his kit for the days threshing, to when everyone went home was always a traumatic experience. Fred was always a noisy worker he couldn't do anything without making the maximum amount of noise, and of course the machines he operated were also noisy. The one disadvantage we had however. Our stack yard was adjacent to one of the milking sheds, so the cows could hear as well as see through the windows, the equipment as it worked all through the day. The noise must have sometimes frightened them a bit, as we would end up having a lower yield of milk to go to the dairy the next day.

Every single job associated with threshing was heavy, difficult or dusty. I always considered the heaviest job was carrying the bags of corn from the thresher to the corn chamber. The difficult jobs were carrying the bales of straw to a new stack or forking up the sheaves from the corn stack onto the box to feed the threshing drum.

For years I always seemed to be the youngest labourer on threshing days. So I was always allocated the mucky dusty jobs associated with youth.

Such as keeping the chaff clear of the threshing box or carrying chaff into a building for storage or changing the rubbish bags at the side of the drum.

But I did eventually progress to being allowed on to the corn stack moving sheaves to where they were wanted, and from there I went on to the job I had been envious about for a long time. That was feeding the drum!

That job suited me down to the ground and I loved it so I did everything in my power to be allocated either cutting the string on the sheaves or feeding the threshing drum whenever the job selection was being discussed.

Everyone was pleased when a threshing day had come to an end whether the job was finished or not. If the job had been completed Fred would be around early the next morning as usual to crash and bang everything around, as he prepared his kit to move to the next farm on his list.

Fred next move could be to our neighbour Spencer Steward or a little bit further just over the hill to Willie Hague's farm so in effect we would only have one day to recuperate before we had another heavy days work. The day would be slightly easier for us because it was someone else's farm, but we weren't envious at all for we knew what they had to go through just as we had at Garlic House.

I can't recall exactly when combine harvesters started to come on the scene for they alone caused the death of threshing machines. Much easier and more expensive no doubt but they did away at one stroke most of the traditional farming rituals at one go. One would have thought that introducing the combine onto the local farming scene would have made things easier for the farmer?

But no. Some new crops came onto the farmers growing agenda such as maze or rape seed needing expert machines to plant them and special machines to harvest them as well. Then silage making became very popular. Because silage was so popular with the livestock and the farmers themselves it meant having to buy or hiring special machines to cut, and harvest the grass.

So all in all farming is almost as hard as it always has been but in a different way, changing from all manual labour to virtual all mechanical.

It certainly has moved on such a lot since I was a farmer's young son living on a Farm in the Yorkshire Pennines.

Now we move on to the winter jobs. For December and January were the months when the potatoes stored in the buildings had to be riddled not once but twice.

The first time was to select the size the buyer wanted to sell in their shops (sometimes the size differed from year to year) so we had to select a suitably sized riddle before starting the job.

One buyer was G.C. Knowles & Sons of Manchester Road Stocksbridge; the other was Jackson's of Shay House lane Stocksbridge. The eating sized potatoes were carefully poured out of the riddle into 112lb Cwt Hessian bags, placed on the big weight scales. Where father ever so carefully made sure the bag weighed slightly more than 112Lbs before the top was tied and then stacked onto the growing pile, until we had done enough for the Greengrocers to collect. Jackson's or Knowles came with their respective lorries to collect the bagged potatoes usually a ton at a time every week or so, until we ran out of stock.

Father had to calculate what we may need in the house for our own use, too many and they would go soft, not enough and we would be buying in, a delicate balance.

The second riddle used was a much smaller size, that riddle was used to separate the pig sized potatoes, from the soil and debris that always came with the spuds from the field.

The resulting small potatoes were bagged and stored for feeding to the bacon pig or the laying hens in the bad weather.

The rest consisted of rubbish and soil. This was shovelled to one side waiting for time to spare when it could be loaded onto the cart and dumped back on a field somewhere.

All this work is now done by machine; the potatoes are planted by machine. Picked, riddled and sized by machine, even washed by machine ready to package in small quantities all done by machine, the only manual part seems to be the final user actually eating the potatoes.

In certain years when there was a glut of potatoes the ministry of agriculture would buy from the big producers any excess stock and sell them on for feeding stock. I can remember father buying some when they were cheap where we found they had been dusted with a bright blue dye so they could be identified I suppose from normal eating potatoes. The stock always loved potatoes in their rations we just had to be careful we didn't feed them with too many at anyone time, as in the long run it didn't do them any good.

What I considered to be one of the hardest jobs in the winter months was when we started to haul hay in from the various haystacks' that had been built outside in the fields. The way we did it was to cut the hay into trusses using a hay knife.

Hay knife! This was/is a thin steel blade sharpened on three sides.

Shaped I suppose like a large table knife measuring something like three foot tall standing upright with a handle at the top set at a right angle for the operator to exert pressure to cut the slabs of hay.

'Hay trusses'. These were slabs of hay cut straight from the stack weighing I suppose a cwt each, the trusses had to be tied up tight with binder band/string so they wouldn't fall apart, whilst they were being stacked on the trailer to be hauled back to the farm.

When the haystack had been built in the first instance the hay was of course loose, but as the stack settled it compacted so the hay became more or less solid.

So ones hay knife had to be very sharp at all times to cut the trusses, and we had to be constantly sharpening the blade with a stone to get the best effect from our efforts. There's no doubt about it cutting hay by hand from the stack was very hard work.

I must relate here the story about one particular haystack we were cutting up and hauling. As we gradually worked towards the middle we suddenly discovered a black perfectly round area of rotten hay which we eventually discovered went right the way through the stack down to the ground. The wet patch hadn't spread, as it was the same size at the bottom as it was at the top. I should say the rotten patch was as thick as a broom handle, about 1½" a bit difficult to imagine really how the water got into the top of the stack in the first place as the stack had a waterproof cover over it

But going all the way down without spreading in a fifteen-foot tall haystack. Well it takes some believing!

The farmers year however continues, once Christmas and New Year celebrations are over the farmers have to start thinking which fields are going to be used for next year's crops, as it would soon be time to start hauling manure out before the fields are ploughed for the prospective planting.

Discount offers on fertilisers are sometimes available if ordered early enough. The potato seed need ordering as does the swede, kale, oats and wheat or barley, new crops such as maze can now be added and of course rapeseed. In some ways the farmers year is the same as it always has been with one important difference there are less workers around, it now only needs a small workforce to operate the machines which have taken over 'The farmers year'.

Twenty five

Back of Beyond

Usually the first words of exclamation any new visitor to our farm uttered was 'Whatever made you come to live at this place for Walter, it must be like living at the back of beyond'.

These words were said of course when they came visiting Garlic House Farm. Over time father became so used to visitors' remarks he could almost recite the exact words before they even said them. In a way they were right, we did live at the back of nowhere or even further still 'at the back of the moon', as some of them added.

Garlic House was situated well away from any populated area right by the side of a rarely used road that didn't go anywhere in particular. Although we did have regular visitors such as friends or relations who braved the elements who came to see us. But first they had to make the decision whether the visit was worth the effort. For at some point they would have to walk a fair few miles when they came visiting our back of the moon location, they came from a place that we didn't know much about. Civilisation!

If it were summer time some of our visitors would stand and stare across at the Broomhead moors and sigh, 'Oh what a view you have'. But for us who lived there, we didn't take much notice of the view as we had work to do, but I have to admit the Broomhead moors did look good when the purple heather was in full bloom.   But I know for a fact if the same people had come to visit us in the winter months, they would have looked at Broomhead moor in quite a different way.

Where our farm was situated was right in the path of the bad weather coming across the moorland whether it was wind, rain or snow we got it bad.   Our nearest populated area was Midhopestones; a small village located several miles away, just off the main A616 Manchester to Sheffield main road. But there wasn't a lot to do even when we went there, for Midhope only had a little shop that sold groceries, and had a small post office area. Across the road from the shop was a public house known at that time as the Club Inn, with an infant's school across the road, and a few houses scattered around completing the picture.

We had to prepare early for the winter months at Garlic House buying in everything we thought we needed to be self contained, not knowing beforehand how long our next winter was going to be.

Coal for instance. Was delivered by Colin Marshall our regular supplier from Stocksbridge. The coal came loose usually in a two-ton load; tipped into a pile behind the coalhouse delivered a few weeks before winter was due to set in. Most of the coal was easy to shovel through the little door into the coalhouse but some of it was so big we had to smash it up with the sledgehammer so it would go through the small hatch. Outside right next to the coal house hatch, was the midden where all the household rubbish that couldn't be burnt on the house fire was deposited. We never had a dustbin or a refuse collection service whilst I lived at Garlic House, so the contents of the midden consisted of such things as tins and jars and broken household stuff. When the midden was full, it was a case of backing the horse and cart, or later the tractor and trailer, as close as possible to the midden. So we could shovel the collection of rubbish from the walled area into the cart and take it down to the bottom of the rye field to what one might call our private tip.

That is where the entire contents of the midden were unceremoniously tipped down into a hole on the other side of our boundary wall where it joined all the rest of rubbish, some of which had been there for decades. One of our essential winter commodities was paraffin or lamp oil, as some preferred to call it. Father had to keep an eye on the big paraffin/oil tank in the buildings to make sure it was full enough to keep the mantle lamps in the house and the storm lamps we used in the buildings outside supplied, through what might or could be a long winter.

It was a daily ritual checking, topping up and trimming the wicks of all the lamps used on the farm whether they were in the house or in the buildings, each and every one of them had a job to do, essentially to light up where we lived and worked.

We knew everything was going to be all right when father declared 'It can snow na if it wants tha nose'! Flour was another essential we couldn't do without, flour was always white bought in a big 112lb bag and stored in

230

the house. As I remember it had to be kept somewhere dry for if flour was allowed to become damp or stored in non-ideal conditions it could become infested with weevils.

Not that I can remember seeing any weevils, but that's what we were told could happen.

We always killed our own pig just before Christmas each year providing enough bacon and ham to last through the worst of winters.

We had a few cows and these supplied the milk for making our own butter. We churned this down in the cellar fresh every week, I know because I was the one who regularly turned the handle on the wooden butter churn, and believe me, turning a butter churn handle continuously for hours can become very boring after a while. Whilst churning a pinch or two of salt had to be added for taste. The best about churning butter was when the finished product was scraped out of the churn to be patted into a rounded lump on a wooden butter pat. Our butter pat had thistles and acorns carved into the surface so when the pat was pulled or shook off, the butter had a nice pattern showing on its surface.

Did I mention the cellar?

When the pig killing day was approaching, Henry Mitchell our grocery supplier brought a very heavy slab of rough white salt. This was I suppose about three-foot long and twelve inches square wrapped in waxed paper to keep it clean.

The slab of salt had to be laboriously carried down the narrow stone steps into the cellar for us to break it up. Breaking salt up was a ritual which had to be done on the big stone slab, and sometimes the salt was very difficult to break up as it varied such a lot in quality.

We had to reduce the salt into small pieces and then keep rolling and rolling with a wooden rolling pin until it was all nicely granulated. The newly crushed salt was finally scooped into a big bag or basket with a cover to keep it clean then placed somewhere near the open fire in the kitchen to help stop it from setting solid again.

Salt is an essential ingredient used to cure the sides of bacon or hams of the newly killed pig to help the curing process. After a few weeks of curing on the stone slab, the bacon sides and the hams were bagged / wrapped in muslin cloth and taken up into the living room to be hung on hooks in the centre of the ceiling by the paraffin lamp to finish the process of curing.

On the hams in particular we used another form of salt which was much stronger this was known as saltpetre. We rubbed it into any holes in the meat and around bones sticking out such as knuckles, but one had to be very careful with saltpetre not to get any in our eyes for it could make them very sore for a long time.

While we are still on about the cellar. I should tell you about something that happened down there in the cellar when quite a renowned carpenter lived at the farm, sometime in the more distant past.

He apparently built a complete full sized wooden horse cart or trap down in the cellar only to find there was no-way that he could get it out. He had, so local legend recorded, to completely dismantle the new cart/trap so he could bring it up from the cellar and rebuild it again outside before he could enjoy his labours to the full.

There's an old saying that goes like this -

'You never miss the things you've never had'. This topic cropped up many times during conversations especially when anyone asked specifically what we didn't have.

The things we had to manage without were quite numerous in those early days. We didn't have what are now considered by almost everyone to be essential everyday things such as Electricity, Gas, Mains water, a Bathroom, a Water closet, or even a Telephone at Garlic House Farm during my early years of living there.

Water came from a spring the same water the cows drank from the stone trough in the yard.

Our only toilet was a 2-seater affair known as an earth closet.

The toilet bin was collected and emptied once a week by the Sheffield Corporation water works lorry. To alleviate or reduce the stink we sprinkled some strong smelling powder down the hole occasionally it certainly helped to disperse lingering smells.

The coal house and the toilet were in fact housed in the same stone building near to the house a few yards along the outdoor flag stones. When it was lashing down with rain we obviously became soaked before we even got there whether it was toilet or coal we were going for.

We had to rely on paraffin lamps for light, and the lack of a telephone didn't concern us that much for we had never had such a luxury.

I was a teenager when Bertram Shaw the builder from Bolsterstone came to remove the old black range in our kitchen, he was going to replace it with a similar but more modern tiled version complete with a back boiler. So we could have hot water on tap for the first time. During the operation Mr Longden a plumber from Stocksbridge came and installed the water pipes for Bert to complete his work. A carpenter came to install a wooden stand to support the header water tank and hot water cistern upstairs in a corner of my bedroom. Then the plumber installed a long white enamel bath in the corner of the bedroom directly over our kitchen, as far as I could recall I had never seen a proper bath before.

From then on I remember when we had a bath we had to have candles or a storm lamp hanging up in the room to see what we were doing.

But, and it's a big but, because it was our own spring water supplying the house there wasn't enough pressure to feed the newly installed water tank upstairs. It could have been a mistake in the planning or just a miscalculation but all the water that was needed to fill the tank had to be pumped by a hand by a device affixed to our kitchen wall.

I remember either my brother or me had to man the pump if we wanted a bath, and because my brother wasn't quite tall enough he had to stand on a box to operate the handle, It needed 1000 pumps or so to have enough water to have a bath.

The water pumping ritual could be done by anyone who offered, anytime. Even washing up the pots could take more hot water than some people imagine it all had to be pumped by hand up to the header tank with the pump affixed to the kitchen wall!

However on washing days the sett pot in the back kitchen was utilised to heat the water for us to use in the washing tub. On those occasions mother used the three legged posher to clean the clothes or the corrugated rubbing board, then the old mangle to finish then off before hanging them on the line to dry in the corner of the back field.

My mothers sister Auntie Mary was one of the visitors who insisted in saying that we lived at the back of beyond, when she came to help my mother bake a few cakes, and she always came with her own kitchen scales to weigh all the ingredients precisely. She followed exactly what it said in a recipe book, she also brought with her when she came to do some baking. Not like my mother who didn't possess any recipe books or weight scales she just added as much as it took and did without all the fiddly bits.

233

Aunty Mary always walked to our farm, but she wouldn't walk home again on her own, she insisted in being escorted either by my mother or father or evens me, when I was big enough.

She could have rode home on the back of a cart horse, but she hated horses so she wouldn't hear of the idea. And there was one thing that was guaranteed to make my father mad and that was Auntie Mary calling him 'Coddles'. How fathers hated that expression.

If Auntie Mary used that dreaded word, there was no way my father would do anything for her. To keep the peace and any chance of a lift home Auntie Mary would have to refrain from uttering the word 'Coddles', even though she would have liked to do as she liked just to wind father up.

Later when we acquired a tractor she insisted on being taken home standing in the link box much to fathers' annoyance. Later still when I became a motorbike rider the task was transferred to me to take Auntie Mary home. I always rode much too fast for her liking, so she would say when I dropped her off 'That's the last time I'll ride with you young man'!

On many occasions when it was time for Auntie Mary to go home, father had mysteriously vanished or couldn't be found, so she had no option but to entrust me once again and ride on the back of my motorbike, or walk. As she wouldn't even consider walking, she was more or less forced to experience my fast riding skills yet again, it always ended with the same ritual - 'Never again will I…

Another Auntie this time my fathers brother Uncle Albert' wife Auntie May, from Leeds. She also thought we lived at the back of beyond. Leeds is quite some distance from Garlic House, so when they came to see us at the farm it must have been a difficult thing to plan. They always came as a family, and the journey involved various buses, so it must have been a relief to finally arrive at Midhopestones even though their journey hadn't finished for they still had to walk the 5 miles or so to Garlic House.

They always wrote beforehand to say when they were coming, calculating the time they would arrive and when we could expect to see them. When the day came we watched excitedly for them to wave from the top of the steps up on the skyline of our top field signalling that they wouldn't be long, as it was only half a mile or so from there down to our farm. There were quite a few of them as a family. Uncle Albert; Auntie May with Jack, Irene, and Colin their children.

I shall always recall those occasions and the fun we always had when the

Couldwell Family from Leeds came visiting our farm at the back of beyond! Uncle Albert always got stuck in straight away helping my father, his brother, with any work going on. And he always said he enjoyed it. Auntie May helped mother in the house while us kids excitedly galloped about outside or in the buildings. What was different was their accent they all spoke with quite a pronounced Leeds accent which to my brother Lewis or me sounded quite strange. But I suppose they thought ours was strange too.

When it was time for them to go home they just accepted they had to walk back to Midhopestones to catch their appointed Bus. I suppose on reflection the family would have had to make sure their journey back home to Leeds would be as trouble free as possible by forward planning, and by making sure the various buses were running on that particular day.

I remember when my brother Lewis and I were older we walked with them to the top of our hill before waving goodbye as they carried on towards Midhopestones to catch their bus home.

I must recount here some of the happenings associated with visitors to our farm and that big field, the field that went all the way up to the skyline where there is a stile onto the road.

If some of the visitors had youngsters in the party I/we knew for a fact the younger ones would take a look down the field towards our farm, with the idea of using it as a short cut. We would nearly always be right, and we could predict what the following move was going to be. There they go my brother and I would shout as we excitedly watched the youngsters climb over the stile and begin the walk down the field. It didn't matter how slowly anyone started to walk down that steep field, they always finished galloping flat out trying madly to keep their balance striving to reach the more level area two or three hundred yards lower down, without falling full stretch on their back or face.

As for myself, I knew all about how steep it was for if I started to run I couldn't stop. In fact trying not to fall my strides would become enormous with the effort involved trying not to trip and fall full length.

Many are the times have I tried to walk slowly down the field only to slip, albeit slightly and away I would go, and I would finish up running so fast I had to continue down the next steep slope careering through an open gate into the next field below. And there I could loose all my speed quickly coming to a stop absolutely winded. I remember on one occasion, when the five-barred gate wasn't open.

235

I collided with it at speed, I hit the gate so hard an area of the surrounding wall collapsed, and I had to rebuild that up before I could continue my journey home. Albeit somewhat painfully because I had badly bruised my shoulder. Over the years I have quite regularly finished up walking with a limp, through twisting an ankle or knee during a headlong dash down that steep field.

There's another thing about that top field. This time something rather unusual or even strange!

So bear with me for a moment whilst I set the scene.

Imagine if you will – a balmy midsummer's evening just before dark when the skyline at the top of the big pasture field becomes vague, as the light fades. Everything is still and quiet when a strange wailing sound can be heard echoing around the area. We gathered in the yard to listen. As we listened we all agreed it sounded like a Scottish reel. We listened harder to try to determine where the sound was coming from. Finally we all agreed that it sounded as if it was coming from up near the top of our highest field near to where the public footpath ends at a dry stone wall where there is a stile onto the road. But we weren't quite sure.

So father said to mother 'Fetch mi glasses lass so ahh can see oop theer'.

With the glasses father studied the area for a moment then declared that there appeared to be someone standing on the stile with a set of bagpipes or something similar.

The noise err- tune, went on for ½ an hour or so before peace finally returned to the countryside. But we were intrigued, surprised, and amused at the same time; in fact we all thought it was highly entertaining.

I remember we formed and agreed on a cunning plan. If, or better still when, the figure appeared again we reasoned because I was the quickest I was going to walk as fast as I could via the road to get behind the fellow to see who it could be. But nothing happened for the rest of that year.

We began to think maybe it was someone having a laugh, or whether it had happened at all, particularly after mother suggested there might not have been anyone there anyway?

So was it an illusion! But we stuck to our plan.

Towards the end of the next years summer on a balmy evening after a hot day there it was, the wail of the bagpipes, father declared he could see the figure as plain as day, even without his glasses.

So off I went running at first then slowing to a trot, finally walking as my legs tired all the time accompanied by the sound of bagpipes.

236

I clambered over the wall into the wood higher up the hill to get behind whoever it was but when I arrived at the position where I could actually see the steps there was no one there! I looked down the road, up the road across the fields on the other side of the steps but there was no one there at all.

I was very disappointed, all that effort for nothing.

When I arrived back home I was accused of scaring him off, but I had been very discreet about my every manoeuvre. So we were no wiser we didn't know whether it was a myth or a jape or even a ghost. Over the following years it continued, the sound of the bagpipes played by someone standing on the steps at the top of our field. It only happened once a year on a barmy summers evening just before nightfall.

As far as I can remember we never went to have a look again, we just enjoyed listening to it instead whether the person was real or an apparition it didn't matter anymore.

Twenty-six

Rabbits

During all of the fifty or more years my Grandad Fred Dyson worked for Captain Reginald Wilson he lived in an estate cottage named hungerhill. Hungerhill cottage situated a mile or so from Bolsterstone village along Heads lane just a little bit further on than Low Flatts where the Hague family had farmed for many years. Fred's cottage was perched precariously on the very top of a hillside, from where it commanded far-reaching views in all directions.

It was quite obvious why the Broomhead estate had built the cottage in that location, for Fred only had to venture outside and stand in the lane to see the town of Stocksbridge, and the village of Bolsterstone. Most importantly he could see the extensive Broomhead Moors stretching into the far distance. All these were visible to anyone standing in the narrow unmade track/lane that went past the cottage where my Grandad lived, the unmade lane went on for another mile or so before petering out. The lane provided access to two or three small farms further along but he couldn't see these from his house. Stepping out further Fred could look over the boundary wall into the old rabbit warren. This was an area of land probably well over a hundred acres in total area mostly covered in bracken and fern, where Fred as a young Gamekeeper had helped in the organising of an annual week long rabbit cull. It was a task that had to be done to keep the rabbit population down.

The resulting bag of rabbits were sold to a ready-made market providing cheap and tasty meat to the populace of the surrounding townships.

When the time came to conduct the cull, parts of the extensive bracken covered areas had to be mown manually by the Gamekeepers using scythes leaving what were known as 'Rydes' (Paths) all leading to a point where a long net was stretched across and secured by the gamekeepers.

The rabbit net was about fifty yards long something like five foot high, brown in colour made from a very strong string with holes just small enough to stop a full sized rabbit from squeezing through. The idea was for the rabbit beaters to scare the erstwhile feeding rabbits, so they ran along the newly mown Rydes straight into the waiting net to become securely entangled in it.

The waiting Gamekeepers and assistants dragged them out to kill them. No shot guns were used, it was all done by hand.
I have the official figure here as to how many rabbits were killed during a weeklong session in 1904;it is recorded as 4,894 rabbits killed in the rabbit warren belonging to the Broomhead estate.
Somewhere here at home I have a length of that very same net that was used over a century ago delicate now I know, but a bit of history all the same.

Wild rabbits played or plagued a big role during my own early years. For when I was still in short trousers, my Grandad Fred Dyson, taught me how to catch rabbits using traps or snares, how to establish which way the rabbits ran and why they ran that way. And where to place the snares in relation to any imperfections in the rabbit run and surrounding terrain and how to place the snares in a precise position to gain maximum effect. As far as traps were concerned he taught me how to disperse any man made smells, how to disguise the newly set trap's position and where to place traps so as not to endanger other animals that might be wandering in the locality. And how to gut rabbits correctly to prepare them for use in the household.
I learnt quickly bringing home a regular supply of rabbits for use in our house, and I can vouch for the fact there's nothing better than rabbit stew to make a tasty meal especially in the winter. I visited my dozen or so snares twice a day to check if they were all there, and check they were still correctly set as well as checking if I had caught anything.
When I say
'Check if they were all there'! I mean just that, as if something big and strong had become caught in a snare it wouldn't have been difficult for it to pull up the entire snare and just run away with it. As father didn't believe in paying me any cash/money for my labours on the farm I had to find ways of generating an income on my own, one way to generate money was by catching rabbits.
I sold most of the ones I caught to housewives in places such as Stocksbridge and Deepcar on a Friday when I accompanied father with the tractor on his egg and potato run. On other occasions when the work wasn't busy at home

240

I had a Mid - week run selling rabbits to housewives in another area.
I transported these with my bicycle to sell door to door; the big ones were
priced at 2/6 (Halfcrown) whereas some of the smaller ones were only worth
1/- (Shilling). To carry rabbits safely on a bicycle, I used a nice long smooth
strong hazel stick tied to the cross bar long enough to stick out behind my bike
for five foot or so.
With the rabbits back legs crossed I was able to slide them on to the stick
making a nice neat row of ready gutted rabbits for my potential customers to
view and choose which they wanted. It only took a moment to undo and hand
the selected rabbit over to the buyer. If it was a wet day I had to cover them
of course but that didn't pose a problem to me.
I could and did carry several rabbits maybe eight / ten or more by that
method.
I knew beforehand of course that by carrying such a large number of full
grown rabbits, my bike was going to be heavy, I also realised I would have
to push my bike more than normal, but there you are. My biggest worry
was the possibility of having to take any unsold ones back home again, for
rabbits want to eaten more or less the same day as they are killed for the best
flavour.
Fridge's and freezers and such weren't around or much in evidence at that
time especially in a working household.
Normally I didn't have much trouble selling all I had with me, I think
housewives realised at that time they were good value for money, and as I
have said before, they always made a good tasty meal. If I did finish up taking
a couple of unsold rabbits back home it didn't take long for the farm dogs or
cats to dispose of them.

I think I'm right in saying the worst or nastiest animal I ever caught in a trap
was a full sized fox, Oh dear that fox was annoyed, it was so savage I had
to go and fetch father to shoot it before it could be released from my trap. I
have caught quite a few birds over the years, if there wasn't a lot wrong with
them I would let them go. If they were badly injured I thought it best to pull
their neck out and have done with it. Some of you may cringe at the thought
but that's how it was in the countryside, in those days anyway. But saying
that some of the big birds were nasty and it was very difficult to release them
without having my eyes clawed out.
Lets move on again. To when I had my first shot gun it was known as a single
barrel 410, Grandad Dyson gave my brother Lewis and me to share. Not

much good really but that was all we were allowed to have or use for a while until I progressed to a double barrelled 12 bore. Courtesy of Grandad Dyson again. I tried an air rifle but I only ever managed to kill one rabbit with it all the time I had it.

In the early 1950's, rabbits became so prevalent around our area they were an absolute pest.
In fact the situation became so bad at one time the sheer number of rabbits could raze a field of corn all the way around the edge to the distance of 30 foot or more just by constantly eating.
As you may well imagine they could almost clear the crop in a small field before it had time to ripen. All kinds of deterrents were tried such as scare's giving off a loud bang!! every so often, but the rabbits soon became immune to such noises.
Gas canisters were tried, and small pest control companies were set up declaring they could clear the nuisance, but they couldn't, so it was all to no avail.

During one period in the summertime, after we had finished milking in the evenings. I started to go out with the twelve bore, and head for what had become my favourite field, the field was one of those behind Cottage Farm, about half a mile up the road from our place where Jim Blyton the Broomhead chauffeur lived.
I had visited the field so many times I knew the best place to climb over the wall from our field, to cross Spencer Stewards lane then climb over the wall on the other side to creep up the first field behind Jim Blyton' house. I was heading for a large bush growing in the wall at the top of the field, once I had gained my usual position behind the bush, I had time to check and make sure my gun was fully loaded, with two more cartridges in my coat pocket readily available.
Then I would wait till everything was nice and settled before pulling both hammers back on my gun as quietly as possible before stepping out from behind the bush into the next field.
All the rabbit's heads would suddenly come up, some would start to slowly lop towards where they had their burrows, and I knew beforehand which direction they would run I even knew where their burrows were in the wood above the field. My first blast would kill two or more, after quickly reloading I could usually get two more before they were too far away and the field

cleared completely.

Not that I made any difference to the number of rabbit population for later in the day they would be back again grazing as if nothing untoward had happened. They still didn't take much notice of me if I went to have another go at them later on.

During the early post war period. Rabbits played a big part in the diet of people living in the countryside. They were easy to catch by whatever means one wanted, they were easy to cook and were very tasty making rabbit pie or stew with our own potatoes, with carrots and onions from the garden. Mmm I can taste it now!

However I did have some complaints from my housewife customers in Stocksbridge, when I started to supply rabbits I had shot with the twelve bore, they complained about finding pellets in the meat. I remember I had to go back to catching rabbits in snares especially to satisfy my valued very discerning customers.

After each of my shooting sessions I took the dead rabbits up to edge of the wood at the top of the field where I gutted and cleaned them before carrying them home.

My Grandad Dyson always told me to clean the rabbits well away from home preferably close to where you had killed them. So any marauding Foxes could have a feast on the entrails, if they were satisfied with their meal they would forget about terrorising any hens, pheasants or killings cats around the farms and go back to their lair to have a sleep instead.

I remember further up our hill there was/is a banking absolutely infested with rabbits, with holes everywhere. At the time our tractor was a petrol-powered Ferguson where the exhaust pipe was like a car, fixed underneath the engine and gearbox to emerge at the back. Father came up with what he thought was a brilliant idea!

He managed to buy or borrow a length of flexible hose from somewhere. Somewhat similar to the ones fitted to vacuum cleaners. Fathers idea was, if we filled in most of the rabbit holes on the banking, just leaving, say a couple open for us to push one end of the hose down and fill the earth up around it, and then affix the other end to the tractor exhaust. Start and run the tractor engine at half throttle for 15 minutes or so before pulling the tube out, then quickly filling the hole in to stop the gases escaping. Father was convinced we would gas and kill some of them inside that hole at least.

Did it work? No I don't think it did, for within a couple of days there were just as many rabbits in the adjoining field as there were before! So I'm sure it didn't work one little bit.

To my mind a complete waste of time.

The rabbit population became so tame we could walk across the same field as they were feeding and some of them would just watch us without scampering off like they're supposed to do.

There was a big field across the Ewden beck directly across from our farmyard called 'New pieces'. About 40 acres in size belonging to Broomhead Home farm, in the mornings or better still late in the evenings there were absolutely hundreds, or even thousands all feeding in the grass field.

With glasses we could have actually counted them from our house doorway.

Yes the rabbits were ruining the countryside ruining the crops and ruining the small farmer's income. It was a very welcome development when myxomatosis was introduced into the countryside that consequently cleared the lot.

Rabbits did come back into the area after a while, but they never became the pests they once were. It seemed as if myxomatosis could reinvent itself and clear the lot every so often that was good. But no one will ever forget the time when rabbits almost took over the countryside.

As you will have gathered Myxomatosis also ruined my income; I wasn't able to supply my valued customers with fresh rabbits anymore on my own account.

As far as fathers Friday potato round was concerned the lack of rabbits on his list of goods supplied was a disappointment to some housewives but they had to get over it. We were reliably informed that rabbits showing the disease should not be eaten under any circumstances.

However I had moved on to other things by then, and I didn't have to rely solely on rabbits anymore for my measly income, so to speak.

By then of course I had almost finished my night school and I ventured into part time electrical installation in the areas where the mains supply had been recently connected. I was doing all right too carrying out work both in Midhopestones and Bolsterstone villagers and further afield if requested.

However, it was quite some time later probably the late nineteen fifties before mains electricity was introduced into the area where our farm was situated. I remember in the beginning farmers or their landlords were asked to estimate the amount of electric they thought they might use.

Then the Yorkshire Electric Board sent a memo around potential customers suggesting their own figure of what they wanted the farmer to use. That was before they would even consider connecting the property to the mains distribution system.

I had of course to rewire our farm completely- yet again, to the latest British standards specifications prevailing at the time. In due course my work was tested and I was issued with a certificate of correctness from Yorkshire electric board before the supply was switched on.

To finish this chapter on a different note but in a way it was still associated with the newly supplied electrical supply.

The new mains electrical supply was brought to all the farms in our area by the installation of tall wooden poles with the two/three wires strung from pole to pole. Each house or farm had its own transformer to reduce the voltage to normal supply.

The new poles intending to supply us, and our neighbour Spencer Steward passed quite close to our house, and within a week, even before the supply was switched on we discovered a full-grown cock pheasant with a broken neck underneath the shiny new wires.

All the time my parents had lived at Garlic House they had never even thought about catching pheasant either to sell or to eat, so they didn't know what to do with it. Eventually mother came to the decision the best thing was to have it for our dinner.

So mother prepared it as she would a chicken and placed it in the oven to cook for our Sunday dinner. She had forgotten it was Sunday and Grandad Dyson turned up as normal, after a while he started sniffing then he declared,

'That smells good whatever have you got int toven lass?' No doubt Grandad Dyson knew very well what mother had in the oven and he also knew that one of the prime requisites of the farm tenancy that father had agreed not to catch kill or eat an estate pheasant.

My mother decided to come clean as to why she was cooking a pheasant, and how we had come by it. Fred accepted the explanation after some tut tutting, and when mother somewhat sharply declared would he have left it there to rot in the grass or take it home and use it to feed his family, he somewhat reluctantly had to admit he would have done the same.

So nobody won the argument or who was to blame so we had our first Sunday dinner of pheasant. I must admit I wasn't all that fussed anyway I would have much preferred a nice fat hen.

I remember mother and father living for a while in fear that somehow the landlord Capt Reginald would come to hear of the misdemeanour but nothing happened and it was forgotten.

Chapter 27

Bounty of the Countryside

One of the biggest advantages of living in the countryside, were the different varieties of seasonal fruits and pie fillings almost literally growing on ones doorstep, so to speak. For when I was of school age mother would regularly request I take my little brother Lewis with me to go and find some fruit for her to use in the kitchen. Father had a few soft fruit bushes growing in the garden consisting of red currants, black currents, raspberries and various varieties of gooseberries not forgetting of course the huge rhubarb patch.

Both my brother and me relished the idea of getting away from home for an hour or so scrabbling amongst the bushes or trees, so we went suitably prepared with strong clothing and footwear and armed with a large container each.

Blackberries

Blackberries, are the most common wild fruits found in and around the countryside, such as along the roadsides or the wall bottoms surrounding fields.

They also grow profusely in dense thickets, where given the chance they would rip your hands and clothes to shreds in a short space of time.

If we were intentionally going to pick blackberries it was a must to take a bowl or bucket. But in an emergency ones flat cap was quite acceptable.

There were some exceptionally large blackberries to be found on the Nether

House farmland quite near to the public footpath that starts in our bottom field.

But saying that just below our farm buildings, in the field over the wall from the Croft, grew the biggest juiciest blackberries anywhere, so if mother wanted some in a hurry that was the place to look first of all.

Bilberries

Bilberries are to my mind the most delicious wild fruit to be found in the Pennines. Mostly growing in large areas amidst the heather or along the roadsides bordering the moors. Grouse feed on Bilberries and obviously they have the first pick, and they pick the best, so what we got to pick was the remains. One big drawback with Bilberries is they are so small it makes the job long winded, very tedious and sometimes even boring. One has to be picking for hours to make any effort of filling even a small container.

However those of us who lived in the area had other rivals. Every year the countryside was invaded in the evenings or weekends by hordes of people from towns and cities, with their bowls and bags bending over bushes that had already been stripped of the best by the grouse.

But at the end of the day they still appeared to be enjoying the outdoor activity.

I could pick quite a lot myself when I put my mind to the task, but I always had to be very careful not to eat more than I was putting in my container they were so delicious and hard to resist.

However I always held the opinion one has to be in the right frame of mind to go Bilberry picking for it can certainly be a boring job, especially if one could or should be doing something better.

Elderberry

The elderberry tree, is a remarkable if annoyingly intrusive tree, it grows in profusion almost anywhere sometimes making a nuisance of itself. One of its two redeeming attributes is the creamy white flower that adorns the tree in the spring. These flowers can be made into an exceptionally strong homemade wine. To the home wine makers the picking of elderberry flowers is a yearly ritual. Everyone should be warned however if one is testing someone else's 'home made' brew be careful not too over indulge in the amount actually consumed for it quite renowned for its falling over powers.

248

Secondly later in the year the home wine makers have another bite of the cherry – so to speak – for the resulting fruit after the flowers have become spent also make a resoundingly good wine and this too has the attributes and falling over powers if one over indulges.

I remember being told by a ardent home wine maker that the best time to pick the huge bunches of black elderberries is when the stalks that support the berries turn red as that is a sure indication that the berries are fully ripe and ready for picking.

Blackthorn

You will have to wait until the blackthorn bush sheds its white flowers and the actual sloe berry start to form before making any decision about whether that particular bush you are looking at is what you consider may produce the best fruit. For even at that early stage you will be able to tell by looking at the blackthorn bush whether it is going to produce sound fruit or useless wizened sloes not really any good for anything.

The actual Sloe berry itself is more or less inedible, even when it displays the typical blue bloom, as it slowly begins to ripen.

Don't be tempted to pick the fruit at that stage for you will find them so tart and dry the juice will dry your mouth up immediately, and give you a severe bout of bellyache.

If you are picking the fruit to make Sloe Gin, the best time to pick them is when the leaves go brown and start to fall when the actual fruit appears to be overripe.

I have learned from good authority that this is definitely the best time to pick sloes, and yet another tip someone once told me, is to make sure you pick them just after the first frost of winter.

Blackthorn has another sometimes-annoying side to its existence, and this is its ability to accurately forecast the foreseeable weather.

Above I have mentioned the bushes having white flowers; these become naturally in full bloom in early April. Some years however they can linger in the full bloom - state for many weeks.

In fact until the end of May, and then suddenly almost over-night the petals will turn brown and fall off. From then on the air temperature will soar heralding the start of spring. It's quite true.

It's known throughout the countryside amongst the farmers as a 'Blackthorn winter'.

It doesn't happen every year, but when it does its very noticeable.

Crab apples

Another wild fruit guaranteed to give you instant bellyache if you indulged is of course the crab apple. We didn't have a single apple tree on our farm Garlic House either in the garden or anywhere else. So if we wanted apples, we had to buy them from the shop or somewhere else. But saying that, there were quite a number of crab apple trees in the Ewden beck area.

Crab apples are normally and naturally a very tart fruit somewhat similar to the Sloe I have just mentioned try a bite from a crab apple and you will feel the effects straight away.

But saying that just below Nether House farm I had discovered a crab apple tree that was to me quite palatable especially late in the autumn when the fruit had fallen.

According to historical books well over 6,000 varieties of crab apples trees were growing around the world at one time not too long ago.

Also according to historical records the crab-apple tree trunks were used for making tools such as set squares or handle for woodworking equipment. Nowadays it's just the fruit that's used for making excellent table jellies or wine.

Wild Strawberries

Wild strawberries could be found growing in profusion in and around the old rabbit warren not far from where Fred Dyson my Grandad lived at Hungerhill cottage.

The wild strawberry fruit are much smaller than the propagated variety but they taste so much sweeter, definitely a fruit to be eaten straight from the bush especially if one is hungry. I can remember them growing alongside a rough lane called 'mucky lane' which I had to walk along when I had been on a visit to Stocksbridge on my shanks' pony.

Medical theory suggests that by eating wild strawberries reduce the risk of certain cancers whether it is true or not I could say.

250

Nettles

I remember well, making batches of nettle beer. A long swig of nettle beer was very welcoming, after unloading a cartload of loose hay by pitchfork through a pitching hole into one of our stone buildings. The ones who were doing the stacking inside the building especially welcomed an occasional swig of nettle beer. For that is where it is always stuffy, dusty and hot?
The best nettles to use when making the nettle based brew, are the shorter young ones, before any flowers are showing on the top, I never used the tall mature dry ones.
Nowadays though I cannot recall in the slightest how I made it.
But I remember it could become quite potent as it matured in the pantry.
I had to use good quality bottles to withstand the pressure as the brew matured.
One of the regular sounds we could hear from the pantry especially in the warm weather was the cork' popping out from the bottlenecks of the maturing beer bottles on the shelves.
However if the cork was tight and remained secure the resulting crash which we sometimes heard could be a bottle exploding?
Making quite a mess in the pantry as you can well imagine.

Gooseberries

In our garden at home we had quite a number of gooseberry bushes. Some were sweet and some were sour. They were supposed to be for making pies for everyone to enjoy but as far as I can recall not many ever made it into the house to be used in the way intended.
My brother and I loved gooseberries. If we had been delegated a job somewhere, such as doing something in the corn or hay field the first port of call we did was to collect a few gooseberries, storing them in our pockets and they would keep us going as we carried out our allotted task.
I have to tell you a tale about gooseberries; it's quite true.
At the time we always referred to the incident as the prickly bush mystery.
It happened probably around 1945.

On the farm we had a pair of working shire horses. This story relates to one horse in particular born during Queen Victoria's reign named Jubilee. Known to us all as Juby.

There was in our farm yard a huge stone water trough where all the farm animals were allowed to drink there fill once or twice a day. The horses were always allowed to drink first as horses can be very stubborn and be reluctant to drink especially after a cow or other animal has been there before or if the water level had become so low the sediment or sand had become stirred up in the bottom. At the back of the water trough was the garden retaining wall and over the wall was a gooseberry bush. In fact the gooseberries on that bush were the sourest in the whole garden.

Anyway! My brother Lewis and me had to do our share of work in the fields and we found a few gooseberries or a stick of rhubarb in our pocket helped to pass the time whilst we were doing work away from home.

Obviously we picked the sweet gooseberries first until they were all gone but avoiding completely the sour bush over the wall from the stone trough in the yard.

Father wasn't daft he knew where all the gooseberries were going.

But one particular day he berated both my brother and me for picking the ones on the sour bush, which of course we strongly denied!

It was only by chance that soon after we had been scolded by father, my brother and me was in the garden doing something when Juby the shire horse' head suddenly appeared looking over the stone wall. But he obviously hadn't seen us. We watched spellbound as he slowly stretched his neck to reach into the sour gooseberry bush, he carefully selected a fruit from the maze of sharp spikes, and pulled it off its stalk then crunched it slowly with an expression of sheer ecstasy on his face. When he had finished Juby lowered his head to continue drinking at the trough as if nothing had happened. Of course father was informed immediately of this new development but to our surprise he declared.

'Let the bugger have em, they are far too sour for us to eat anyway'.

That let us both of the hook and effectively solved the prickly bush mystery.

Rhubarb

Rhubarb was somewhat similar I suppose. For rhubarb grew profusely in our garden at the farm and it wasn't thin stringy rhubarb either! Oh no, it was big and fat and luscious, it grew in a huge patch just over the wall from the farm yard, where the occasional shovel full of cow muck was thrown over the wall onto the rhubarb patch in the winter months.

Most of the mature rhubarb in our garden, finished up in the house for making pies. Or given away to visitors to take home with them. But as I have

252

mentioned above a stick of peeled rhubarb with a spoonful of sugar in our pocket bottom to dip into went a long way to elevate feeling hungry when out in the fields.

Sweet chestnuts

I remember now that there was a huge sweet chestnut tree growing down in the wood below Ewden-bridge. However one thing the tree lacked was consistency. It had good years and bad.
On its good years the chestnuts were wonderful and sweet, big and luscious. But in complete contrast on its bad years it was absolutely hopeless bearing small-wizened nuts not fit to consider eating at all. During the good years they were definitely the best to be had around the area, and it was always worth filling ones pockets to take home to roast on the fire or in the oven.

Conkers

Talking about conkers? I collected hundreds if not thousands of conkers from under one particular tree in long bank wood. But disappointingly some years these were not top class either! During good years the horse chestnuts lying about on the ground under that particular tree were huge. I took them to school to use as bargaining power for swapping items or used in actual competitions in the playground when the conker matches were in full swing.
However I never managed to have a champion with the ones I had collected. I always strongly suspected the ones that did achieve that honour had probably been doctored somehow.

Last but not least, Wild Roses

Wild field roses (Rosa Arvensis), when in flower always looked nice in a vase on the sideboard in our house, they didn't last long however, before the petals all fell off.
But the best as far as we boys were concerned was later when the bushes were adorned with rose hips instead. Rose hips were a cheap souce of making our own fun from nothing if you see what I mean? You just had to wait until the hips were nice and ripe, then with a knife cut open the hip to scrape out the little pips, dry them carefully before crushing them into a fine powder.

253

The resulting powder was secretively sprinkled down the collar of some unfortunate victim's shirt, and then stand back for the result.

One didn't have long to wait for a reaction. That was when the victim started to scratch.

One of the most important things one had to do at the time was to make sure no one else saw you do the dirty deed, or friendships were very likely to suffer in any resulting recriminations.

The end.